2ⁿᵈ EDITION

A
COACHING JOURNEY
IT'S IN THE
"FILE CABINET"

Dick Lien
970-217-4654
dicklien1943@gmail.com

1

To My Head Coach, Loretta,
and our team:
Brent, Darin, Marybeth,
Michael, Wyatt
Kate, Sarah, and Eli

PREFACE

I started coaching in the 1960's that's a long time ago. I have lived in a lot of places, 17 to be exact. Done a lot of things and seen a lot of things in the coaching world. I have enjoyed every stop along the journey and would not trade these coaching experiences. I have head and assistant coaching experiences at many levels: junior high school, high school, junior college, NCAA Division 1-2 and internationally as a head club coach and National Team head coach.

During a coaching career of nearly six decades, self-learning has always been JOB ONE. A "Spin Off" from the goal of developing players and winning games; I collected a large "File Cabinet" jammed with all things coaching. This collection includes information from every conceivable source: Clinic notes, magazines, newspapers, scraps of paper, billboards, marketing slogans, podcasts, videos, speeches, collaborating with fellow coaches throughout the decades, et.al. The more I dug into this collection of information, it became apparent there were lots of great things in this over-stuffed "Cabinet" that would help other coaches in all sports with their teams to help win games.

The result is this anthology from many sources and professions; all meant to help persons in leadership positions, as well as athletes, and others move forward in the realization of goals.

Although this book comes at coaching from a basketball perspective, in reality it is a human interest read including wisdom from many sports related people: 1. Pre - postgame speeches. 2. Speaking engagement "Ice breakers." 3. Coaching stories to inspire players and coaches. 4. "Winning and Losing" in the coaches own words. 5. Getting to "YES" in the recruiting game. 6. A "Playbook" of learning techniques used by successful coaches. 7. Team and player motivational ideas. 8. Statistical tools to measure team efficiency. 9. The invaluable "Grinder" mentality and more...

CONT. PG 5

This is a unique look into the "File Cabinet" of a nearly 60-year coaching journey. The pages of this book were collected and filed through the decades for one purpose, "to find a better way." A better way to: teach, communicate, motivate, understand, and develop a culture of grit /pride and in the process earn the right to pursue success. It is believed that by studying the wisdom of coaches and successful people in and out of the sports world, it will inspire the reader to be an inspiration to others to become more than they believed possible.

It's all "In the File Cabinet."

Etc.: THINGS THAT DON'T LAST

1. *Dogs that chase cars.*
2. *Re-capped tires.*
3. *Teams that can't make free throws*
Benny Dees, former Hd. Coach, U of New Orleans,
U of Wyoming

*** Many years ago, recapping tires was a failed attempt to slap new rubber on worn out tires to get more miles from worn out tires.

IN MEMORY

JIMMY TUBBS – BASKETBALL COACH

1949 - 2009

Jimmy Tubbs coached the Kimball Knights High School basketball team to an eight year 232-42 won-loss record and a Texas Class 5A state championship. Coach Tubbs was named Texas High School Coach of the Year. An 88%-win total is what the mountain top of success in the athletic arena looks like.

Jimmy coached at SMU for 12 years.

But the real Jimmy Tubbs story goes way beyond being a championship basketball coach; it was his humility, loyalty, work ethic, friendship and winning personality that was the essence of who he was and how he lived his life.

We may have come from different world experiences, but the time shared on the Southern Methodist University coaching staff was the best of times. Jimmy was a great friend; I think of him often like everyone who knew him. Coach Tubbs, always missed, and forever remembered.

CONTENTS

Etc.: Success comes from stepping beyond what
you think you can do, it takes
courage to sacrifice comfort.

"THEY SAY ENTHUSIAM IS WASTED ON THE YOUNG AND EXPERIENCE IS WASTED ON THE OLD

BUT _IF_ YOU CAN MAINTAIN YOUR ENTHUSIASM

AND NOT GET WEARY
YOU CAN BENEFIT FROM BOTH"

TERRY VENABLES – ENGLISH FOOTBALL

The above by Terry Venables was discovered in a Jeddah, Saudi Arabia bookstore while Coaching the Kingdom of Saudi Arabia National Team. Circa 2001

This is a truism coaches eventually must confront; Terry Venable's verse perhaps explains why many coaches continued to coach well into their 70's, like Leonard Hamilton, Fla. St.; Mike Krzyzewski, Duke; Jim Boeheim, Syracuse; and Bob McDonald, Chisholm HS (MN) who coached for 59 years and others who coached long after many of their contemporaries moved on to other things for many reasons.

SECTION I

"THE BANQUET CIRCUIT"

A FEW "ICE BREAKERS"

FOR

YOUR NEXT SPEAKING REQUEST

LOU HOLTZ

FORMER NOTRE DAME FOOTBALL COACH
CLOSING REMARKS TO GRADUATING CLASS AT
FRANCISCAN COLLEGE

Want to be happy for an hour? **Have a steak.**

Want to be happy for a day? **Play a round of golf.**

Want to be happy for a week? **Go on a cruise.**
(For me a cruise is like going to jail only you have a
Chance to drown.)

Want to be happy for a month?   **Buy a car.**

Want to be happy for a year? **Win the lottery**

Want to be happy for a lifetime? **Put your faith in
Jesus Christ.**

Etc.: "THINGS I HAVE NEVER BEEN ABLE TO UNDERSTAND?"
How can a team be full of chatter and conversation prior to practice beginning and then once
practice starts the whole team goes "stone cold silent" and that silence allows an unsuspecting
teammate to get knocked "silly" on a screen because not one word was uttered to alert the
teammate? AND how is it possible for a player/team to know every word of every "rap" tune on the
planet and YET is unable to remember the yesterday's new play.

THE LIGHTER SIDE

- ✓ Our leading scorer had 2 points at halftime and then scored 22 in the second half – I told her she needed to work on her first half scoring.
- ✓ We have great outside shooters – too bad we play all our games indoors.
- ✓ We can't win at home, we can't win on the road, I have no idea where to schedule the games.
- ✓ Left hand – right hand it doesn't make any difference, I'm amphibious.
- ✓ Coaches always say nobody is perfect and then they say practice makes perfect – I wish they would make up their mind.
- ✓ The secret is to have eight great players and the rest cheering like crazy.
- ✓ The person who complains how the ball bounces is most likely the one who dropped it.
- ✓ A hypocrite is a guy who complains about sex, nudity, and violence on his DVR.
- ✓ The danger of forgiving people is that you do not have anyone to blame.
- ✓ I can keep a secret; the problem is telling it to people who can't.
- ✓ Be careful in this business, if you stop working, you can go from hero to zero in a heartbeat.
- ✓ At the first team meeting, I asked the team for a 100% commitment, they countered with a 50% offer AND no weekends.
- ✓ Where I grew up, preventative medicine was directly related to how fast I could run.
- ✓ I got two letters during my college career: one telling me I was being cut and a second telling me to turn in my equipment.
- ✓ As coaches we've all had them: a turd, brown and tapered on both ends.
- ✓ I once had a player who claimed that his trust issues were a result of raison cookies that look like chocolate chip cookies.
- ✓ We were on a road trip; the team attended a Baptist Church on Sunday. In true Baptist exuberance the preacher came down out of the pulpit and with godly authority demanded of one of our players, "Young man are you a sinner." The player uneasily before replying, "No sir I'm a guard.

THE WIT OF JIM VALVANO

- At N.C. State, in basketball, I coach all the positions – in football they have all these specialists. I couldn't believe they even had a coach for "down" offensive and defensive linemen. He works with them when they are feeling "sad or unhappy."

- The football team gets slammed 36 – 0. Coach meets the press and says he must see the film before he can answer any questions. When I get beat by 36 points, I don't need a film to know that we just got our butts kicked.

- I flew into Las Vegas to speak at a clinic, a lady of the night comes up and says, "I'll do anything for $200. I said, "Paint my house."

SO YOU WANT TO BE A . . .

TRUCK DRIVER – It takes 120 hours to be licensed.

"NAIL" TECHNICIAN - It takes 600 hours to be licensed.

BEAUTICIAN – It takes 1500 hours to be licensed.

MECHANIC – It takes 2 years to be licensed

MEDICAL DOCTOR - It takes 12 years to be certified.

COACH - It takes one three semester course or less to coach. . . Go Figure?

MIKE LEACH, MISSISSIPPI STATE U. COACH

DATING TIPS

You want someplace casual on the 1st date. I recommend Colton's Steak House. Its casual and there is very little salad, and the girl will be forced to eat in front of you, which is something women hate, but if you can get them do it, the earlier the better – the more they'll conversate and the more they'll show their true self.

I am a big movie guy, if you want to do a movie like I did when I was your age you can go to the Bijou Theatre. The movie theatre is pretty good, but you want to end it in some cool coffee shop type of place. Where there are bizarre looking characters going in and out, so if conversation isn't going too well you can reference some of the different characters coming and going into the place.

If it is a huge night and you are really having a good time, you can trade computer schemes, twitter accounts, emails and all that mischief people are up to these days, which I know nothing about.

NEVER TRUST . . .

- a guy who wears sunglasses in a dimly lit room.
- a guy who wears his "T-shirt tucked into his boxer shorts and the boxers are showing above his trousers waistband.
- a guy who's after shave reaches you before he does.
- a guy who claims loudly so those nearby can hear that he is a world traveling entrepreneur flying back from a six-month assignment in Rome and Paris, has thick foreign accent and is in the middle seat of the last row on the plane.

THE POWER OF POSITIVE THINKING

It's baseball season, and a young person is alone at the ballpark, with their trusty ball, bat, and glove.

With the ball in one hand and bat in the other, he tosses the ball into the air and takes a haymaker of a swing that would make a big leaguer take notice – but misses.

Unfazed, the lad tosses the ball again takes another monster swing and misses.

For a third time, he tosses the ball and takes another lusty swing and again whiffs mightily.

The young ball player looks around at the empty ball field, hesitates momentarily and then confidently declares, <u>"WOW, I DIDN'T KNOW I WAS SUCH A GOOD PITCHER."</u>

.

Etc.: "Be what you <u>is</u> because if you be what you <u>ain't</u>, is what you i<u>s</u>."
Kids can spot a phony or con man a mile away.

PAT CROCE

AUTHOR AND FORMER GM 76ERS

"HAVE YOU EVER SAID TO YOURSELF. . ."

- "I <u>should</u> have said studied last night . . ."
- "I <u>should</u> have worked out today . . ."
- "I <u>should</u> have told mom I was sorry . . ."
- "I <u>should</u> have thanked dad for fixing my car . . ."
- "I <u>should</u> have apologized for not calling . . ."

If you "SHOULD" or you "SHOULD HAVE," I am telling you TODAY, "DO IT" AND "DO IT NOW."

- Don't smell like <u>"SHOULD. "</u>
- <u>"SHOULD STINKS."</u>
- <u>KICK the</u> <u>"SHOULD"</u> out of yourself.
- And we all know that <u>"SHOULD"</u> happens – but do not let it happen to you.
- I am telling you, <u>SEIZE THE DAY</u>, "CARPE DIEM" even when the day is trying to seize you.

Etc.: "Take that "Cool" out of your game. "Cool" ends up freezing.
"Cool" has nothing to do with winning.

SECTION II

MOTIVATION:
TO PROVIDE AN
INCENTIVE TO
ACTION

American Heritage Dictionary

"I FAILED"
MICHAEL JORDAN #23
CHICAGO BULLS

. . . 9000 TIMES BY MISSING SHOTS.

. . . BY LOSING 300 GAMES.

. . . 25 TIMES TO MAKE THE GAMES WINNING SHOT.

. . . I FAILED OVER AND OVER AND OVER AGAIN.

. . . AND I THINK THAT MAYBE THAT IS REASON I SUCCEEDED.

Etc.: Success is having a chance to win every game.
It is my job, as the coach is to give the players a chance to win
and have their character and their drive to win determine the outcome.
Pete Carril, Princeton University

PEPPER RODGERS

TALKS "PERSEVERANCE"

Listen and take action

Pepper Rodgers was a Georgia Tech quarterback and placekicker and led the Yellowjackets to an undefeated season in 1952 winning the Sugar Bowl and was named the game's Most Valuable Player. He was the Head Coach at Kansas, UCLA and Georgia Tech. Later Rodgers coached in the professional ranks in the USFL. <u>*He made many speeches and one thing he always talk about was winning and being successful is to simply persevere, get started, don't quit, never give in.*</u>

"I say the reason I'm standing before you is because when I was the 3rd string quarterback at Georgia Tech, <u>I DIDN'T QUIT</u>. When I was a 2nd string quarterback as a junior, <u>I DIDN'T QUIT</u>. And when I was a senior, I got injured and <u>I COULD HAVE QUIT.</u> I persevered and ended my career quarterbacking an undefeated Georgia Tech team and was named MVP of the 1953 Sugar Bowl. So, everybody thought I was a great player, but I wasn't. **But I was great at not quitting.**

> *Etc.: "How dull it is to pause, to make an end*
> *To rust unburnished, not to shine in use!*
> *As though to breathe were life!"*
> *By Alfred Tennyson, on retirement*
> *Walter Cronkite CBS, news anchor retired at age 65. He later said,*
> *"I made a serious mistake. I've missed every minute.*
> *And then he added, "Keep going!"*

THIS IS A TRUE STORY:
THE AMAZING RAMS OF 2007-2008

The Colorado State University 2007-08 women's basketball team with a mostly "New" team began the season with great enthusiasm and anticipation. The season began with four consecutive losses before a welcome 59-53 win over Navy. Eleven days later the Lady Rams won their second game with a nicely played 84-77 victory over the University of Pacific.

The next Ram victory would come 97 days later.

During these 97 days the Lady Rams lost 20 consecutive games by an average of nearly 15 points per game: hitting a season low point v. Utah scoring a meager 28 points on their way to a 40-point loss. Utah's overall record would be 27-3 (with Mountain West Conference with a 16-0 record. CSU would do the same, unfortunately in reverse going 0-16 finishing dead last in the league and ending the regular season with a 2-27 won-lost record. Under this dismal backdrop of a "lost season," The Colorado State Rams checked into the Las Vegas South Pointe Hotel pondering if there was a need to unpack their bags.

CSU was to play Nevada-Las Vegas in the appropriately named "Pig Tail" game for the right to get into the post season MWC tournament. UNLV had already defeated CSU twice during the season.

IT'S 2:00 PM MST, GAME TIME, **UNLV V CSU** – UNLV FAILS TO MENTALLY ARRIVE AT TIPOFF TIME. THE RUNNIN REBELS NEVER RECOVER AND THE CSU RAMS CRUISED TO A SURPRISING 69-48 SCORE, WINNING THEIR THIRD GAME OF THE SEASON.

NEXT UP – MWC QUARTERFINAL #11 NATIONALLY RANKED UTAH (27-3) V. CSU - NOW 3-27. This game was widely advertised as a non-event turned out to be a GAME FOR THE AGES – CSU stayed in the game early avoiding intimidation and the very real "Blow out" possibility. And in the process the Rams realized not only could they take a "punch" but also "dish out" a few and fight on. CONT.PG 24

In the second half and down the stretch, the nation's #11 team uncharacteristically abandoned their training – quick shots, bad shots, weak rebounding effort, missed key free throws and frantic defensive play. Conversely, the Rams continued their gritty and determined play, staying dialed in playing moment to moment on both ends. Colorado State completely out classed Utah in the final minutes that produced little drama and the Rams won their 4th game of the season and 2nd in two days after going 97 consecutive days without experiencing the thrill of any win. FINAL SCORE 60-52 COLORADO STATE.

The Lady Rams lost to a fine New Mexico team in the semi-finals - season over.

WHAT COULD HAVE CAUSED THIS RENAISSANCE? WHY DID THIS HAPPEN? WAS THERE A REASON? 1. Maybe Utah took the Rams too lightly and then it was too late. 2. Maybe it was the Ram players who refused to submit to "Facts on the ground" and just kept pounding the rock for 97 days – it finally broke. 3. Maybe it was Coach Warden who kept enough of a positive "vibe" around the program regardless of the "scoreboard." 4. Maybe as a group in this moment the Rams, rose to the level of their season long training & team character to do something very special. 5. Serendipity, perhaps. 6. Maybe it was "All of the Above."

Coaching points: Give players deliberate, Knowledgeable instruction and then work hard to motivate a replication of this training in game competition.

SIDE STORY – There was an off-day between the Utah win and the New Mexico semifinal. CSU practiced in the Cox Center that is attached to the Thomas & Mack Arena. After practice, in order to get to the team bus the players had to walk through the Thomas & Mack Arena where a men's tournament game was being played. As the Lady Rams filed down the steps to the arena floor and walked to the bus exit – the fans during live play of the men's game gave the 4-27 Rams a nice ovation, a sign of earned respect.

GOLF ANYONE

<u>A GOLF BALLS LESSON</u>

At one time in the history, the golf balls were not nearly as dimpled as they are now. The golf ball was much smoother than in today's modern game. It was discovered that once the smoothness of the ball became dented and roughed up from being hit many times – it actually went farther. <u>It had greater distance.</u>

Going through life is like a golf ball being banged around and getting dented up. As we think of the dents we deal with in our life as bad things – but it is just another way nature is redesigning us so we can go farther.

Coaches who are into motivational "Wrist bands" consider giving the players a dimpled wristband, with the saying, "Designed to go farther."

Etc. The Green Bay Packers Team Motto the year after winning Super Bowl XVL

"THE TITLE IS THE ENEMY."

"COACH. . ."

CAN YOU TEACH YOUR TEAM TO BELIEVE IN THE FOLLOWING? IF YOU CAN, IT WILL HELP YOU TO BECOME THE COACH YOU ASPIRE TO BE AND YOUR PLAYERS TO BECOME EVERYTHING THEY HOPED FOR WHEN THEY JOINED YOU AND THE TEAM. HOW? <u>1. WITH DELIBERATE PRACTICE THAT INCLUDES DAILY AFFIRMATIONS/REMINDERS. 2. IMMEDIATE CORRECTING OF BEHAVIOR THAT FALLS BELOW EXPECTATIONS. 3. CATCHING AND RECOGNIZING BEHAVIOR THAT IS ABOVE EXPECTATIONS. "GOOD JOB" THAT'S WHAT WE MEAN BY BEING "TOUGHER LONGER."</u>

- Be where your feet are.

- Under pressure, you do not rise to the occasion, you sink to the level of your training!

- When things get tough out there run to your teammates-not away from them. You are always better together.

- Be the one who never has a bad day and if you do – make sure no one will ever know it.

- Be Tougher Longer.

- Don't do it until you do it right Do it until you cannot do it wrong.

- Winning requires many things. Losing requires doing nothing.

- If you <u>can't</u> believe in yourself Believe in me because. I believe in you, it's my job and I love it.

THE GREAT DEAN SMITH
UNIVERSITY OF NORTH CAROLINA
HALL OF FAME COACH

In 1979, as a younger assistant coach at the University of Minnesota, my first recruiting assignment for Head Coach Jim Dutcher was to attend Howard Garfinkel's Famous FIVE STAR Basketball Camp in the Pocono's in Honesdale, PA. In those days, all the top college high school prospects would "eat glass" to get invited to "Five Star." Hubie Brown, the great NBA coach was a guest lecturer and made a presentation to the campers using a 6'10" high school freshman named Patrick Ewing as a demonstrator. Who was Patrick Ewing? I had no clue. In 1979 no one knew about Patrick Ewing . NIKE's EYBL is the closest equivalent in today's youth basketball industry. During " FIVE STAR," I had lunch with two of Coach Smith's assistants, Roy Williams and Eddie Fogler: I did not know them, but it was a small restaurant in a small town invaded by coaches from virtually every Major conference in the country. Eventually, it seemed like everyone got to know each other.

My Dean Smith takeaway from that casual lunch a long time ago with two Tarheel assistants was: 1. How easy, and comfortable "Coach speak" flowed between unknowns'. Since "FIVE STAR," Coach Williams has had a welcoming greeting whenever our paths have crossed. 2. And more important, during casual conversation there was something special in the way they talked about Coach Smith and his coaching style and everyday way of living. It was in larger-than-life terms, almost biblical in nature – difficult to adequately explain but still memorable 40 years later.

THE CAROLINA WAY

PLAY TOGETHER: <u>The whole is greater than the sum of the parts. This synergy creates camaraderie and team cohesion.</u>

1. Basketball is a game dependent on togetherness.
2. <u>Seldom if ever does the nation's leading scorer on a ranked team win a championship</u>.
3. Help each other to become a better player. CONT PG 28

PLAY HARD: <u>That means "compete." Competing is the highest level of play.</u>
1. You control your own effort, never be outworked.
2. We immediately penalize effort that is lacking.
3. No team should ever compete or play harder than the Tarheels.

PLAY SMART: <u>To win consistently, proper execution of the fundamentals must be demanded every day.</u>
1. Attention to the "smallest detail."
2. "Think the game," know what to do, when and how to do it.
3. Repetition – 1000 X 1000 times to get it right.

Etc.: Failure is not a destination.

SOMETIMES IN LIFE. . .

Sometimes in life you are not rewarded for your hard work, dedication, and sacrifices in the pursuit of a worthy goal, and it is hard to escape the "The why me" or "why us" regarding those life events.

But life is "Motion" not all good or bad, but simply "motion" and what is important is that you do not allow the lack of "motion" in life grind you to a standstill.

Nurse and rehearse your unrewarded efforts "flush" them and get back in "motion"– because the opposite leads to despair and quitting. Life requires the opposite – "motion" and what's NEXT is what counts.

Finally, success delayed is different than success denied.

The inspiration for this piece was a newspaper article about Mario Cuomo, Gov. of NY (the father of the former NY Governor and TV Cuomo.) Mr. Cuomo was known for his "Noon Hour" basketball playing well into his 50's.

EVERY MORNING . . .

Every morning in Africa. . . the gazelle wakes up – he knows that he must outrun the fastest lion.

Every morning in Africa . . . the lion wakes up knowing he must run faster than the slowest gazelle or he will starve.

It does not matter whether you are a gazelle or a lion – when you awake in the morning you better be on the move.

THE ALABAMA BEAR BRYANT

"HERE'S HOW YOU CAN WIN."

This is the legendary Head Football Coach Bear Bryant's address to the incoming freshmen at their first team meeting; prior to fall camp beginning.

Here's how you can win. Little things and a little bit extra, you'll hear a lot about a "little bit extra" as long as you are at the University of Alabama.

Let's suppose for the sake of discussion that the most ability that a player can have is a 100 and here you are with a 75 ability and over there is a guy with an 85 ability and now you are going to play against this guy on Saturday. Now it takes everybody, but now we're just talking about you as an individual.

Now on game day, based on the fact that you have paid the price, you have learned the lessons about working on the little things and you are willing to give a little bit over your head and we expect you to – you play at an 85 level on game day.

Now here you are an 85 on this day. The guy you are playing against is an 85. Now this could happen, it doesn't always happen – but maybe (your opponent) hasn't paid the price, maybe he hasn't learned these lessons. He is not as dedicated as you are and he doesn't play as well as he is supposed to and falls off to let's say a 75. Then you, because of your preparation you can beat the other guy and we do these 11 men at a time."

"IN FOUR YEARS FROM NOW, YOU'RE GOING TO WALK OUT OF HERE AS NATIONAL CHAMPIONS – AND I WILL EXPECT NOTHING LESS."

"BACK IN THE OLD DAYS WHEN I WAS TRYING TO FIGHT FOR MY LIFE AND WIN. ALL I EVER THOUGHT ABOUT WAS HOW TO WIN GAMES." COACH BRYANT

THE ANT PHILOSOPHY

Jim Rohn

"Over the years, I have been teaching kids about a simple but powerful concept---the ant philosophy. I think everybody should study ants. Ants they have an amazing four-part philosophy and here is the **1st**: <u>ants never quit.</u> That's a good philosophy. If they're headed somewhere try to stop them, they look for another way. They'll climb over, they'll climb under, they'll climb around. <u>What a neat philosophy, to never quit looking for a way to get where you're supposed to go.</u>

2nd <u>Ants think winter all summer.</u> That's an important perspective. You can't be so naïve to think that summer will last forever. So, ants are gathering their food in the middle of the summer. An ancient story says, "Don't build your house on the sand in the summer. Why do we need that advice? Because it is important to be realistic. In the summer, you've got to think storm. You've got to think of rocks as you enjoy the sand and sun. <u>Think ahead.</u>

3rd <u>The ants think summer all winter.</u> That is so important. During the winter ants remind themselves, "This won't last long and soon will be out of here" – <u>they have a positive attitude.</u> And the 1st warm day the ants are out. If it turns cold again, they'll dive right back down again, but they come out on the next warm day. They can't wait to get out.

4th <u>How much will the ants gather during the summer to prepare for the winter?</u> <u>All they possibly can.</u> What an incredible philosophy – the **ALL – YOU – CAN PHILOSOPHY.** The ant attack – **Never give up** – **Look ahead** – **Stay Positive** – And **Do all you can.**

Etc. "Shot fakes take away the athleticism of the defender.

PAT DYE, HEAD COACH
AUBURN UNIVERSITY
"IN VICTORY AND DEFEAT"

Pat Dye coached Auburn University from 1981 – 1992 building the program into a power in the Southeastern Conference (SEC.) He won 71% of his games at Auburn. Coach Dye passed away in 2020.

(In Victory) Pat Dye in his own words

"Tonight, is what our goal was all about. I want you to think about it and let it sink in real deep. This is why you work in the summertime and in January, February and in the Spring. This is the reason we push you beyond what you think you can do to experience moments like this. Ain't no easy way in life. It wasn't easy out there tonight, but you were prepared for the test.

To every one of you players, I ain't smart enough to put into words to tell you how I feel about you – it's family every one of you know it. Sure, I'd like to be 11-0 but I am goin to tell you something, I wouldn't swap this year for any year that I have been at Auburn because I have watched you struggle, and I've watched you grow and become men.

You remember me standing in front of you and telling you that when you become ONE, you'd know it and you know it now – It don't make any difference who is carrying the ball' don't make any difference who's catching it; who's rushing the passer; who's making the tackles as long as he has a blue jersey.

(In Loss)

"There are going to be a lot of days when you lay your guts on the line and you come away empty handed. Ain't nothing you can do about it but it lay it on the line again and again.

Life: "You are going to be in a lot of tough battles in your life, including battles with yourself and you won't have teammates with you, but If you will just look back at this Sugar Bowl victory – it'll help you down the line."

THE "ALL BLACKS" AND A BLACK BOOK

The All Blacks, New Zealand's National Rugby Team are the premiere rugby team in World Cup competition with a long history of dominance – The New York Yankees of rugby. This is about the rituals and indoctrination of new players who have been selected to join the team for the first time. It is meant to ingrain in the rookies there is much more to being an ALL BLACK than having world class talent. The ALL BLACKS are shrouded in a glorious mystical history that is on the line in every contest and it is the job of the present team to preserve and try mightily to surpass the ALL BLACK history of dominance.

When a player makes the All-Blacks roster, they receive a book. It is a small black book bound in fine leather and beautiful to hold.

The first page shows a jersey of the 1905 ORIGINALS, the creation date of the All Blacks. That team began the long "Whakapapa," (a Māori term for traditions, culture, mores.) On the next page is another jersey, that of the 1924 INVINCIBLES (The team slogan) and on the page after, another jersey and so on until the present day.

It is a visual "Whakapapa" layered with meaning, a legacy to step into and preserve the All-Blacks tradition, its "Whakapapa."

The next pages of this All-Black Handbook remind the new players of the principles, the heroes, the values, the standards, the code of honor, the ethos, the character of the team.

The rest of the pages are blank, waiting to be filled. It's time to make <u>your</u> own mark. <u>Your</u> own contribution, it's time to leave a legacy, <u>your</u> legacy is to leave the 'jersey' in a better place. It's <u>your</u> time.

Etc. By studying the All Blacks "black book" philosophy and with a strong dose of imagination and creativity; coaches can develop their own "Black Book" for their program with pictures, of uniforms, teams, players, facilities, mission type statements, etc., etc. And if you don't have an All-Black legacy to work with, better yet you can start your own "Whakapapa" and take it in any direction you want.

SECTION III

COACHES AS STORY TELLERS

COACHES NEED TO USE A VARIETY OF

METHODS AND MEDIUMS

TO "REACH" THE TEAM, STORIES HELP.

GOOD STORY TELLING ALLOWS

THE COACH TO COME AT THE

PLAYERS/TEAM FROM ANOTHER ANGLE. IT'S

A LONG SEASON – KEEPING THE TROOPS

ALERT AND ENGAGED IS CRUCIAL.

COACHES SHOULD PRACTICE STYLE, DELIVERY

AND EVEN INCLUDE A LITTLE THEATRICS

IN THEIR STORY TELLING.

WINNING COMES IN MANY SIZES, SHAPES AND FLAVORS,

INCLUDING WELL TOLD STORIES.

"WHEN IT'S TOO TOUGH . . . "
MARV LEVY, BUFFALO BILLS (NFL)

It was an extremely hot day, and we had a terrible practice. The team could not wait to get off the field. I was very angry that they didn't come back fighting better than they did in the heat.

I called a meeting and told the team a story that was told to me by my father who had been a Marine in WW1. He fought in the Battle of Belleau Wood (France.) The Marines were exhausted with little food and rest for several days. In addressing the troops, the Marine Commander said, "We are going to attack." The troops were unbelieving. The Commander looked them straight in the eye and said, "WHEN IT IS TOO TOUGH FOR THEM, IT'S JUST RIGHT FOR US!"

So, I relayed that story to the players. I said, "Tomorrow it is going to be hot and you're going to be tired, and I am going to be tired, but at least I am going to give it all that I have and if you don't, I'll know when it is too tough for you, it's just right for me."

"TENNIS ANYONE"
THE MIND OF A CHAMPION
"(ROGER) FEDERER MAY WIN"

BUT

"I WILL NEVER BE DEFEATED."

Rafael Nadel

"AUSTRALIAN SHEEP DOGS"

COACH WESTERHOFF NY JETS SPECIAL TEAMS COACH AT PRE-SEASON TRAINING CAMP COACHING "UP" HIS POSITION PLAYERS

An American writer went over to Australia to do a story on the Australian Outback. He went to a farm in the Outback and asked the rancher what was his most important tool? The rancher said, "The Dog – the sheep dog." OK, where do you get them? We go to the breeder and pick the smallest one of the litter – the "runt." We "mark" him and we come back in a couple of months. If he is still alive that's the one we want.

He started out, not at the top of the heap but we know he had to be one of the toughest, he had to be a hard worker and have moxie to figure it out in order to survive.

Now the most interesting to me is that the rancher brought this "runt" back and put him with all the other dogs. The rancher gave the "runt" ONE DAY to see how he does with all other dogs. If he doesn't make it, by that I mean he gets bullied by the other dogs and ends up cowering in the corner of the pen or worse; the rancher destroys him, kills the dog. They drown the dog. (Following is said in jest-but part of the message to the players) *"Now we are not going to put any of you guys in a sack and throw you in Annies Whirlpool, although it has been discussed."*

Coach Westerhoff, hesitates for a moment, scanning the room getting every players full attention (many of the special team guys are undrafted rookies just trying to earn a roster spot); and spoke, "Some guys are recruited by every school in the country and that is fine, but you tell me what is the difference between a top recruited player and a guy who starts out on the bottom of the heap and makes it because he has the qualities of toughness, hard worker, has a great attitude and figures out what needs to be done to get to the top and he wants to make it and be a PRO."

"INCHES"

This is a rewrite of a transcript from the Al Pacino movie "Any Given Sunday."
A nice read, coaches using this plus some theatrics will be remembered at "game time" and at the team reunion 10 years later.

Inch by inch, possession by possession, we play until we finish. To win, know your job. It is always about "the Team," "The Team," "The Team."

In the end it will come down to all the little things that happen in high level competition. "Inches, half seconds, those teeny, weeny, little things" that even the trained eye will miss:

- A cut that was not a half second to soon or a half second too late.
- A pass on target and on time – not an "inch" too high or half second too late or too soon.
- A "help" defensive position that is six inches to the right or left stops the offensive players drive to the basket.
- A pass that is made instead of a shot taken.
- A shot taken instead of a pass made.
- A hustle play that saves an "inch" allowing for a basket.
- A solid screen set at the precise time and correct angle.
- A half second too fast or an "inch" too high or too low and the play breaks down.
- A pass an inch too far right or left and the play "blows up."
- A perfect pass not too high, low, right, or left allowing for what looks like an easy full speed layup, that only a professional eye can recognize the degree difficulty.
- A solid block out that allows a teammate an open lane to get a rebound.

The inches and half seconds we need are everywhere around us and we need to fight for all those inches and seconds. And when we add them up at the end of the game that is what is going to be the difference in between winning and losing. And those willing to fight for every second and every inch one at a time won't beat themselves.

SISU AND 1980

The Miracle on Ice, Feb 22, 1980 "a remember where you were moment" in the history of American sport.

"Great moments are born from great opportunity, and that's what you have here tonight, boys. That's what you have earned here tonight. One game, if we played them ten times, we might win one. But not this game, not tonight. Tonight, we skate with them. Tonight, we shut them down because we can. Tonight, we are the greatest hockey team in the world."

In Finland, there is a phrase – dating back hundreds of years which refers to extraordinary determination, courage, and resoluteness in the face of extreme adversity. It's called **SISU**. In other countries, since there is not a translation of the word, **SISU** might be referred to as "having grit." And the 1980 US Olympic Hockey Team was full of "GRIT."

Head Coach Herb Brooks knew it would take a complete team filled with passion and grit to defeat the far superior USSR team. Two weeks prior to the Olympic Semi-Final game with the Soviets; in front of a sold-out Madison Square Garden, the Americans were soundly beaten 13-1 by the Russians. **After that humbling ass beating Brooks went to work. His practices emphasized communication, toughness, conditioning and playing unselfishly. Brooks was willing to forgo natural talent for hard work and grit. He knew that no matter how much talent his team possessed they would never be as talented as the Russians. Brooks knew the Gold Medal was not obtainable <u>only</u> with talent, he needed a fresh approach, a different path. Therefore, Brook's devised a new way to compete and give himself an advantage over the mighty Russians. <u>He thought divergently, not creatively.</u>**

Most coaches/leaders during a problematic situation, facing a challenging opponent believe they must put on their creative hat and find the solution when CONT PG 40 in reality the situation calls for a divergent hat. Being creative means: relating to or involving the imagination or original idea, especially in the production of artistic work. Being divergent means: tending to be different or develop in different directions. The difference?

Divergent thinkers take a fresh approach to an old idea. Meanwhile, the creative thinkers imagine a new way. Let's face it in most sports there are no new ways. In chess, the pieces have moved in the same direction for centuries, yet chess masters find divergent ways to play.

Stop thinking you must be creative to discover a new path. Examine your teaching and leadership methods and find a divergent way to do it better. Just like Herb Brooks did.

*Note: Remember where you were when "**IT**" happened? Or maybe you weren't with us yet? The collector of this book was at a hotel sports bar in San Antonio TX with two fellow assistants from TCU and SMU. We were recruiting and had just finished attended a high school game and happened to be lucky enough to witness history. (Truth is – we didn't even know there was a hockey game being played.)*

Etc. ***The Nature of Being a Coach***

"Coaching by nature is a confrontational experience between athlete and coach. As a coach, you are trying to take a player to places they have not been before or do not necessarily want to go or may fear the process".
COACHING:
"IT'S CHANGING BEHAVIOR,
THIS IS THE CHALLENGE."
Stew Morrill, an excellent coach,
Utah State University
Winner of 620 games.

THE "DEVIL" AND DISCOURAGEMENT

COACH WESTERHOFF, SPECIAL TEAMS COACH, NY JETS.

This is a great approach (story) to developing and fostering encouragement by defining the effects of discouragement when things get tough.

The Devil was having a going out of business sale. He was moving his workshop from old town South to the Harmony Ave area. A guy comes in and asks what the Devil was selling. "I am selling everything that's ever worked for me. All my tools are for sale." The guy then asks, "What's your best seller." The Devil looks at the guy and says, "**DISCOURAGEMENT**, because as soon as people get Discouraged everything else goes down the drain and all my other weapons work to defeat them."

- When you get **DISCOURAGED**, you look around and say, "Aw geez, I don't know if I want to do this?"

- When you are **DISCOURAGED**, you don't focus on your job.

- When you are **DISCOURAGED**, you don't study as hard.

- When you are **DISCOURAGED**, you don't practice as hard.

- When you are **DISCOURAGED**, you don't run as hard.

- And the list continues and on . . .

"GO AHEAD AND GET A LITTLE "DISCOURAGED" AND YOU WILL NEVER, EVER BE ANYWHERE NEAR ALL YOU CAN BE OR WHAT YOU WANTED TO BE. IN FACT, YOU MAY NOT BE AROUND HERE MUCH LONGER."

KOBE BRYANT

From the Las Vegas Review Journal

This "read" displays Kobe's unequaled and legendary work ethic. It takes a look into Kobe's competitive mind providing a snapshot on what it takes to be one of the best ever. It isn't so much the time because <u>TIME MEANT nothing to Kobe. It was all about purpose, the intensity of his practice was meant to satisfy his personal needs. That was nothing new or unique for Kobe, he was known throughout his career for being extremely dedicated to getting himself Ready.</u>

I was invited to Las Vegas to help **TEAM USA** with their conditioning. I had worked with **Duane Wade** and **Carmello Anthony** in the past. But this would be my first interaction with **Kobe**.

The night before the 1st scrimmage, I had just watched the movie "Casablanca" for the first time and it was about 3:30 AM. A few minutes later, I was in bed slowly fading away when I heard my cell ring. It was Kobe. I nervously picked up. Kobe says, "Hey Rob, I hope I am not disturbing anything, right." I say, "No, what's up Kob?" He said, "Just wondering if you could help me out with some conditioning work." I looked at my watch, it was 4:15 AM, "Ya, sure I'll see you in a bit."

It took me about 20 minutes to get my gear and get out of the hotel. When I arrived at the main practice floor, I saw Kobe alone, he was drenched in sweat as if he had just taken a swim – it wasn't even 5 AM.

We did some conditioning work for the next hour and 15 minutes. Then we entered the weight room, and he did a multitude of strength training exercises for the next 45 minutes. After that we parted ways. He went back on the floor, and I went back to the hotel and crashed. Wow, I was expected back on the floor at 11:00 AM. I woke up feeling sleepy, drowsy, and having pretty much every side effect of sleep deprivation – thanks to Kobe. I had a bagel and headed to the practice facility. SEE PAGE 43

The next part, I remember very vividly – all the **"Team USA"** players were there, **LeBron** was talking to **Carmello Anthony**; **Coach "K"** was explaining something to **Kevin Durant.** On the right side of the practice facility, **Kobe** was by himself shooting jumpers. I went over to him – patted him on the back and said, "Good work this morning." He looked at me and said "Eh, I repeated, "The conditioning work." "Oh, ya thanks," Kobe said, "I really appreciated it."

"So, when did you finish," I said, "Finish what?" Kobe said, I responded, "Getting your shots up – what time did you leave the facility?" **Kobe** said, "Oh just now, I wanted 800 makes, so, ya just finished."

If you are keeping score that is about 6 ½ hours of work <u>before</u> practice.

Etc. Along with Kobe, Magic Johnson had a tremendous work ethic, both knew the difference between working hard and being a competitor. In the end, it is the competitor who surpasses the opponent who thinks they are simply working hard.

"MIRACLE ON THE HUDSON"
FLIGHT 1549 OUT OF LAGUARDIA (NYC) – FEB. 2009
CAPTAINED BY CHESNEY SULLENBERGER

The first 180 seconds of the takeoff from LaGuardia was uneventful. The next 218 seconds was "Life and Death" when the aircraft hit a flock of geese incapacitating both engines.

While LaGuardia scrambled to free a runway for an emergency landing, Capt. Sullenberger determined he could not wait for LaGuardia, he calmly announced that he would be landing on the Hudson, not the airport, the river – which he did saving all 155 lives aboard.

When asked about his thoughts during those 218 "Life and Death" seconds, he said: **"No distractions. I did not agonize about crashing and everyone getting killed or about my family. That was it. I compartmentalized my thoughts totally concentrating on executing what I had been trained to do."**

1. **"Nose up."**
2. **"Wings level."**
3. **"Stay on the glide path as much as possible."**

More Capt. Sullenberger:

1. "Be a long-term optimist and a short-term realist."
2. "Never stop investing in yourself, never stop learning."

Editor/Collectors Note: Capt. Sullenberger received intense training: "Nose up, Wings level, stay on the glide path" that served him well as he guided Flight 1549 to safety. Similarly, coaches train their athletes to perform in a laboratory that teaches performance under pressure in the athletic world. This training transfers to life experiences.

THE "BEAR"

Paul "Bear" Bryant, the legendary football coach at the University of Alabama. An Arkansas native who got nicknamed "Bear" by actually wrestling a live bear at a county fair as a teenager.

This is a speech Coach Bryant gave to his team before the Tennessee game; a big rivalry game, that the "Bear" always really wanted to win.

"Men, tomorrow we come together as a team"

"When Joe blocks – <u>We all block!</u>"

"When LC tackles – We all <u>tackle!</u>"

"When Joe runs – <u>We all run!</u>"

"Now remember this – the game is over, it's maybe 5:00. You are back in the dressing room, <u>and you pass a mirror and looking in the mirror, you realize, it is only you and the mirror that know if you did the very best that was within you.</u>"

"Now you walk out of the dressing room and into the nearly empty stadium.

<u>You see a friend,</u>

<u>Someone else you know</u>

<u>A family member</u>

<u>You get a hug</u>

<u>You reach out and touch the hand</u>

<u>of those you care about and care about you</u>

<u>The emotion is real – it's from the heart.</u>

<u>And still you and only you and the person in the mirror really knows if you did the very best that was in you.</u>"

MENTAL TOUGHNESS:
"IT'S WHAT YOU FOCUS ON."

You have a choice, focus on "Petty" thoughts, or focus on a "getting it done "mentality. Petty counter-productive thinking includes:

- "Ball has too much air."
- "Ball doesn't have enough air."
- "Floor is too slippery."
- "Gym is too hot."
- "Gym is too cold."
- "After getting fouled hard, miss both free throws – "my leg was still hurting from the foul."
- "Coach yelled at me again and it was not even my fault, why is he/she always picking on me?"
- "And the list goes on and on. . . <u>"Mentally tough "get it done type people – actually get confidence from an opponent who acts in "petty" childish whiny ways:</u>
- "Ball has too much air" – mentally tough player simply says – "It's what it is – "Game on!"
- "Ref doesn't like me" – "That's the ref's problem – "Game on!"
- "Floor is slippery" – "That's a janitor problem – "Game on!"
- "Gym is too hot." – "Good, let's see who is going to 'blink first' – "You or me."
- "Coach is yelling at me, and it was not my fault – "No big deal, we are still on the same page, we both want to win, sometimes he/she just gets a little too excited."

Bottom line, take pride in having a "Get it done" attitude. Gain confidence from your opponent's "snowflake" behavior. **"Pettiness" is a lot of things, and they all scream weakness – look for it in your opponent – guard against it in yourself.**

"MAKING THINGS EASY"

Fred Astaire, one of the greatest dancers of all time, to his partner Ginger Rogers...about long grueling practice sessions, "Ginger, my dear, we practice to make things easy."

What does this mean?

Remember the best saxophone player in the band, best math student, tennis player, golfer, basketball player, etc. Why were they the best? Maybe the answer is found in the following:

As a kid, I lived next to the "Midway Bar& Grill," a local joint, that sponsored the Sunday afternoon horseshoe pitching tournaments. The "Midway" was a busy place in our little village. It was owned by my best friend Howard's dad. I spent a lot of time at the Midway. I learned a lot of things at the Midway.

My Uncle Walt was really good at pitching horseshoes. He won a lot of money from the money collected in the "grass pot" on Sunday afternoons at the Midway. Why was Uncle Walt the best of the best at "horseshoes?" How could he MAKE IT LOOK SO EASY?

Interesting thing about Uncle Walt, nearly every night, after work he would be outside in his backyard pitching "shoes" by himself. I know because I could see his house from where I lived and hear the metal on metal "clanging." Uncle Walt pitched horseshoes night after night until after dark. The cold weather would come and forced him to spend more time inside the "Midway" shooting pool with the same dedication he had for pitching "shoes."

Looking back, I think Uncle Walter just practiced more than all the other guys in our area and because of that practice he became the best horseshoe pitcher around. . . "He practiced, to make things easy."

Etc.: "Today, I gave everything I had, what I kept I lost, forever." Players for sure, but how about us too, coaches.

47

DON'T CONFUSE DISAPPOINTMENT
WITH DISCOURAGEMENT

DISAPPOINTMENTS are daily and mostly annoying life events:

- Alarm didn't ring this morning.
- Key broke off in the lock.
- Didn't do as well as I should have on the test.
- The final test was yesterday, not today.
- Missed a "Big" free throw.

DISCOURAGEMENT is a condition that creates failure:

Remember the Devil loves discouraged people. (See Pg. 41)

MAKING A POSITIVE OUT OF **DISCOURAGEMENT:**

After a disappointing outcome, the moment of your greatest

courage will be when you simply to decide that: "Tomorrow I will do better."

The opposite is to "let" your DISAPPOINTMENTS spiral into the "Devils Delight - "DISCOURAGEMENT."

"ONE SECOND"

A lot can happen in one second.

(Note in locker of each MO S&T player the morning after the Drury game)

In ONE SECOND:

- Sound will travel at 1,226 feet.
- A car will travel 88 feet at 60 mph.
- The fastest man in the world Usain Bolt can run 24.7 feet in one second
- AND Annie Armstrong, Drury University's great guard can launch and make a three-quarter court shot with one second or less on the clock.

<u>A teachable moment:</u>

With three seconds remaining in the first half, Missouri S&T misses a field goal attempt and starts to walk/jog to the dressing room for their halftime orange slices and Gatorade- BUT Drury's Annie Armstrong realizing it "ain't over til it's over" rebounds the ball - takes two dribbles and launches and a basket seeking missile as the half ends -- with the S&T players literally looking back at the court as the horn sounded to witness the splash of the ball swishes through the basket.

This "one second" in the life of a season screams the importance of taking nothing for granted not even for "one second."

<u>The lesson is:</u>

Be careful when you wave the "white flag" and give up. It is really hard to tell if maybe on the next swing cracks the rock, or the next application gets the job, and after 1000 X 1000 repetitions it comes together and you become the player/ nurse, doctor/ teacher/business owner you think and dream of being.

Train yourself not to have enough sense to give up by remaining in the present moment or "Second." If you choose not to, basketball and life will "smack" you around like "rag doll."

49

OPTIMISM, PESSIMISM, & REALISM

The only way to prevent bad things from happening is to anticipate them. I can only be optimistic after I have studied and analyzed the worst possible outcomes.

Optimism must be tempered with realism for optimism to be tolerable and reasonable. We all know the Pollyanna claim, that "God himself could not sink this ship." Yet, the Titanic lies at the bottom of the North Atlantic. We have all met this type of annoying mindset – better to do what we can so the ship does not sink.

Be optimistic about your effort, but the outcome is never guaranteed.

"The <u>optimist</u> keeps hoping

The wind will change.

The <u>pessimist</u> curses the wind.

The <u>realist</u> adjusts the sail."

Etc.: IFITISTOBEITISUPTOME

"AN ATHLETE FACING THE FIGHT OF HIS LIFE"
MATT LONG – NYPD

A 17-year veteran of the New York Fire Dept., Matt Long tells his courageous story. Mr. Long's bicycle / bus accident physical injuries were horrific, but a greater challenge was the severe depression Mr. Long experienced in the recovery phase. The severe debilitating depression that came to a head when he was confronted by his mother. <u>This is an inspirational read.</u>

- <u>*Newscast report*</u> *– "A city firefighter riding a bike to work was hit by a private bus this morning. 39-year-old Mathew Long is in critical condition.*
- <u>*Mayer Bloomberg's TV comment*</u> *– "his condition is grave, and I ask all New Yorkers to pray for him."*
- <u>*Medical staff*</u> *– "with brutal injuries. . . he had about a 1% chance to live!"*

I ask everyone in the audience before I speak "Would you have the will to carry on?" Would you have the will to continue to fight, to want to compete again? In a race that doesn't have a clear finish line but when done it will define you as a person for the rest of your life!

For me, after the days of September 11, 2001 (the day the twin towers were attacked,) I did a real check about my life. I like to call it an inventory check. I did not like the way my life was going. I was slightly overweight; I was drinking more than I should have to depress what really happened on that day (9-11) the memory of friends and family.

I decided I needed to start setting goals for myself. I needed to take care of my body. As a fire fighter, fitness is our best tool. <u>We have a slogan at the academy,</u> <u>"Let no man's ghost come back to say his training let him down."</u> I didn't want my training to let me down. If something happened to me and it was my day to go – I didn't want it to be because of my shortcoming. Now as we grow up as children, we dream. I remember dreaming as a kid. I remember going to bed every night with a dream in my head whether it was to play college basketball; high school basketball; or date the girl around the block. CONT PG 52

As you become adults, those dreams become goals, but if you want to achieve your goals there are 3 important things you must do:

1. You have to set a plan that is going to get you there.
2. You have to commit to that plan.
3. And you will make sacrifices.

After September 11, I remember setting two goals for myself. One day I wanted to be a Boston Marathon qualifier. I wanted to run the NY Marathon. In the NYC Marathon, we have a race within the race, police department of NYC v. the firefighters. I wanted to be part of that team for the fire department. We always want to beat the Cops. They only tally the 1st five scores – the 1st five runners that cross the finish line. That was one goal I set for myself in 2004.

In 2004, I also said that if I pushed myself this hard, I wanted to compete in an Ironman. An Ironman is: 2.4-mile swim and 112-mile bike ride; and a 26.2-mile marathon, with a time of under 17 hours. 17:01 and they say better luck next year. You don't get a T-shirt; you do not get a medal; it's been a long day.

Now I am 39 years old, I was not an endurance athlete; I was a college basketball player. I ran around the streets of the "City," I ran 2 or 3 businesses – so the action was fast.

I enlisted a coach, together we devised a plan and I committed to him and that plan. I would make very workout count. Sacrifices came in the way of nightlife in the "City;" family functions, getting to bed at 9:00 on Thursday because on Friday morning I had to get up at 5 AM and ride the bike 100 miles and then run 8 miles afterwards. My family thought I was crazy, and they were right.

Because of my training I was on top of the world. I was in the best shape of my life. 39 years old and I had made the commitments and sacrifices for the two moments in my life, the Marathon and Ironman.

Five weeks later, I am struck by a 40,000 lb. bus on the streets of NYC. It took the rescue workers 20 minutes to lift the bus and remove the bicycle from my abdomen and get me to a hospital. There was not a gentleman or women at the scene that thought I would survive the night. I received more than 68 units of blood in the first 10 or 11 hours. I think at some point the nurses in the room CONT PG 53

thought they were wasting blood – and I was not going to make it. It turns out that those commitments and sacrifices I made all throughout that year
played a big role in saving my life. I spent 5 months in the hospital, lost more than 55 lbs.; had 42 different surgeries in a 14-month period.

When I talk to people about my accident, the pain I went through; the broken bones; and the torn skin is nothing compared to the mental battles with depression. Why me? Why did this happen to me? Why was I going through this? Why did I not die? Why was I meant to survive? Why was I meant to carry on and continue to try and race?

It turns out that all the training I was doing wasn't for Boston and it wasn't for the Ironman in Lake Placid. I was training for life.

As the battle with depression came so did a search for a reason, I sunk deeper and deeper into depression. It was at that moment with my parents after a doctor's visit, I said, "Mom, I am glad you prayed and your prayers were answered and I lived, but you should have prayed for me to die.

There was a moment of silence at the table as tears came out of my dad's eyes, my mom's and mine. I expected her to reach across the table and hug me – but she put her hands down on the table and said, "Enough is enough, we may not have gotten hit by that bus, but we are suffering alongside you, and you do not need to tell me to tell you that you are not the only person in this world going through a tough time.   You are not the only person suffering. Matt, you need to pick up the pieces. You need to make your life the best you can possibly make it."

Not only am I dealing with physical challenges, but mental challenges and the mental fights, and my own mother has just challenged me to get my "stuff together." CONT PG 54

Etc.: "Are we all in this together or is someone going to let go of the rope?"

I wasn't finished because I told you I was a little bit crazy. I eventually worked my way to finishing the Lake Placid Ironman. I finished 1 min. 55 sec. before I would have been disqualified. The best part is I did not finish last.

Now I no longer ask why I survived when I got hurt: instead, I embrace it. I use it to visit people who are going through what I am going through, I tell them, here I am, I am with you. I was where you are."

What got me through was not only a strong Irish Catholic mother, but the power of the human spirit an incredibly powerful tool that we all under use at some point in our lives.

Etc.: oneinarow
Any success takes one in a row
Do one thing well. then another.
Once, then once more.
Over and over until the end,
Then it's oneinarow again.

MORE KOBE BRYANT. . .

An in depth look at the incredible thought process of a world class athlete. Learn to work and think like Kobe and you will never want to go back to anything else.

Mike Krzyzewski, – "Kobe was all about the art of preparation."
Kobe shot 4 consecutive air balls in the 4th quarter of the final game and overtime v. the Utah Jazz as a rookie. Kobe, "I should have made those shots what did I do wrong? **Kobe was always asking questions**. Kobe overcame his failures by thinking tactically rather than emotionally. On Kobe's 4 airballs in the playoffs, he asked why? He concluded that his legs were tired, as a rookie he had never played that many games in one season. Kobe created his own reality and then made plans to eliminate the problem.

Kobe answers question. "Do you love to win more than you hate to lose? Kobe, "Neither, I play to learn and figure things out. Playing to win or lose is a weakness either way." The only way you can lose in Kobe's world is to STOP. If there is progress, there is no failure. You need to find a middle ground regarding winning and losing. Then it doesn't matter – this allows you to stay in the moment and not feel anything other than what's in front of you.

Kobe on the fear of failure – The fear of failure, how do you overcome it? <u>It doesn't exist – it's not there. It's a figment of your imagination.</u> Everyone wants a happy ending. Snow White has a happy ending riding off into the sunset with her man wonder. But two months later he's sleeping on the couch and the story continues. If you fail on Monday, the only way it is a failure is if you STOP and decide not to go on Tuesday. Therefore, failure is non-existent because if I fail today, I am going to learn something from that failure and I am going to try again on Tuesday. And try again on Wednesday using what I learned from Tuesday. I have goals and if I don't accomplish them, I am very disappointed – but I have to ask myself." WHY?" And then analyze and apply the solutions to what is NEXT in my life.

If you do not take the lessons and apply them to what is NEXT, that is the worst thing that can happen. **Kobe on his legacy. <u>"I want to be remembered as someone who left not one stone unturned. I tried and learned as much as possible. If people said I was a talented overachiever, I'd be OK with that."</u>**

THE GREAT PAT RILEY

1. University of Kentucky, All- American 2. Played on Los Angeles 1972 NBA Championship Team. 3. Coached five NBA teams to NBA Championships; Four with Los Angeles Lakers and one with the Miami Heat. 4. Two NBA Championships as an executive with the Miami Heat.

"If I needed one player to win a game, I'd take Michael Jordan"

"If I needed one player to save my life, I'd take Larry Bird"

"THE JORDAN RULES"

During the competitive and brutally physical Pistons/Bulls Eastern Conference finals of 1988–90; Detroit had a special series of defensive rules tabbed the "JORDAN RULES" targeted solely on stopping Michael Jordan. Detroit claimed the so called "Jordan Rules" were mostly psychological to throw the Bulls off their game. Never-the-less, the rules gained notoriety and were designed to contain the explosive and "greatest of all time," Michael Jordan.

Isaiah Thomas: "Jordan, when in the air we had no shot – when everything was on the floor we could hold our own."

The Rules:

#1 on the wing the Pistons forced Jordan to the "elbow" where there was help. We did not allow him to go baseline.

#2 when Jordan had the ball on the top the Pistons influenced to the left.

#3 when Jordan had the ball in the post, Detroit doubled down from the top.

The Piston locker room "rules":

- ✓ "We had to stop him before he took flight because you know he is not human."
- ✓ "When he got to the paint, we knocked him down."
- ✓ "When he got to the basket, we knocked him down."
- ✓ "If he did go baseline, Laimbeer or Mahorn were to knock him to the floor."

<u>In reality it came down to a test of Jordan's physical and mental courage. How willing #23 was to risk injury to score points?</u>

10,000 HOUR PRINCIPLE

The 10,000-hour principle tells us that it takes 10,000 hours of Deliberate practice/training to excel at the highest expert level of performance

PRACTICE HR	WEEKLY HR	ANNUAL HR	YRS TO 10000 HRS
1 HR	7 HR	364 HR	27.5 YEARS
1.5	10.5	546	18.3
2	14	728	13.7
2.5	17.5	910	11.0
3	21	1092	9.2
3.5	24.5	1274	7.8
4	28	1456	6.9
4.5	35	1820	5.5
5	38.5	2002	5.0
6	42	2146	4.6

What is deliberate practice?

"It isn't work and it isn't play, but something entirely onto itself."
It is: 1. Designed specifically to improve performance.
2. It demands "game-like" concentration and repetition.
3. Highly demanding mentally and physically.
4. Must enjoy the process & satisfaction of seeing/feeling improvement.

"THIS CANNOT BE DENIED"

I heard you say you wanted to get better, didn't I?

This fundamental law of learning cannot be denied and is universally accepted intellectually, philosophically, and scientifically. Nor can it be simply dismissed as invalid. In the 21st century, just like the 20th century, 19th century, et.al. the science of learning demands that:

"You will only get good at what you do and the more you do something the better you will get at whatever you are doing – this includes making baskets."

Unfortunately, the laws of learning also work in reverse:

"One who does less than he / she is able or less than the competition to improve at their craft, this includes making baskets – unfortunately will get just that, <u>less."</u>

Etc. ***ARE YOU WORTHY,*** *(This is edited from Pete Carill's, book, <u>"The Smart Take from the Strong,"</u>: Various national events from time to time promote an outgrowth of patriotism with the wearing of US flags on team uniforms? During these times this is what I thought: Maybe it's far-fetched to think that a young (high school/college age) soldier in a far-off land on the front line taking "incoming fire" is concerned about whether our players are acting in a proper way as a college student-athlete. BUT I think that it is a part of what they are fighting for, what good is it to wear a flag on your team uniform and then play and practice like a dog and not go to class. This "Me first" attitude is letting the whole country down. This kid who is taking enemy fire, he is not wearing on his uniform anything to honor you, instead ask yourself, what are you doing in your life to make sure you <u>are worthy.</u>*

JIM STOCKWELL (POW 1965-73)
"THE OPTIMIST"

James Bond Stockdale, the Vice Admiral's A-4 Skyhawk jet was shot down over N. Vietnam on September 9, 1965. Mr. Stockdale was the most senior naval officer held captive until his release on February 12, 1973. That's 2619 days of without a single day of freedom.

This read is a response to a researcher's question: <u>"Which prisoners did not make it out of Vietnam?"</u> Mr. Stockdale's answer:

"Oh, that is easy, THE "OPTIMISTS" didn't make it." Once he said that you immediately think, "Hey, wait a minute here, you are taught all through life that everything is going to be OK." But Stockdale said, "The optimist would say, I'm going to be home by Christmas, Christmas would come and go; I am going to be home by Easter; Easter would come and go; I am going to be home by summer, summer would come and go and eventually the optimist's spirit would be broken, and they would quit and die of a broken heart."

This is a very important lesson. You must never confuse faith that you will prevail in the end – which (faith) you can never afford to lose – with the discipline to confront the most brutal facts of your current reality, whatever they might be."

Derek Dooley, the new football coach at the University of Tennessee, a team struggling to find relevance in the SEC presented the above story to the team as a way of mapping out a path to move the program forward regardless of the present circumstances. The point of this (Stockwell story,) is you never lose hope, you never lose faith in what the story is going to be, even if it is not clear, YET.

Derek Dooley:<u>*" I do not have any doubts that Tennessee is going to be what Tennessee expects to be – but we also have to confront some tough brutal facts that we are facing right now, and it is going to be tough – you darn right it is. We/you are presented with a set of circumstances every day. You cannot change what happened in the past. You cannot worry about what might happen. You cannot say if this would have happened then that would have happened, etc. These are the circumstances we are faced with, and you've got to go after it as best you can and never lose faith in the end of the story."*</u>

SECTION IV

THE COACHES

"TO THE EXPERIENCED COACH,

THE CHOICES ARE FEW.

FOR THE INEXPERIENCED COACH,

THE CHOICES ARE MANY."

ATTENTION! ! !

"There have been no studies conducted showing coaches should be more conservative in their coaching."

Coaches have a natural aversion to losing. It manifests itself in coaches being less likely to be aggressive in their decision making. *This aversion to risk taking can show up not only in games, but also in recruiting, discipline, and other decisions in the program.*

Etc..: "WE OVER COACH BECAUSE WE LOVE WHAT WE DO – BE CAREFUL."
Denny Crum was long time assistant to John Wooden at UCLA. He became the head coach of the University of Louisville where he won two NCAA National Tournament Championships, 70% of his games and was inducted into the Naismith Hall of Fame in 1994.

ADOLPH RUPP
"THE BARON OF THE BLUEGRASS"

The colorful and legendary Adolph Rupp, head
coach of The University of Kentucky
876-190 W-L record for a .882-win percentage, winning
28 SEC Championships and four NCAA championships

Coach Rupp's Classroom

During a particularly listless Wildcat practice, Coach Rupp, strolled out onto the court, and in a deep Southern drawl said, "Cease and desist this disgraceful exhibition. These hallowed halls have never seen such a display of total ineptitude." With the players looking on in wary silence, Coach Rupp, abruptly stopped glancing at the floor and bending carefully to one knee, he meticulously studied the floor and then dramatically with his finger, picks something off the floor, studies it and says, "Well looky, looky, what I have discovered, by god I believe it is a drop of "sweat," I don't believe it, where on God's green earth did this come from, it must have come from a working man, a janitor while he was cleaning the floor, it certainly did not come from anyone on this sorry, non-working, non-playing team."

"Message sent – message received!"

Etc.: <u>A Coaching Journey:</u>
"This game has given me a few scars
I have been good at it
And
I have been not so good at it
But
But it's been a pleasure, all of it – <u>either way.</u>"

DICK BENNETT
HEAD COACH
"THE UPSET WIN."

HEAD COACH, Eau Claire Memorial HS (WI,) U of WI. Stevens Point, Green Bay, U of Wisconsin, Washington State

Coach Bennett is one of the outstanding coaches of our time. Successfully coached high school basketball in Wisconsin. Head Coach at WI-Stevens Point, Green Bay, Washington St, and Wisconsin, leading the Badgers to the Final 4. Coming from a Wisconsin coaching family, brother Jack, daughter Kathi and son Tony all college coaches with Tony currently the head coach at the U of Virginia.
This is an important read for coaches that requires consideration.

You have to want to win more than your opponent. It comes down to a possession battle. That means, on every possession you must want to stop them more than they are willing to run their offense. And offensively you must be willing to run your offense and get the shot you want more than your opponent is willing to defend.

This is the easiest way I know to shrink the talent gap between you and your opponent. You take it possession by possession that is the way it is done. If you want it more on each possession and put that into action you can cut the gap. All you want is a chance to win the game down the stretch.

It is important for a team to have humility and through this humility the team knows who they are – because once you know who you are, you know what you can and have to do.

You have to take it upon yourself to play every possession – if it doesn't go well on one possession, get up for the next and the next. . . there can be no roller coaster – your effort is consistent if you are battling to win one possession at a time and then one game at a time.

Etc.: Leaders Create Leaders

BILL BELICHEK – THE G.O.A.T.

I coach all the players, if I favor one, then I am neglecting the other 52.

- I give everyone what they have earned.
- Tom Brady on Bill Belichek: "He makes practice harder than the game."

What a player needs to learn if he wants to make it in New England:

- Dependability
- Improve – work hard understand what you need to do to be a better player.
- Consistency
- It is not what you know – it is what you know every time.

Good players cannot overcome poor coaching – it is impossible.

- Personnel decisions: eventually you must go with the most dependable player.
- Young players have all sorts of transitioning issues into the pros. It is the organization and the coach's job to take care of these issues early.
- Players and coaches: "Every battle is won before being fought." Sun Tsu
- We are prepared when everyone knows what they are supposed to do.
- Players and coaches need to know that "the battle plan is great until the first shot is fired." Gen. D. Eisenhower
- Coaches and players: sometimes it comes down to, "Just figuring it out."
- "Winning is always the goal."
- "Never be afraid to use a good idea."
- Players need to: <u>Do your job</u>. <u>Be attentive to details</u>. <u>Put the team first</u>.

PAUL "BEAR" BRYANT
UNIVERSITY OF ALABAMA

"I'm just an old Plow head" from Arkansas.

But I have learned how to keep a team together.

How to lift some up and calm others down until you finally have one heartbeat as a team.

Three things:

1. If things went wrong – **I DID IT.**
2. If things go semi-good – **WE DID IT.**
3. If anything goes really good – **THEY DID IT.**

MORE BEAR . . .

The story goes . . . Coach Bryant at practice on occasion would reach into his

pocket and pull out a crumpled piece of paper and read it and

put it back in his pocket. He did this 3- or 4-times during practice.

Finally, a reporter asked him what he was reading, Coach Bryant slowly

Pulled the worn piece of paper from his pocket and gave it to the reporter, it read:

"IT'S THE ITTY, BITTY, TEENY THINGS THAT GET YOU BEAT."

THE SEVENTY'S, A HAIR CUT AND "THE COACH"

UCLA was in the midst of its 11 consecutive NCAA national championships during the 60's and 70's. Almost as well known as the NCAA championships, was Coach John Wooden's firm dress and appearance demands during the season. In the off-season, the players would literally let their "hair down" afros, mutton chop sideburns, facial hair in various states of length and style. But once the season started, clean shaven, hair no longer than two inches was Coach Wooden's "Rule" as representatives of the University.

Enter Bill Walton, the National Player of the Year on the National Championship UCLA team, and a team in the middle of what would be on an 88-game winning streak.

Bill Walton was known as the freest spirit of the free spirits in a chaotic era of self-expression during a time of national activism, to the point of Bill being arrested while participating in a protest that was blocking a downtown LA street.

He was an upper classman by this time. It is the day of the first practice beginning another National championship journey. Bill comes to practice, Coach Wooden looks disapprovingly at Walton's appearance. Bill immediately explained to Coach Wooden how he (Coach Wooden) did not have the right to dictate how long his hair should be, his sideburn appearance and if he could have facial hair. It must be remembered; Bill Walton was the best player in the country. Coach Wooden looked at Bill and offered the following, "Yes Bill you are right, I do not have that right, I just have the right to determine who is going to play AND, Bill we are going to miss you this year. In 15 minutes, you won't be on the team if you do not get upstairs and get that taken care of." Bill raced out of the gym and returned shortly to the approval of "THE COACH."

*John Wooden and Bill Walton would become very close until the day of Coach Wooden's passing. John Wooden: "Youngsters test you, don't get upset, but don't give in, gracious sakes, don't give in, if you start giving in you are "Whipped." But at the same time stay open minded. Times change and you need to make changes too and change is needed for progress but be aware, **all change is not progress.**"*

DOUG BRUNO, HEAD COACH
DePaul University
A proven winner. A master Coach

MAKE YOUR PROGRAM BETTER

- <u>Recruitment</u> - Get better players – we recruit the best players in the country.
- <u>Player Development</u> - Make the ones you have better.

We try to get the best players in the country. But we have a philosophy. It's not about the players you did not get, it is making the ones you have better – it's the ones that say "Yes" to DePaul. <u>Cherish the players that you have.</u>

THE "SEASONS" OF A BASKETBALL PLAYERS LIFE AT DEPAUL

A. **SPRING** – conditioning after 3 to 4 weeks off. The first skill workout is to teach the team how to work out on your own. They need more than the NCAA two hours. It drives me nuts when kids hire a trainer. If our staff is not good enough to teach them how to get better – we should not have our jobs. I sit in the gym and watch people from NBA come in and the skills trainers basically rebound for their clients. Jimmy Butler of the HEAT works out better by himself than when he has his training "Guru" with him.

TEACH YOUR PLAYERS HOW TO GET BETTER ON THEIR OWN. Why should they need to pay a guy/gal $20 or more an hour to be a rebounder? We teach drills they can do on their own in the gym by themselves.

1. **Strength and conditioning**
2. **Open gym** – must work out after season is over as a team – it will tell you what kind of team you will have next season – leadership is mentored during this time.
3. **Mental conditioning – team building.** You must re-develop your team during open gyms in the spring w/o your seniors. CONT PG 70

B. SUMMER –

1. Require kids to be with us one summer session. I think it is healthy for them to be home during the 1st session. During the second session everyone must be in school, and they can work out. After the 2nd session they get to go home for 2 or 3 weeks.

FALL / SCHOOL STARTS -

C. **Pre-Season Conditioning - after schoolwork.**
D. **Pre- Season games**
E. **Conference games**
F. **Post Season**

THE FIVE STEPS TO SUCCESS: These five steps are timeless, regardless of cultural changes, privilege or poverty.

1. **MAKE A DECISION** – People have a hard time making decisions. What do you want to do? Where do you want to go? What do you want to achieve?
2. **DREAM AND VISUALIZE** – Never stop dreaming – know the difference between a dream and a fantasy. Don't be afraid to dream that you can be a starter, all conf., WNBA, etc. Don't be afraid to think you can do it. See yourself doing it before you have done it.
3. **WRITE DOWN YOUR GOALS** – Harvard Business School did a research project and they found out that: 85% of graduates had no goals. 14% had goals but did not write them down. And 3% of the study had goals and wrote them down. The 3% group out earned, out produced, and out achieved all the others by a significant amount.
4. **Mental conditioning** – We become what we think about – what you want to achieve takes positive mental practice. CONT PG 71

Etc.: NVRGVUP!

5. PHYSCIAL DISCIPLINE – a. Wake up with a smile b. Thank God you have one more day to live. c. Thank God that you can work your butt off to be the best you can be.

Steps one thru four requires no sweat equity.

Defense is nothing more than offensive behavior on defense
Offense is a "Party" earned through hard work on the defensive end.

WHAT IT TAKES TO BE A PRO

1. Basketball intelligence – Basketball IQ – "Think the game."
2. Competitiveness
3. Combativeness
4. You must have a specific "Game." What is your specific "go to skill?" Is it:

- Physical Talent
- Visual athleticism
- Quickness Speed
- Strength / conditioning - how dedicated are you to the weight room. A stronger player is a better player.

5. Work ethic – playing professionally is your job.
6. Leadership talent

Etc. Keys to success in any endeavor: 1. Be On Time. 2. Pay attention
3. Each day, "Empty your bucket." (Give an honest effort.)

"WHO CLEANS THE BUILDING?"
JOHN CALIPARI
HEAD COACH, UUIVERSITY OF KENTUCKY

Hall of fame Coach Calipari imparts an important message in the Art of Coaching that goes beyond recruiting and X's and O's. It's about people and how you treat them.

The Business Administration professor handed out the final exam and it was on just one piece of paper, which surprised everyone because they had anticipated a test with dozens of questions.

One side of the paper was blank when students turned it over, so was the other side. The professor then said to them." I've taught you everything I can teach you about Business Administration in the last ten weeks. But the most important lesson, you should have learned in this course is this one question final examination:"

Question #1 **WHAT IS THE NAME OF THE LADY WHO CLEANS THIS BUILDING?**

Etc. "I pulled out this Visa Platinum card I am so proud of, when my lunch partner said, "I got it, I let him win, even though, I love to win."

G. Blair, Texas A&M, Hd. Coach

JIM CALDWELL
NFL HEAD COACH

a classy professional
and respected coach much
in the mold of this mentor, Tony Dungy

SIX PILLARS OF EFFECTIVE LEADERSHIP

1. **Be competent in your craft**. There are lot of "hippy-dippy" people in leadership who by-pass this pillar for other cosmetic aspects such as public relations, branding, etc. All are important, but none have "competent in your craft" type status.

2. **Commit to be an expert**. Be really good at a few things. John Wooden: "Attention to details is the difference between champions and near champions."

3. **Humility**. Leaders match humility with professional will. Leaders are more plow horse than show horse. Leaders praise the team without flattery. Leaders regard success as an entitlement enabled by hard work and effort. Leaders are humble without engaging in self-deprecation.

4. **Be comfortable in your own shoes**. I have lived in mine for a long time. Dr. Ruth Simmons, President of Brown University, "Strive to be a good role model." I am who I am. My life experiences make me unique. Emotions on the public stage will strip away a veneer and expose phoniness. BE WHO YOU ARE. As a head coach I cannot hide.

5. **Motivation**. The good lead through hard work and sustained effort. Resilience is a need – because of disappointment – resilience and grit are leadership keys with intrinsically motivated people. With them all you have to do is fuel their desire – Persistence, "I will try until I succeed."

6. **Passion.** Passionate teams, have great morale, excited and believe in what we do. Gen. Patton, "Take care of your men." Coaching is a service business. CONT PAGE 74

<u>Coach Caldwell - Bonus notes</u>: <u>A young person's mind is not cultivated</u> <u>enough to understand the consequences of their deeds.</u> <u>Integrity is who</u> <u>you are.</u> <u>I believe in second chances.</u> <u>You cannot have a long-sustained win</u> <u>streak</u> <u>without high character people.</u> <u>I don't care how hard you push my</u> <u>daughter – but first you must care about her, and she must know you care.</u>

Etc. I was so slow, the coach thought I was a traffic pylon.

JACK CLARK
HEAD RUGBY COACH

University of California-Berkeley
Former US Rugby Team Coach
Entered 2019 Season with 671 wins – 95 losses – 5 draws

This is a great read that explains the need and purpose of developing a system and its importance to winning.

Constant evaluation of every function in your operations: travel, budget, practice on the road, and at home, equipment, etc. There are no wins in this "bucket" – just redundant but necessary work.

OUR MINDSET: GRATEFUL FOR EVERYTHING – ENTITLED TO NOTHING.

There is certainly not enough gratitude in the world and definitely not enough in athletics. "You put your dirty clothes on the little loop and the next day they come back clean., It's amazing." I just want us to be thankful for little things and the big things. We believe that we must, and we are willing to work for everything we have – that makes us more resilient.

CREATING A VALUE SYSTEM

It is not enough to say we believe in this stuff. We must "box car" what we believe in together as a unified group. With a combination of values means - we have a system – and that system allows us to process the transactions that come before the team on and off the field collectively/individually. It allows us to process all those decisions in a principled way based on our value system. **The system needs to be all encompassing. Think of any possibility that could happen that the student-athlete could walk into the office and ask about. What possible situation could our team be in on or off the field – your value system has to be able to have answers. The system must have an answer for every situation that can come up. All of your values must be complimentary to each other, and none can contradict another program value.** CONT PG 76

Leadership. Our value system includes:

1. Selflessness 2. Constant performance improvement. 3. is merit based 4. Toughness.

1. Selflessness - We just believe in the team first – self last. The declaration is that we will process every decision with what is best for the team.

2. **CONSTANT PERFORMANCE IMPROVEMENT** – I do not mean results – its constant performance improvement that is a value. "We are working too hard at this not to demonstrate we are getting better." A lot of stakeholders i.e., fans, administrators, etc. Interpret this as more wins. Sometimes we do get results, but not always. **Results follow performance – performance does not follow results**. We must concentrate on performance that is how you get results. If you have been coaching for a while you realize results, follow performance so if we can keep getting better – we can begin to win. Winning always comes last. If you say this in a business setting someone will always say, "ya, but at XYZ company we have to produce immediately." I wanna laugh. We get fired too for not winning. But winning is not a value – getting better every day is a value.

3. **MERIT** – Merit is a value. When you really study high performance teams you find they are meritocracies. If a player's voice resonates with the team, people are going to listen to him and people are going follow him and collaborate with him. it is because he is getting it done on the field. It is not about your seniority (although that is good to have.) Seniority is your intellectual property – if you can't put your experience to good use in the moment it is useless. Seniority in and of itself means nothing. CONT PG 77

Etc. John Chaney, the great Temple coach and leader, "I am not going to stick a lollipop in your mouth. I am going to coach you like a man."

4. **TOUGHNESS** - is the ability to concentrate on the next important thing. You need to become resilient (mentally tough) by not expecting too much from the following:

a. not from your opponent
b. if you are playing both halves against the wind, that's just the way it is.
c. not from the referees
d. Don't expect lucky breaks
e. Do not spend much time on what just happened
f. Just go on to the most important thing. This approach makes you tougher and it's easier to win and harder to lose.

Etc.: If your best players love to be Coached – you are going to win a Lot of game.

MIKE DUNLAP
NBA, DIV 1, DIV 2 COACH

*Former head coach of Charlotte (NBA), Loyola-Marymount (CA) & Metro State (Denver)
Coach Dunlap is a coaches – coach. Highly respected as one of the top X & 0
Technicians in the game.*

You must use math / statistical information to support and assess the effectiveness of your instruction to your team.

1. Measurement provides facts.
2. The eye test is an opinion / perception has built in biases.

 This is an important point: Do not destroy a compliment to a player (or anyone for that matter) with the **"BUT"** conjunction.

"Joey, I thought your defense in the second half on #24 really made a difference, **"BUT"** you need to cut down on your turnovers."

What you have is a player stewing about why the coach is always picking on him about turnovers – "everybody makes turnovers – why doesn't he/she say something to them."

Etc. Assistant coaches practice rules: 1. No Assistant Coaching poses (arms folded.) 2. Bring "it" every day. 3. Don't idly "chat" with other assistants at practice.

Jim Harrick, UCLA Head Coach, Head Coach at Pepperdine, Rhode Island and UCLA. At UCLA Coach Harrick won the NCAA National Championship in 1995.

"GENO"
GENO AURIEMMA, Head Coach UCONN

Apparently because of his incredible success and known for having several of the top recruited prospects on his team every year; that his biggest challenge is to get the team to the game on time in order to win National Championships. Nothing could be further from the truth. Geno Auriemma, in addition to being a great recruiter, he is a master coach by every measurable criteria.

Coach Auriemma is in the team huddle, here he gives us a snapshot of his genius, if we read carefully.

"OK, we are up 25 points, is it because we are just that good and we are executing and playing much harder - than a good opponent. OR do we have a 25-point lead because they stink, if that is the case, then we are just a little better than someone who is not any good. Is that what we are in the game for (just to be a little better than a poor team) or are we trying to be and do something special."

More Geno on Process:

"If we are getting better each day we will get to a sustainable level of success. The process is the same. The process shows improvement every day. The process says that improvement is there whether you are winning or losing. The game cannot be played perfectly in practice or competition. But the key is how long can we sustain perfection in our effort, execution, and team attitude (yes, attitude is a skill.) We are not just a regular team, are we?

Etc. Questions: 1. What do I have to offer? 2. What will I sacrifice?

GENO AURIEMMA – TALKS
WE NEED TO LISTEN AND LEARN

RECORD: 1091-142 - Winner of 11 NCAA CHAMPIONSHIPS

Recruiting enthusiastic kids is getting harder than it has ever been. Every kid watches the NBA and use what they see in their school games acting like they are really good players. You see it all the time at every AAU, WNBA, NFL, MLB game and what you see are players being really "cool", so high school players think that is how they are going to act, and they have not even figured out which pivot foot to use and they are going to act like they are really good players. You see at every AAU or high school game.

So, recruiting kids who are really upbeat, loving life, loving the game and have tremendous appreciation for when teammates do something well; that's really hard on our staff when evaluating prospects. We put a large premium on body language. If your body language is bad, you will never get into the game, NEVER. I don't care how good you are. Some will always say, "You just benched Breanna Stewart (the best player in the country and the #1 draft pick in the WNBA) in the Memphis game for 35 minutes, that was to motivate her for the South Carolina game the following Monday, NO I didn't, Breanna was acting like a 12-year-old, so I put her on the bench and said, "Sit there."

Other coaches say you can do that because you have three other All Americans you can put in, I get that, I understand, but I would rather lose than watch some of these kids play the way they play. I'd rather lose than watch kids get away with thinking about themselves it's all, "me, me, me." "I didn't score so why should I be happy". "I am not getting enough minutes, why should I be happy?" That is the world we are living in today, unfortunately kids check the scoreboard because they are going to get yelled at by their parents if they do not score enough points.

When I look at my team, they know how I feel. I watch game film, I am checking what is going on, on the bench and if someone is asleep over there, someone is not engaged in the game, they will never get into the game NEVER. And they know I am not kidding.

80

TOM IZZO, MICHIGAN STATE UNIVERSITY

INDIVIDUAL MEETING WITH PLAYERS

I MEET WITH EACH PLAYER:

1. "We write down on a note card five goals our players want me to help them achieve at Michigan State, be selfish list your biggest dreams. Things the players usually write down are: <u>graduate</u> – <u>be the best player I can be</u> - <u>starter</u>- <u>All Big Ten</u> – <u>Big Ten Champions</u> – <u>NBA draftee</u> – <u>win NCAA championship.</u>

2. Have you ever done any of the above things you listed? Player ans. "No."

3. I know how to get you where you want to go because, I have a blueprint that will get you to where you want to go.

4. Do you believe this coaching staff can get you where you want to go as a student-athlete? Player ans. "Yes"

5. The minute the player says, "Yes," he believes in the MSU coaching staff and they can help him achieve his student-athlete goals, I know I have got him. "My job is to hold you accountable to your goals, they are not mine, they are yours."

FINALLY, as a staff we can challenge him if issues/debates should arise. I tell him to just refer him to his agreement with the coaching staff.

Etc. Hubie Brown, former NBA Head Coach: "I hope young coaches lose early in their career. So they will have to figure out that the game is about the kids and teaching."

JOE JUDGE
HEAD COACH, NEW YORK GIANTS

This is a Press Conference transcript on the announcement of Coach Judge's appointment to the Giants Head Coaching Position. Joe Judge was a position coach, a defensive backfield coach in the New England organization. He had no head coaching experience at any level. This was a gigantic professional jump over coordinators and former head coaching candidates for a head coaching position in the NFL. Coach Judge is very direct, with a "tell it like it is going to be" interview style. This interview approach seemed to be a major factor in his being named head coach.

This is a <u>very</u> <u>informative view that should be studied by coaches in every sport at any level</u>.

<u>Joe Judge, Introduction as Head Coach of the NY Giants Press Conference. January 11, 2020</u>

I would like to thank all those who have made this opportunity possible. I do not take lightly the position I am in, the city, and region I represent. I would like to thank the Mara family, my family, and all those close friends who have made this step in the process possible, which is just another step in the process in where we want to go.

Thank you to all my former coaches, Bill Belichek, Nick Saban and others and the players I have worked with for building in me a foundation of fundamentals that have allowed me to teach and instruct at a high level and put me in this position.

Coaches Belichek and Saban and the other coaches in my background taught me that you hold those you expect the most from to the highest standard. I want to thank the players, they gave everything, that's what I expect, I am very demanding and will continue to be demanding. I expect the players to be held to a certain standard for all those who have played under me in the past. This is just an opportunity. I have to make the most of it. That starts today.

<u>There is a question out there. Who is Joe Judge? Maybe what is more relevant in this conversation about the new coach of the NY Giants is,</u> **what is Joe Judge about?** CONT PG 83

- I am about "Old school" physical and mentally tough play. We are going to put a product on the field that this city and region can be proud of, this team will represent this area.
- We will play fast, we'll play downhill, we will play aggressive, we'll punch you in the nose for 60 minutes.

- We'll play every play like it has a history and a life of its own with a relentless competitive attitude.
- We'll be fundamentally sound.
- We will not beat ourselves. That is our mission.
- I am about caring for the players in the locker room.
- Let's not forget the human element in this game.
- Let's not forget that because we pay a check to a player, that allows an absence of empathy.
- We need to make sure we take care of the players in the locker room, and we treat them the right way.
- It's vital we teach them the correct techniques and we put them in the right situation to be successful on the field.
- We are going to ask these young men to come and give everything they have every day. We are going to demand it and we will appreciate everything they give us.
- It is our responsibility to take care of them on a daily basis and make sure that when they are done with the game they are prepared for the rest of their life as a father, husband, and a career.

What this team is going to look like?

I want this team to reflect this area. I want the people to pay their hard-earned money in the neighborhoods NY, N&S Jersey to come to our games and know the players on the field will play with the same attitude they do every morning on the job, that's blue collar, it's hard work, it's in your face. CONT PG 84

We are not going to back down from anybody. We are going to come to work every day and grind it out the same way the fans do every day in their jobs and they can invest their money in our program knowing it is worthwhile to put on a Giants jersey or a Giants hat, that it is not just representing the 53 on the field but it is representing their neighborhoods, communities and their families with the same values they have instilled in their children.

Right now, I have an outside view of this team. I've competed against the Giants; I have studied this team from the outside in preparing myself for this job and opportunity. But I must make myself fluent in the language of the building.

Building the Coaching Staff

I have to evaluate the players and the coaching staff, give everyone a fair evaluation and make sure we make the right decisions and have a clear vision of what the right path going forward needs to be in order to help players progress the correct way relative to direction by the staff. I do not have a staff in place yet. I do have some names in mind, but we'll talk to everyone. We will take our time.

My priorities are to put the right men around the players, that the players come to work every day, they can be coached hard. They can be taught. I want good. People. Before anything, if you are going to work in our organization, you are a good person. I don't want alternative agendas. I am making that clear right now. There's not going to be a coach in our organization who doesn't have the players best interest at hand and is going to come to work every day and put their "butts" on the line for the players who are going to work for them.

I want teachers. I want old school people who can get to our players and give them a mental image of what it is supposed to look like. I want them to demonstrate on a daily basis what it is going to take to do it successfully day in CONT PG 85 and day out; because over the course of a six-month season it takes day in, and day out work to be successful. The margin of error in the league is too small.

Getting started, teaching and commitment

You cannot win with some kind of a magic scheme, or a new gimmick and you think you have to re-vent the wheel. The same things win football games that have always won football games; it's fundamentals and those fundamentals will start for us in April in the classroom. We will start our meetings on time. We will be on the field on time in proper dress. We start with knowing your play book. On the field, we start stretching in the right way, we warm up your body the right way, so you prevent any unnecessary soft tissue injuries on the field. All this carries over to the fundamentals on the field, teaching ball security, it's running, it's teaching. It is a contact sport you can't get around that. It is meant to be a physical game. It's for tough people. We will practice live tackling, not to make a statement that we are trying to be tough. We are going to practice live tackling because I believe in doing it safely. You want to make your players safer. You start by instructing them how to do it. We are going to work on everything we ask the players to do.

Everything we ask of the players at full speed on Sunday at a competitive level; we are going to make sure we have practiced, corrected and re-practiced before they must do it at a live pace. There will be no short cuts in what we have to do. It is a tough division in cities with tough people and they expect to see a program, a product that represents them.

I am going to do everything in my power every day to make sure the people of this city and this area can turn on the TV or sit in the stadium seats and are proud to say we are their Giants.

 UPDATE: The NY Giants finished 6-10 in Coach Judge's first year. He is credited with a cultural change in the Giants persona as an aggressive, hard-working team that he promised in this first press conference.

BOB KNIGHT
ARMY – INDIANA – TEXAS TECH

A legendary, championship coach, often referred to as the "General." A winner of 902 games as a head coach. In his brilliant coaching career Coach Knight Won 11 Big 10 championships, Olympic and Pan American Gold medals and winner of three NCAA championships.

PATIENCE & DEMAND

Bob Knight talks about the need for two competing coaching techniques that must co-exist in order to advance the teaching / learning process

Coaching is a balance between demanding and patience. A coach who **only demands** – a constantly demanding style is not particularly successful.
A coach that relies on **patience only** and is extremely patient is not particularly good either.
There is a **balance** between the two that is important to the learning process.
Patience allows for development. **Demand** brings about development at a rate that is needed to be successful.

Collector/editor's note: During the 70's I worked several Bob Knight Summer Basketball Camps. The IU camps had between 400 & 500 campers weekly for six weeks each summer.   It was a 12-hour car ride to Bloomington leaving Saturday night and arriving at noon on Sunday for afternoon sessions. The Coach Knight camps went from Sunday to Friday night. This was a totally serious teaching camp. Two-and-one-half hour station teaching sessions morning and afternoon, one or two games per day in the late afternoon and into the evening with lights out at 10:30 pm. Coaches working camp were instructed in the exact teaching methods and drills to be used by an IU staff member. Camp coaches were not allowed to sit down at any time; they coached and refereed their team's games. Coach Knight spoke to campers three times per day. Camp was physically demanding on campers, not to mention the coaches. For the coaches, Coach Knight set aside Thursday night after lights out for a pizza and beer coaching clinic during which he answered any and all the camp coach's questions. This Q & A usually lasted until there were no more questions which usually did not happen until after the beer and pizza were gone around 2:00-2:30 AM.   The chance to connect and get coaching tips from the biggest name in college coaching was the big draw for nearly all coaches working camp. I don't believe too many coaches, if any, came for cafeteria dining and no air conditioning in the dorms and $125 for the week, myself included.

GENE KEADY
PURDUE BOILERMAKERS
"THE MAGIC LEVEL"

An intense competitor, Coach Keady coached the Boilermakers to 18 NCAA
tournament appearances and winning at a 66% clip. In 25 year career.

It has often occurred to me that all members of the human race are striving for a special sense of satisfaction and success, i.e., the **"The Magic Level:"** this is that upper level of success that puts you in a special class. Only a few experience **"The Magic Level"** of success. I don't think that one is considered a failure if they don't reach their **"The Magic Level,"** but it is special for those who move to that level of achievement. Thus, I believe it's really important to want and strive to succeed at **"The Magic Level"** in all areas of your life. The foundation for reaching **"The Magic Level"** is:

DDT – Discipline – Dedication - Toughness

1.**Discipline** – having a plan and doing what has to be done to successfully complete the plan.
2.**Dedication** – Commitment.
3.**Toughness** – Overcoming obstacles – never giving up.

If you really want to win at all things you endeavor to be successful at, you'll follow **"the Magic Level"** ideals:

  A. Have the right attitude. Never be negative about yourself and never be negative about who can help you reach **"The Magic Level."**

  B. **"The Magic Level" Philosophy**: be a good person, good student, good athlete, be on time, go to class every day, and try your best. We expect that you are here to get an education and to do everything you can to graduate. You are here to help us win as many games as we possibly can and bring credit to the University and yourself by your actions on and off the court. So, you must have character, want to win, and want to graduate.

Thus, really there isn't any magic to "The Magic Level" philosophy. It's:

1. Hard work, 2. Attitude, 3. Faith – in yourself – in the people who care about you – and in God.

MIKE KRZYZEWSKI
DUKE UNIVERSITY

Led the US to three Gold Medals. Coached Duke to three NCAA National Championships with a career win total of over 1157 wins.

OLYMPICS AND STANDARDS

Before the first practice for Team USA, we did not talk about basketball we talked about, how we were going to "live" as a basketball team. Coach Krzyzewski wanted to have a set of standards as to how they were going to live as Olympians. How the team was to play would come later.

To set this up, Coach K met with a few of the team leaders. Kobe, Jason Kidd, and Lebron James. Coach K explained to them what he was planning to do and what did they think and if each would bring a "Standard" to present to the team like an "Ice breaker" to create a flow of conversation. These mega star NBA players were all in; this made it, not only possible, but greatly enhanced the chances of success. The team met and made a list of <u>standards</u> – these were not considered team rules A few are listed here:

- Not being late.
- No excuses.
- Looking each other in the eye.
- Always acknowledging each other on and off the floor.
- Being Flexible.
- Always telling each other the truth.

Notice not one standard was directly related to basketball.

When you set a standard, that draws a line as to what is acceptable and what is unacceptable. Award <u>above the line behavior</u> address <u>below the line behavior.</u> The Olympic team created their own standards, with only guidance from Coach K. Successful standards:

1. Set clear standards, with no gaps in interpretation.
2. Reinforce above the line behavior by acknowledging players that do it.
3. Below the line behavior is addressed amongst the teammates

TOMMY LASORDA
MANAGER – LOS ANGELES DODGERS
HALL OF FAME 1997

Tommy Lasorda passed away in January of 2021 of a heart attack. It was heart issues that forced him to retire from managing the Dodgers in 1996. He managed the Los Angeles Dodgers for 20 years. Winning two World Series Championships.

"Managing is like holding a dove in your hands. Squeeze it too hard and you suffocate it; not hard enough and if flies away."

"When Orel Hershiser came to the Dodgers, He had a Reputation of being the kind of guy that did not have that real desire when times were rough. I think through endless hours of being (working) with him . . . he began to believe in himself."

Orel ended up winning a lot of games (204) for the Dodgers and became a "tremendous competitor."

The Lasorda Approach:

1. They (players) know I care because I do.
2. They believe I can help them because that's my job and I love it.
3. My success at working with players is based on one principle: "I am never the one to give up on a player, that decision is on the player as to when he's had enough and decides it is not worth the work and effort and decides to give up - quit.
4. PRESSURE equals the fear of failure.
   Thinking of failing equals PRESSURE.
5. **Be Optimistic:** You must believe you are going to win every game. I'm the 2nd greatest optimist in America. The greatest optimist was Custer; with 50 soldiers surrounded by 4000 Indians and he yells to his men, "DON'T TAKE ANY PRISONERS."

TONY LARUSSO
MANAGER
Chicago White Sox-Oakland A's-St. Louis Cardinals

At age 76, Named Chicago White Sox manager for 2021

Leadership – Putting Players in a Position to Succeed

During the steroid area, when we went on the road, they packed the blenders right along with the bags.

I won't talk about my career. Lots of time the manager just told me to leave my bat and glove at home and just bring the pompoms,"2 bits, 4 bits, 6 bits a dollar come on team stand up and holler."

In the 2011 season: 1. We had the historic comeback, down 10 ½ games with 32 to play. We get into the playoffs on the last day. That was step one. 2. Now you are in the eight-team playoff, and you must find a way to be the last team standing. Whenever you get to a point where you think you're a pretty good leader, remember you are not leading anybody unless the team responds. When I think about 2011, I think about those players because they are the ones that are competing and having the ups and downs and they're in the actual competition. Those of us that lead try more than anything else is to put them in a position to succeed.

What I have felt is gratitude. I have never worked a day in my life. I signed a contract at 17 and have been in baseball for 50 years, that's not working. Once I saw my baseball card, they had crossed out prospect and replaced it with "Suspect!"

So, you go into managing. You get these mentors, and they teach you and the lessons have been incredible it's like going to grad school.

Our St. Louis goal was to create an atmosphere that was POSITIVE. Because negativity is for losers. HONESTY, which means at times you point out what is wrong so you can get better, then the players need to play. CONT PG 91

Now what's today like that makes this so challenging. I really believe that leadership is more important than ever. That is because times are changing so fast. In the old days, things were simpler. Now there are so many distractions; distractions of fundamental values that used to be automatic when a group got together that you were going to lead. They were there and they were not confused and there was not a lot of nonsense from their peers. They were not totally thinking about getting "mine." They felt family, the team was a family and it carried over onto the field.

It is different now. If you don't understand that then you are missing a key part of being a leader. Be careful what you are communicating because what you think you are saying may not be coming back the way you meant it.

We brought Dennis Eckersley over from the A's, he is a Hall of Famer. He is a very colorful guy with his slang type language. A very cool guy who speaks in a very cool way which for a lot of us who are not cool don't understand. He would say things and I would have no clue what we were saying. Now what do I do if I tell him I have no clue - I'm not cool.

Now Eckersley is on the mound and getting beat up pretty good. I walk out to the mound. I am not going to pull him. I am just going out to talk to him. "Hey, it's not going right," I say, he says, "ya I know, I'm just salad." Now he looked concerned when he said it. So, I looked concerned and gave him the old standby's, tuck your shoulder, arm up, stay back, all that stuff. "OK dude," I get back to the dugout and there are two-line drives. So now I go out to get hm. I say, "just not your day." Eck says, "Why did you leave me in? I told you I was salad." Finally, I decided it is better to be "not cool" than stupid. I finally said, "Hey I have no idea what you are saying." Eck says, "Geez dude, I am just tossing salad up there." "Eck you are telling me that just because you don't have, your good stuff, I am supposed to understand you are tossing the ball like salad instead of throwing the ball. Ya dude, what's so tough about that?"

This whole style of leadership at St. Louis is based on communication. You pay attention to what you are saying and what is said back to you. The verbal and the non-verbal. CONT PG 92

Everybody that touches our team, we include in our leadership group. Coaches, equipment guy, trainer, strength, and fitness, video guy anybody who even touches our team on a partial basis. We got together and what we wanted to create was an environment where players come to the ballpark and were excited to be there and anxious to put on a professional performance.

Etc. Hank Aaron, Baseball Hall of Famer. "My motto was always to keep swinging. Whether I was in a slump or feeling badly or having trouble off the field. The only thing to do was keep swinging."
Hank Aaron, Baseball Hall of Famer
(Yes, never stop swinging – editor/collector note)

MIKE LEACH
HEAD COACH, MISSISSIPPI STATE UNIVERSITY
An outstanding coach, an innovator who is known for coaching "outside the box."
COACH LEACH REACTS AFTER A LOSS

While the head coach at Washington State U., after a devastating upset loss to Boise State, Coach Leach stated what practice would look like in the coming week:

- More plays repeated
- Significantly louder verbal instructions from coaches
- Lineup shuffling
- Post practice drills
- More coaches talking in meetings – less talking from the players. The players have proven their input is flawed

As coaches we have misjudged the players ability to judge situations and respond, we teach them all this stuff and we see a concerned look and the heads nod as if they have understanding, then on the field the body doesn't move. We, as coaches have got to be smart enough and prepared enough to know that the players do not know anything.

Right now, we are a JV softball team just trying to have fun. We are not competing. This kind of stuff has contaminated America. We don't keep score and every kid gets a trophy. I think that the entire thing has retarded the competitive spirit in America and as coaches we have got to take that into account.

Bad Teams – nobody leads
Average teams – coaches lead
Elite team – players lead

MIKE LEACH
MISSISSIPPI STATE UNIVERSITY
"THE PIRATE LEADING THE CHARGE"

Coach Leach known as the "Pirate" for his interest in Pirate lore as one of his many interests. This piece is a wide-ranging perspective of the "The Pirate's philosophy on all things. This read will give coaches ideas they can use to help them in their coaching.

Reading personalities is one of the trickier jobs you have as a coach. There are so many variables at every level of coaching that it is important to encourage the creative process rather than try and impose some sort of one-way, my way or the highway, assembly line tactic. I've found that keeping the door creativity open helps problems get solved better and faster. At the same time everyone needs to understand that decisions need to be made quickly, because a bunch of people second guessing their way around a solution is not doing anyone any good.

As a coach or as anyone leading a group of people will understand, people are fickle, and you have to be ready for just about anything. You're always thinking about how you can reach someone to get the most out of him because conditions are bound to shift, they always do. A guy who was "up" is going to be "down," another guy who's "down" is going to be "up." Somebody thinks they're getting screwed. Somebody's really coming along, but you're just not sure if he's ready. You haven't seen him get enough reps, so do you start him ahead of the other guy? He's more talented and more explosive but you're wondering, can he do the job consistently?

Michael Jordan wasn't picking up baseball good enough for the cynics. He left basketball to play baseball because he wanted to see if he could play baseball. We have too many "non-tryers" these days. They're afraid of how things may look. Rather than experiencing the journey, they're worried about how they'll be perceived. It is very unfortunate. In my eyes MJ was an incredible success in baseball. He had the opportunity to test his abilities in a different field and to see where starting from scratch would take him. You had the greatest athlete in his

CONT PG 95

sport at the time, riding buses playing minor league baseball. In that alone there is something noble. This was a guy that craved experience, wanted to test himself and see what else he could accomplish. Just having the desire to be more, that's a big part of the reason why he is MJ and that's why I think his baseball experiment was an incredible success.

You never know who you really are until you get out of your comfort zone. Michael Jordan is a great inspiration to all of us.

When I was at Kentucky our strength coach, Rob Oviatt, had a Jordon quote from his playing time with the "Dream Team" hanging in the weight room: "I saw some "Dream Teamers" dog it in practice before the Olympics. I looked at them and I knew that was what separated me from them." He could tell from one practice that it was the difference in his preparation, in his work ethic, that made him the best of the best. It was focus and mindset.

I've always believed that you will succeed if you have an unobstructed mentality, as opposed to being a dithering Barney Fife type frightened of adversity. Don't let fear of failure cause you to hesitate. Hesitation is just like a busted play. It's the same when calling a play or giving a direction. When you tell the guys what you want them to run, you have let them now 100% you believe in the play you are calling. Otherwise, you diminish your chances of success. When it comes to taking chances and sizing up risk, there are certainly some wrong decisions that get made, but they happen less often than you'd think. What affects an outcome more than anything else is effort and attitude.

When I was the offensive coordinator at Kentucky, we'd go for it on 4th down about 40 times a year. The aggressive attitude you're stoking within your players is the key. Especially if you're coaching at a program where most of the recruits repeatedly hear how they're not as talented as the opponents. When we're going for it on fourth down, we're making a statement: "You have to stop us." The team philosophy becomes "We're going for it." The guys take a lot of pride in that spirit. They also know if they're unsuccessful too many times you're not going to keep give them chances. Almost every player wants to go for it, they don't want the privilege taken away from them. In their minds they know that if CONT PG 96 they don't make it they are responsible. They're determined to find a way to make it work.

Certainly, any decision needs to be evaluated, but just because "conventional wisdom" suggests something is too risky doesn't make it so. You think it through, if you believe the benefit outweighs the risk, then you need to do it. Life is a series of risks and how well you manage them. Every great thing that has ever happened in my life is the result of taking a risk. Ask yourself, "WHY NOT ME."

You just want good value. Do the best you can and once you make the decision, live with it and go forward because if have regrets or second guess, you are going to hurt yourself. "Don't coach unless you can't conceive of doing anything else." Bear Bryant, U of Alabama

I have a saying: "I was always smart enough to be naïve enough not to know what I couldn't accomplish." When I started out in the business, I didn't think, "Oh crap, I can't compete with these guys with all of their resources, instead, it was 'Screw it, why not us?' My feeling is that anything I would've gotten into, I would have worked my ass off to succeed. Overcoming your fears and whatever other nagging resistance you may have is always the first step to solving a problem. You have to defeat yourself before you defeat someone else.

One of the big mistake's coaches make is over-thinking the playbook. They mess themselves up by constantly tinkering and putting too much in or by trying to run too many different plays and they end up overlooking what they really need to do; football is not about trickery, it's about executing. You need to get sharper running plays in your playbook by focusing on technique. How can you be precise with all the detail that's vital to making a play work properly if you're giving them dozens of different plays to digest? You can't? We need all the detail stuff to become second nature, so the players can just react and do precisely what they did in practice.

OUR 3 OVERALL GOALS:
1. **Be a Team.**
2. **Be the most excited to play.**
3. **Be the best at doing your job**.
   CONT PG 97

Academics have always been important to me. How stupid and tragic it is for somebody to go to college and leave without a degree? When that happens, I think it's due to selfishness, laziness, and a failure of a good support group. In most cases it's because of all three. I felt like I had a responsibility to help the guys through their academic issues so they could be the best people they could be, but as a coach there is always a practical aspect to it; You don't have time to detour for academic issues. It all comes back to holding people accountable for themselves and emphasizing what is important over what is not.

The Tower of London – punishment tower. Too many players were missing study halls. Everyone had to run and crawl carrying cinder blocks above their head from one corner of campus to the other. My attitude was, "You play with this guy. He plays right next to you and he's holding us back. You're going to class but you're not doing anything about him not going. You're sitting having watched this guy not do his part and you haven't done anything to fix it and you are a senior and he may be a freshman. There's not just something wrong with him, there's something wrong with you, too. There is also something wrong with me as a coach and the assistants and our academic people. I had a sign in my office that said, "you are either coaching it or allowing it to happen." Discipline is not just focusing on the negative aspects and scolding your guys when they don't do something the right way. Discipline requires encouragement. Discipline requires support. Discipline requires sharing a new perspective so the person can gain the confidence he needs to be successful.

Obviously, if a guy isn't giving great enough effort, he needs to be called out. There will be times when you have to cut people who simply refuse to change. With every aspect of instilling discipline, there needs to be some reflection on what your role has been as a coach. What could you have done better? How could you have reached that guy sooner? You can't fall back on, "Well I told him a thousand times and he still won't do it." If that is the case, then you're not worth much as a coach. If I had to tell someone a thousand times to do something, he ain't the problem. I am the problem. CONT PG 98

Texas Tech Linebacker Mike Smith: "I missed one class. Every day after practice, one of the coaches read the names of anyone that missed a class in front of everybody. Leach called me into his office and asked me what my problem was. I was a captain he said guys look up to me. He was sending me to the "Tower of London." I never missed another class. It wasn't just because the "Tower of London" was so grueling, but it was the guilt of knowing I let him down."

(Fights) We punished them, but we reminded them how to handle these situations. You don't just throw punches, you leave. If a situation starts to go bad. You leave because the other guy out on the streets doesn't get to play in the stadium on Saturday, you do, when they write about it in the paper, it'll say, "so and so and 'so and so', who plays for Texas Tech, who went to 'such and such' a high school is from 'this town' got into a fight with an unidentified male." The unidentified male doesn't have anything to lose. He just goes back to his job. You have a scholarship to lose. There's a different standard for you – I don't care if it's fair. I don't care what the other guy said, it doesn't matter. You leave. I warn the team about fighting. It was one of the first things I'd talk about every year when I first addressed the team.

This was how I'd breakdown the initial team meeting:

Introductions: New staff, freshmen, and JC players. Explaining there is no initiating of the freshmen. We have freshmen who are going to play, so don't treat them like freshman. If you're a freshman, don't act like one.

Academics: I'd remind them that we have the #1 graduation rate of any public institution in the nation. They were expected to uphold that standard.

Communication: There is never an excuse not to talk to one another. This is critical on and off the field.

Respect: Managers, trainers, secretaries, and all the support staff. No one works hard for less reward. CONT PG 99

Then I would explain the team rules which included no fighting.

The rest were:

No Stealing: If you steal anything you will get kicked off the team. Trust is very important, and a thief can't be trusted.

Don't Use Drugs: Drugs of any kind will get you kicked off the team. Drugs are selfish. No player partying is more important than the team.

No hitting women: People who hit a woman are cowards. You will be immediately dismissed.

No Drinking: no going out after Wednesday night on game weeks.

Be on time: Discipline doesn't have to mean being required to cut their hair, wear collared shirts and taking off their jewelry.

I didn't want them constantly looking over their shoulder worrying about the team policies. The football training complex is their sanctuary. I wanted them to feel comfortable and excited to be there. It's important for them to enjoy the company of their teammates and coaches. <u>Discipline should be designed around necessary results, not unnecessary rules.</u> I reminded the team that no one is entitled, and they earned their position every day.

Coach Leach and Wes Welker:

"I just try to concentrate on what I can control and that is me going out and believing in myself." Wes Welker

Wes' words are simple to understand but difficult to do, because most people don't have that level of focus. Some guys like Welker, are just born with the ability to focus. It is a talent, just like speed, quickness or strength. Wes was able to do things that people a lot more "talented" than him couldn't do because of his concentration. He didn't allow a lot of distractions to get in the way. He

CONT PG 100

didn't worry about how good the other guy might be or what the other guy was trying to do. He was just focused on himself.

Selfishness is like a cancer; football is infested with it. Between players, coaches, and staff, it's everywhere: "Well, I didn't recruit him. . ." "I don't coach him, I'm not his position coach. . ." "They don't know how to use me. . ." "Why did they call that play. . .?" And on and on . . . with the excuses.

It's all just finger pointing. You can't let that attitude find its way into your program. If they say, "me, me, me" or "I, I, I," and complain a lot you need to get rid of them if you can't change the problem. Then you need to eliminate it. If it means firing or cutting people, it's better to do it sooner rather than later. Bo Schembecler: "If you miss on a great player, he will beat you once a year. If you get a kid and he turns out to be a bad apple, he will beat you every day of the week."

Ego is Important. Ego doesn't help you when you win. But it protects you during the losses. When you don't win, and thousands of people are disappointed, and you are getting hammered from all directions. An ego will allow you to stand up and say," I'm the guy that can straighten this out. I am the guy that can make this happen." If you do not have that inside you, then the people around you won't respond with confidence.

Michael Crabtree (great Texas Tech and NFL wide out) as quiet as he was, he had a huge ego. If you asked him, "Do you think you're better than this other receiver, he would tell you without hesitation that he is. But he's not beating you over the head telling you that. Wes Welker is the same way, in his mind, you can see this in his eyes, he is convinced he is the best receiver in the NFL.

I don't think you can be a good coach without having some ego. Often as a coach you find yourself having to draw a line in the sand, and ego and firmness play into your ability draw that line. **John Wooden** was a caring, giving, confident person but he had a huge ego. He was an outwardly humble and a very sincere guy, but he clearly had a lot of presence about him.

A CORE BELIEF: "LET'S WORRY ABOUT US, NOT THEM."   Our product is going to be superior to the point that it'll overcome everyone else's product. Ego shouldn't come off as abrasive. Confidence should be genuine, not artificial. You can't help but respect a guy whose ego manifests itself through focus, determination, and willingness to take his own path. You need a touch of ego to head your own way. You wanna be unique? You wanna be special? I truly believe every present circumstance is preparing you for something else.

Be a team. Be the most excited to play. Do your job. That doesn't stop if you're down 39 or up 30. These are all valuable opportunities. You can't just mail it in. Every chance you get can help you down the road. The buses don't leave until the game clock says 00:00.

Being a great <u>Communicator</u> is something I constantly strive to be. The central role of a coach has to be able to explain to his players how they can get the best out of themselves.

I want a role in the improvement of my players. I don't buy into that whoever has the best players automatically wins. You have to be a great listener to be a good communicator. As tempting as it is to talk, you learn more by listening. You also have to observe body language and mannerisms.

<u>Discovering the ideal way to motivate someone is the ultimate challenge to any leader.</u> There is an art to it. When I was coaching Texas Tech, we had a few players you just couldn't be nice to, when it came to football matters. If you complimented them, they would ease up. I'd say to my assistants, if we're jerks to them for 4 years, these guys are going to have better careers. But you can't assume that approach works with everyone. It won't. Some guys will fold or recoil. With some people you need a relaxed approach because they create enough of their own tension. CONT PG 102

I think everyone needs a push. If you're driven, you might find ways to push yourself, but you still need an outside nudge from time to time. Crabtree could push himself, but he periodically needed a reminder or a challenge. Observe your players, really pay attention to the nuances in their actions and interactions. Observation will tell you what to do.

John Wooden taught me that it's always more important to worry about what you do, not what your opponent might do. He said the thing that's going to impact the score is you doing the best you can, "If you want to change the score you must change yourself." Wooden once said: "Be more concerned with your character than your reputation. Reputations fluctuate based on what people think. YOU can't control what people think any more than you can control the weather. But you can control who you are and get satisfaction in knowing you did your best. The most important question you can ask yourself is, "Is this the right thing to do? YOU can't let what somebody else thinks or might think about your judgement."

"When I was in high school and college, I did the best in classes that I enjoyed which is why it's important to me that my coaches have the ability to make our players enjoy practices and meetings." Rex Ryan (NFL coach) liked to operate by the kill acronym **"KILL" – "Keep it likeable and learnable**." Everybody was excited to be part of his program because they were going to be aggressive and play on the edge.

Something that seems to get overlooked a bit is how important it is to have good energy at practice. The coaches are responsible for that. They shouldn't be out there with slumped shoulders and their hands in their pockets. Attitude is contagious. It's the personalities of the coaches and the players interacting that helps keep things interesting way more than changing up the practice schedule.
CONT PG 103

Themes I remind the team about:

- Respect everyone but fear none.
- Make the routine plays.
- Only play the next play.
- Have a great attitude on the sidelines
- Great body language.
- Don't try to do too much.
- Play with a clear mind.

The same squad can look flawless one Saturday and like a train wreck the next. People may try to attribute that inconsistency to the emotional "ups and downs" of 18–23 year young men. I think that is an over-simplification. The operational phrase is "over-simplification." As coaches can we do something about these "ups and downs," that is our job and our coaching challenge.

Etc. The goal of every young player should be to be a Six Tool Player: 1. Shoot 2. Pass. 3. Dribble. 4. Drive 5. Rebound. 6. Defend. Kyle Smith – Washington State U.

BOB McKILLOP, DAVIDSON UNIVERSITY
"THE BOAT THEORY"

Coach McKillop is a 30 plus year veteran with over 600 career wins. Credited as one of the outstanding basketball technicians in the game, Coach McKillop's teams are well known for not beating themselves and a "tough out" anytime but particularly in the NCAA tournament. Coach McKillop recruited and developed the great Stephen Curry of the Golden State Warriors. This piece takes a unique look at elements of being a "team."

You put the boat in the water and point it in the direction you want to go, two things become obvious instantly. 1. Only the coach(coxswain) can see the destination of the canoe. 2. The players doing the rowing have their backs to the direction and the destination. They must have faith in the coxswain(coach) to show the way.

Now the boat travels through the water, there will be some calm waters, some rough water, there will be wind, rain, and hot sun.

Where you position your team is key:

- You want some guys in the front of the boat.
- You want some guys in the back of the boat.
- You want some guys in the middle of the boat.
- The coach is in the back directing the boat.
- Everyone begins by paddling.
- One paddle out of the water and your team will not go as far.
- A paddle in the water but not working with the others and you will not go as far.
- One paddle going too deep or too shallow and the direction is altered, and you are not going as far.
- And then someone doesn't like their seat in the boat – so they get up and try to change seats in the boat and all of a sudden, the boat is off balance and the boats direction changes and the distance to the destination becomes farther and more difficult.

The Boat Theory has a lot of application to our basketball team.

Think about it. How do we keep the boat rowing in a direct route to our destination?

GREGG MARSHALL
WICHITA STATE UNIVERSITY

This is a transcript of Coach Marshall's pre-game comments to the Shocker team prior to the 16-17 NCAA round of sixteen. A great season in Wichita basketball history winning 31 games and going 17-1 in the Missouri Valley Conference. This Kentucky game was played at a very high level with Kentucky surviving with a 65-62 win.

"If we are sad after this game, we're sad because it's over, not because of the way we played; not because of anything else; because we had so much fun and such a ride and now it's over."

"But are we satisfied? Are you satisfied that we're the last team playing in the state of Kansas? Are you satisfied with the number 31(wins)? Are we satisfied that everybody is saying that we're not going to win this game? Are we satisfied, hey, it was a nice little story, but we're not going to beat Kentucky?"

"If they were to change the uniforms. . . they would be talking about us right now as one of the best college basketball teams in the history of this great game. Do you hear anybody saying that? No, because they do not expect you to come out and win this game. We have proven all year long that we can do this. This is an unbelievable opportunity. You've got to decide if you want to be <u>DAVID OR GOLIATH OR BOTH."</u>

Etc. "There are two ways to live your life.
One is as if nothing is a miracle
and the other is everything is a miracle.
I lean to the latter and am drawn to other people
who believe the same."
A. Einstein

PORTER MOSER, HEAD COACH
LOYOLA UNIVERSITY – CHICAGO
UNIVERSITY OF OKLAHOMA

With the legendary Sister Jean supporting the Loyola Ramblers every step of the journey to the 2018 Final Four for the first time since the 1963 Ramblers were in the Final 4 NCAA tournament. The Ramblers lost in the National semi-final in a high-level matchup with the Univ. of Michigan.

Porter Moser was a former assistant for the legendary Rik Majerus who preached offensive spacing, and the Ramblers are second best in the nation with a 52% field goal percentage thanks to a spaced offense. He demanded a winning culture, to which Moser deliberately recruited to; the Ramblers roster features seven players who won state championships in high school. If you want culture you have to recruit culture. But the biggest Majerus imprint of all comes with patience and trusting the process. After getting fired following four seasons at Illinois State in 2007, Moser came to Loyola with the anxiety that he wouldn't win fast enough. That's what made Saturday's 68-61 regular season finale so full-circle: The Ramblers celebrated their Missouri Valley Conference crown-five years after joining the league from the Horizon Conference by beating Moser's former team, Illinois State.

Coach Majerus helped reaffirm how I wanted to build a program, said Moser. When you go through what I went through (fired at Illinois State,) It'd be easy to come in and get over-anxious and make bad decisions. I have letters in my office from Coach Majerus reminding me to do it the right way– recruit good kids and don't be in a hurry. **Our team has been saying, "There is no finish line;"** and that's the mind-set we must have. We have to play hungrier than we've ever seen." As a mid-major to get into the NCAA tournament we know we have to be the best team in the conference for three days. Recruiting when you're a losing program, that's hard to overcome in the recruiting pitch. The pitch was, "if you're part of a group that changes this, they'll remember you the rest of your lives. You've got to have special kids that believe they can win." It all started with a vision that has evolved in teamwork and a "We" culture that shared the ball like no team I have ever seen.

GEORGE PATTON

US ARMY FOUR STAR GENERAL, WW2

An aggressive hard charging warrior, who's philosophy was to lead from "the front." His emphasis on rapid and aggressive offensive action proved successful and he was feared by the German High command. His ability to inspire troops with attention getting, colorful language speeches were legendary. He loved his troops and they loved him.

In the iconic movie "PATTON" starring George C. Scott as Patton, early in WW2, the US Armed Forces were getting slammed at every turn by the Nazi's.

This prompted General Eisenhower and Allied Command to assign Gen. George Patton to the North Africa campaign. In Patton's first big battle v. the Germans, the allied troops were hammered on the ground and in the air. It was a humiliating defeat for the US Forces and Patton personally, one he would revenge many times.

In the movie, there is a scene where Patton by himself tours the decimated war zone. Smoke clouded the battlefield with still smoldering tanks jeeps and big guns. The stench of dead soldiers, local Bedouins and the carcasses of dead animals including camels, horses and dogs added to the pungent smell of death that smothered the battlefield.

As Patton dismounts from his jeep and for several minutes solemnly surveys the carnage and in a low almost inaudible voice says to himself:

"GOD HELP ME, I LOVE IT SO."

Editor/Collector notes: This might well be the words of the dedicated coach who fights her/his own "war" against the heart break of players losing purpose, gut wrenching final second losses, the long ride home, irresponsible adults, injuries, defections, media ignorance or worse, budget cuts, etc., etc., but still with pride & perhaps not knowing why, repeats the words of General Patton:

"GOD HELP ME, I LOVE IT SO."

NICK SABAN
UNIVERSITY OF ALABAMA
COACH SABAN TALKS "DISCIPLINE"

Discipline is doing what you are supposed to do, when you are supposed to do it and do it the way it is supposed to be done.

SELF DISCIPLINE: Means you do it in any circumstance whether you feel like doing it or not, you make yourself do it.

There is no one that feels like doing what they need to do every day, but you make yourself do it because it's the right thing to do. It's what you want to accomplish that drives you to do what you need to do.

When we talk about people, they are not one kind of character in one part of their life and then another kind of character in another part of their life."

Alabama Nick: **"Everyone wants to be the beast, but few want to do what the beast does."**

Etc. Vision without action is a dream.

JOHN THOMPSON "TALKS" BOB KNIGHT
JOHN THOMPSON "TALKS" JOHN THOMPSON

Coach Thompson, the great Georgetown Coach, won the NCAA Championship in 1984, coached the USA Team in the 1988 Seoul, Korea Olympics. Coach Thompson was a giant in the game. He was the kind of coach that when he made a statement on a lot of things, not just basketball, A common reaction would be, "I wish I'd thought of that."

John Thompson, Georgetown University and Bob Knight, Indiana University. NCAA National Championship coaches and Hall of Fame inductees and two of the most impactful coaches in the history of college basketball both every different and yet very much the same in their approaches to winning basketball games and developing boys into adults.

John Thompson on Bob Knight*:" I have a great deal of respect for Bobby because you know where he stands. You don't have to wonder what he's thinking. He'll tell you. The bottom line that I have looked at with him is beside the fact that he has won, the people who have come under his tutelage have been very sensible people when they've left. His kids tend to graduate from school and do well."*

John Thompson on John Thompson*: Coach Thompson relies on seniors to teach underclassmen about Georgetown tradition and how Hoyas do things comparing it to family. "It helps a lot if the older players are sensible. I think my youngest son goes to my older son for advice a lot more than coming to me not realizing I gave the older child the advice he's giving him." <u>The bottom line is to have players on your team who act and think sensibly</u>*

NICK SABAN
UNIVERSITY OF ALABAMA
AFTER A "WIN"

What our players and our fans need to understand that this was just one game. Our players need to continue to improve and remember how we got to this point rather than think that we can just show up and beat whoever we play.
We have a tendency to think (just show up) around here instead of just kicking peoples butts like we are supposed to and work hard to do it. The mentality that we've got to earn it in the next game seems to get lost in all the after-game celebrating. What we did tonight was great, but it was only one game. We need to improve as a team that's the way everyone should think.

What good does it do if you made a "B" on the midterm and now you take a week off and get a "D" next week for a "C" average. Or are we going to go back to work tomorrow and get and an "A" in the next game.

COACH SABAN ON MOTIVATION

Motivation is achieved on a daily basis. Motivation must be daily, organized, and planned. A charged-up speech the night before the prom about the dangers of underage drinking probably won't go too far. Same thing goes for a pre-game pep talk.

Etc. Mount Carmel, ILL football coach Frank Lenti letter to parents before the season begins. ". . . we appreciate the opportunity to coach and teach your son, but we're not going to have parents involved in playing time or coaching decisions. You're no more qualified to evaluate your child than I would be mine. We want them all to do well."

DOC SADLER
ASSISTANT COACH
UNIVERSITY OF NEBRASKA
"Not Sold on the 3-point shot"

Doc Sadler is a veteran coach, a former U. of Nebraska head coach returned to Lincoln after a head coaching stint at Southern Mississippi University to join Fred Hoiberg's coaching staff.

I have been a head coach for 16 years and it has been a grind.

Defense is competition, if you are a competitor and you want to win, when it comes time to defend, you'll defend.

Sadler is not sold on the 3-point shot. The national average of 3 made point shots made was 7.9 or 7.8 a game. 22 were shot a game, people think 3 pointers beat you, but that is not what beats you. It's points in the paint. Eight 3 pointers per game sounds nice but it is only 24 points. At Southern Mississippi last year, we once gave up 17 3's in a game and we won by 10 points. We did not give up any points in the paint.

The main idea is not to give up any points in the lane. Force teams to build a "brick" house from 11 to 16 feet and if a 3 pointer goes in, that's fine, they won't beat you from there.

The contrast is that Sadler's Head Coach at Nebraska's Fred Hoiberg's offense is designed to take 3-point shots and paint shots closer than 5 feet. Hoiberg's Iowa State University teams led the Big 12 in 3 point attempts all five seasons he coached in the league.

Etc.: There are no passengers on this team. Everyone has a job to do.

BO SCHEMBECLER
UNIVERSITY OF MICHIGAN
"A LESSON FROM BO"

The fastest way to demoralize your entire team is to make exceptions for the stars. Everyone sees it, and everyone resents it. You'll lose your troops, and it doesn't help the stars either. I've heard a lot of leaders give lip service to "no double standards" and the like, but you're not going to fool your people. They know if you're willing to make the sacrifice to enforce your rules or not.

If you are going to build a team, you simply cannot have one standard for the stars and another standard for everyone else – no matter what it costs you, or them. As competitive as I am, I will not compromise my values or the team's values to win a game. I refuse! That means I am willing to lose. And that's not easy.

Leaving a guy standing in the parking lot just once, and you better believe they'll be a half-hour early next time. Once everyone knows I'm not holding the bus for anyone, trust me, they'll get there. They always do. That bus symbolizes the foundation of our values: simple, straightforward, no exceptions. You start cutting corners for this guy or that situation, and before you know it, you're spending all your time playing judge and jury, deliberating over every little incident, when you should be leading your team. It's painful sometimes, but you create lot fewer headaches for everyone, including players, when you simply stick to your guns.

More Coach Schembecler: Coaching Expectations in Div. 1:
1. Fill arenas/stadiums
2. Do not cheat in recruiting.
3. Graduate all your players.
4. Staff and team must be morally superior to student body
5. Create a positive image for the university
6. Win all your games

JERRY SLOAN – HEAD COACH
UTAH JAZZ
(Jerry Sloan died of a long illness in 2020)

- *Star High School player in Illinois*
- *outstanding college player at Evansville University*
- *teamed with Norm van Lear as the most physically & mentally tough guard due in the NBA with the Chicago Bulls*
- *In the NBA, Coach Sloan became the same kind of coach with the Utah Jazz*

Jerryisms:

- "Pair off in 3's"

- "Line up in a circle"

- Pre-game comments to team: "It's time to make a living, Let's go get some groceries"

- "You will never learn what do not want to learn."

NBA great, Bill Walton eulogizing
The passing of Coach Sloan
"When I think of Jerry Sloan, I think of physical and mental toughness. We worked hard, we played hard.
Outside of the game we laughed and enjoyed each other.
He was a wonderful Coach.
He was a wonderful man."

PAT SUMMITT
HEAD COACH
UNIVERSITY OF TENNESSEE

A dynamic pioneer and a major driving force in the development of women's basketball. Never had a losing season in 38 years of coaching and won 1098 games. Played and coached in the Olympics winning two Gold Medals as Olympic Head Coach. Coached Tennessee to eight NCAA Championships.

DEFINITE DOZEN

TO STAY HERE
Take Full Responsibility
Respect your self
Discipline yourself so no one else has to
Develop and demonstrate Loyalty

TO PERFORM HERE
Make hard work your Passion
Don't just Work Hard, work smart
Put the Team before yourself
Make winning an Attitude

TO BE SUCCESSFUL HERE
Learn to be a great Communicator
Change is a must
Accept your role
Handle Success like you handle Failure

114

TOM THIBIDEAU, HEAD COACH
NEW YORK KNICKS

Offensively we try to get:

1. Layups
2. Free Throws
3. Corner 3's

Defensively we are trying to take away:

1. Layups
2. Free Throws
3. Corner 3's

Work on defensive techniques so that you do not foul:

1. Do things to take away the layup, corner 3.
2. Now we want to force offense into a long 2.
3. There are ways to influence the ball, so the ball handler brings the ball back to a defender.

MODERN COACHING IN THE NBA: BALANCE – TEAM AND TALENT

1. Build Trust – coach needs to be around the team.
2. Must keep best players accountable – the head coach and the best player must never have a bad practice.

You want to win games. But you want to put the team in the best environment to get better. We are not focusing on winning. We focus on coming in every day and doing our job. We are focusing on improving basketball players.

We never use age as a cop out. We sign up to be a coach or a player regardless of circumstances in the film room, on the floor, conditioning, it takes total commitment to get better.

Minutes played has a lot of variables that contribute to playing players too many minutes:

1. Age of team   2. Matchups   3. Health – short handed

Not all minutes are the same, shooters in the corner playing end to end. Some sports science people say play fewer minutes. That is not the case, if you need him to play 48 minutes; coaches need to get the players body ready to play 48 minutes.

115

JEFF VAN GUNDY
NBA HEAD COACH
NEW YORK / HOUSTON
When Coach Van Gundy speaks it is good to listen and read

- ✓ You must know what loses games before you know what wins – Bill Parcels
- ✓ Expect your players to repeat what you believe in.

- ✓ Players "On the line" – give a pop quiz to start practice.

- ✓ **Pat Riley always developed coaching confidence (that was respected by players.) Are you confident, knowledgeable, sincere, reliable, trustworthy, if you have these traits anyone will allow you to coach them? Great players don't want you to waste their time just give them a plan for improvement.**
- ✓ Don't be intimidated by any player or situation (KNOW YOUR STUFF.)

- ✓ Do the players understand the concept of "TEAM?"

- ✓ The best players unite and inspire the group. They are thinking only about winning.
- ✓ Coaches inspire with passion, energy and being prepared.

- ✓ You've got to know who can coach well and who can't. Those who can't coach well project softness, selfishness, and stupidity.
- ✓ I love "hungry" scorers, not selfish scorers, there is a difference.

- ✓ Smart play is a talent that we do not value enough. How can you win if you don't know when to do something?

Players don't care if you are short, tall, black, white, a former player, or not. All they care about is can you help them.

116

JEFF VAN GUNDY
NBA COACH

"21ˢᵀ CENTURY BASKETBALL"

"The Golden State Warriors present a lot of problems in their half-court offense – but to me it is the first 6 – 8 seconds that they get you. You are never set and ready to guard because you are trying to get back and are never set in your defense – getting your matchups are difficult to begin with. The Warriors do not come down the floor in a traditional way.

They play as much random basketball as we have ever seen in the NBA. I don't say that in a bad way. They play intelligent random basketball. There is no way to know what is coming. . ."

Etc. Coaching is nothing more than teaching:
"How are you going to make me better?
If you can make me better, I don't care
If you are the 'GREEN HORNET.'
I will listen."
(The "Green Hornet" is a crime fighting "superhero.")

JEFF WALZ
UNIVERSITY OF LOUISVILLE

THE WISDOM AND WIT OF JEFF WALZ

A Final Four caliber coach and perennial National Championship contender

Walz Wisdom:
- ✓ I am a big picture person, many days I do not bring a written practice plan to practice (Resulting in fewer drills.)
- ✓ Just get it done. I really don't care how (fewer rules means more instinctive play.)
- ✓ We do not treat all players the same
- ✓ We stay close to our player's parents.
- ✓ I will reward you with playing time for working hard. What you do with it is up to you.
- ✓ We are not a democracy. The best player needs to take the most shots.
- ✓ Players know I will tell them how I feel and still love them.
- ✓ We do a lot of down and back in 12 seconds for conditioning and a variety of other reasons.
- ✓ We need to hold each other accountable, especially women, what happens on the floor stays on the floor.
- ✓ More rules – more problems.
- ✓ It's not the X's and O's it's the Sarah's and Kate's.
- ✓ If you act like an adult, we will treat you like an adult, if not, we will teach you to be one.
- ✓ I am not paid to be wrong.
- ✓ Anything (elite player, Indy race car, etc.) that is high performance is high maintenance.
- ✓ Must be true to your rules.

CONT PG. 119

The Walz Wit:

Coach Walz and his team have a high level of trust and loyalty in each other. Therefore, a witty communication style is a technique used by master coaches to create a desired team atmosphere. Players learn and remember from pithy type, humor: they repeat it, laugh and giggle about it amongst themselves; it is another coaching tactic to bring and keep the team together.

Coach Walz
- ✓ "If you read books like you read defenses, you'll be a certified illiterate."
- ✓ "Players ask me what kind of cell phone I had in high school; Coach told me practice was at 3:00. I didn't get eleven text messages from teammates telling me what time practice was. I showed up at 3:00"
- ✓ HTM defense, "Hope They Miss" defense.
- ✓ Do you believe in free speech, "yes;" Do you believe in the 1st amendment, "yes;" Good because I have a free speech for you."
- ✓ (Rhetorically speaking) "If you kill someone you are still on the team, lie and you are off the team.
- ✓ Our team thinks Denial defense is a river in Egypt.

Etc. Urban Meyer, former Jacksonville Jaguars Head Coach addressing Colorado State University football team: "Scholarships come with obligations to coaches, alumni, fans and the school to always do your best – those who don't are letting everyone down and the coaches regret recruiting them. I will bet your coaches wish some of you were not here."

COQUESE WASHINGTON
ASSOC. HEAD COACH
NOTRE DAME
TEAM DISCIPLINE THROUGH RECRUITMENT

Ms. Washington is the former head coach at Penn State

I do not want to coach drama – so I do not recruit drama. We work very hard in the recruiting process to make sure we bring into the program the kind of kids who will be a good fit for the program's values, culture, physical and academic environment.

Team rules:
1. Be on time
2. Go to class
3. Attend all meetings and appointments
4. Act with dignity and grace and dress appropriately for each occasion

Expectations align with our rules and what they look and sound like verbally and non-verbally on and off the court is what it means to be a Lady Lion Basketball Player.

Editor/Collectors note: This is a nice concise statement regarding recruiting players that will thrive in the system / culture of the team and University. Recruiting high maintenance athletes is not found in too many programs mission statements; unless this is the student / athlete that appeals to your coaching style and you can coach them; but if you can't coach'em you can't win with'em. And chances are they end up being the team influencer (bully.)

The Collector/editor of this book: As a kid, I lived next to a beer hall. The owner often said, "If you let a bully run the 'joint' pretty soon all the paying customers leave and then the bully leaves, too. This is something coaches need to be aware of.

ROY WILLIAMS
UNIVERSITY OF NORTH CAROLINA
THE FREE LANCE GAME

Coach Williams, a disciple of the great Dean Smith, began his coaching journey as a JV player for the UNC Tarheels before moving to the Tarheel assistant coaching staff. Coach Williams first head coaching job was at Kansas University where he coached for 15 years before accepting the head coaching position at UNC in 2003, going back to where he began his coaching journey. The winner of three NCAA championships and 885 games and inducted into the Basketball Hall of Fame in 2007.

1. It's our job as coaches to take what we want not what the defense gives us.
2. Three passes unless we get a layup – ball must change sides of the floor.
3. When the ball is passed to the top, we back screen, and the passer follows his pass.
4. The toughest screen to cover is the one for the passer.

In Practice:

We play 4x4 if a player doesn't screen for the passer, it is a violation, early in practice sessions we allow only layups

Roy Williams: "Sometimes you lose – sometimes you learn. Nothing in life breeds resilience like adversity and failure."

Etc. The only failure is to not try. Our integrity is measured by how we handle disappointment and how we meet and greet what is "Next."

JOHN WOODEN
UCLA
"IT WAS MY FAULT... "

Widely recognized as perhaps the greatest coach and leader of any sport.

"You have to make a positive out of wherever you are." Coach Wooden.

During my first years at UCLA, I never thought we could win big. We just had too many handicaps: poor facilities, other sports practicing in the fieldhouse at the same time we were practicing. It was very difficult and I kind of accepted all the problems we had.

But one year we had a team I thought might do well. That team won the NCAA championship by defeating Michigan and their great player, Cazzie Russell.

After that breakthrough year I believed every year, we could win the NCAA.

Looking back, now I realize it was not the players or the circumstances, it was me, I didn't believe we could do it. All those bleak years I didn't really feel like we could win. It was my fault, not the players, not the lack of resources. It was me all the time.

Collector/Editor Notes: Coaches are wise to think about this, perhaps the greatest coach of all time admitted it was HIS attitude holding him and UCLA back from winning big early in his career. The lesson: be wary of giving up on your aspirations and hopes for your program and team. Maybe it just requires one more try.

Etc. KNOW THYSELF – and keep it real.

JOHN WOODEN

MINNESOTA – UCLA AND A SNOWSTORM

10 NCAA National championship – seven in a row – 88 game winning streak. Bill Walsh, the great 49er football coach described John Wooden as a "philosopher coach" a man who in the truest sense, whose beliefs, wisdom and teaching go far beyond sports. . . he was an American legend, comfortable with today's citizen's and leaders. . . a very special American."

John Wooden wanted to coach at the University of Minnesota. Being a graduate of Purdue, the Big 10 and being a Midwesterner increased his interest in Minnesota. He had less interest in the open UCLA position. He had interviewed for both positions and arranged for Minnesota to call at 6:00 PM and UCLA at 7:00 an hour later in the hopes that Minnesota would offer him the Golden Gopher basketball coaching position before the call from Los Angeles.

By 6:55 Minnesota had not called. When the phone rang at 7:00 it was UCLA with an offer to coach the Bruin basketball team. Coach Wooden accepted UCLA's offer.

When Minnesota finally called to offer him the Minnesota job, the one he really wanted, it turns out that there was a severe snowstorm in the Minneapolis area and all the telephone lines were down. The rest of the story is history.

There's a second layer to the above account of Coach Wooden accepting the less attractive UCLA position:
1. Keeping one's word. 2. Sometimes fortune is not your first choice.

Etc.: Do not concern yourself with boredom by the players or yourself.
This is Learning not Entertainment.

SECTION V

RECRUITMENT

"RECRUIT LIKE YOUR LIFE DEPENDS ON IT BECAUSE YOUR COACHING LIFE DOES."

RECRUITING

RECRUITING . . . A GUARANTEE

We are going to <u>Help</u> you <u>Help</u> yourself be a better person.

We are going to <u>Help</u> you <u>Help</u> yourself get a great education.

We are going to <u>Help</u> you <u>Help</u> yourself be the best player you can be.

WHAT IF YOU GET THAT "STAR?"

If you really go after a kid and really work hard on him.

And the kid goes to another school, he will only hurt you once a year.

But if you recruit the wrong kid, he will hurt you every day of the year.

B. Schembechler - Michigan

Etc. Why I coach? "Whether my career ended with a better job or getting fired – every stop was a great experience, it was the players, the relationships, they were all great." Unknown

TERRY PETTIT
HEAD COACH, WOMEN'S VOLLEYBALL
UNIVERSITY OF NEBRASKA

Coach Pettit, former head coach of the NCAA champion Nebraska Volleyball team. Coach Pettit is a recognized author, public speaker and coaching mentor. Coach Pettit is a coaching master.

The goal is not perfection but to get better.

You have to recruit as if your professional career depended on it – because it does. Once you have done that. What do you have? You have a group not a team. Now it is up to the coaching staff to transfer this loosely connected "group" into a "team" with singleness of purpose and focus.

There must be fanatical commitment to recruiting talent. The coaching staff has to have a clear understanding of the combined strength of the athlete, the institutional culture of the University and local community and find creative ways to leverage those strengths (In the recruitment process.)

The purpose-oriented coach before they have recruited the right rowers looks out across the bow of the boat and sees farther than anyone else and seems foolish in in her/his confidence. "The National Championship is where we are going" and the coach must continue to say it, "The National Championship is where we are going through, injuries, lost recruits, disappointing losses, and the perception by others that the program is not making headway."

There is nothing so satisfying and rewarding as the coach who chooses to risk as much as refusing to believe that it will not happen clearly acknowledging all the challenges along the way making him/her uncomfortable with their refusal to let go of being great until everything, talent, staff, athletic administration, players and skeptical fans are all caught up in where we are going, "The National Championship."

127

"BE CAREFUL OF WHAT YOU WISH . . ."

Deion Bonner stole IPods and IPhones on a recruiting trip to Georgia. Bonner eventually signed a scholarship offer with the University of Tennessee. Following is Head Coach Derek Dooley's explanation for the Bonner signing.

"When I say we bring in high character that doesn't mean I'm never going to bring in guys who have made mistakes. I can tell you right now, I have made as many mistakes in my life as anybody, but I'll put my past up against a lot of guys.

We did a lot of due diligence on this situation. Deion was incredibly truthful, incredibly remorseful and I do not know of a high school player who had to pay the piper for what they did and what he had to go through. He had an absolute public disparagement. Five games of his high school career taken away and everybody stopped recruiting him. It was tough and it was incredible the maturity level he showed, and I believe he can come in and represent Tennessee and learn from his mistake and be a great example, certainly it is not the norm, but we felt like given the diligence we did on him and of course he is a good football player, let's not deny that and at a key position. We felt willing to take the risk."

Bonner as s freshman player in 9 games mostly on special teams, He was not listed on the Vols roster in 2013, nor was Coach Dooley who was relieved of the head coaching position after the 2012 season. . . You decide.

Etc. MOMENTUM: "Big MO," don't let circumstances control your response.
We do not recognize momentum. What is happening in real time
Is because of what we are doing and what we are not doing.
PJ Fleck, U of Minnesota

JOHN CALIPARI
UNIVERSITY OF KENTUCKY
"RECRUITING QUESTION"

"If you come to the University of Kentucky and in three years, what would have to happen to make you feel happy about your progress or success? (Ask the same question in the negative.")

"If you come to the University of Kentucky and in three years, what would have to happen for you to not be satisfied/happy about your progress or success?"

Now shut up, say nothing, if the prospect does not or will not answer the question, they do not trust you.

If they do answer the question, their answer will probably reveal something

significant.

Etc. The second team can't win the Championship; but they can keep the team from winning it. The non-starters must be held responsible and accountable in practice.

"THE PRO"

By Hank Evans

Hank Evans is a "gung-ho" Purdue Boilermaker. He knows selling, he knows sports, he knows recruiting and he loves the Boilermakers. Mr. Evans would often accompany Purdue coaches on recruiting trips. These were the days when recruiting resembled the "Wild west" – and was a lot more fun.

Joe Tiller, the Wyoming head coach and previously an assistant for the Boilermakers and destined to return to W. Lafayette as the Boilermaker boss in 1997 was friendly with Mr. Evans and invited him to the Wyoming campus to conduct a recruiting workshop. The timing was perfect as Mr. Evans, a liquor salesman by profession was in Denver where he had just closed a $7,000,000 liquor sale with United Airlines.

Hank Evans presented a seminar that was informative and valuable regarding using sales techniques to advance the recruiting process. What made the presentation special was:

1. *Hank Evans knew what he was talking about. He was a seven-million-dollar expert.*
2. *He loved the challenge and competitiveness of his profession and athletics.*
3. *Mr. Evans, a high energy guy with enthusiasm and a degree of theatrics that added to the presentation.*

Reading and studying "The Pro" will help recruit better players and win more games.

Workshop Objectives

Increase coaches' awareness on the use of professional selling techniques for recruiting student-athletes:

1. What to sell and when to sell it.
2. When to close and how to close.
3. How to overcome objections and recognize conditions affecting the sale.
4. Learn how to use questions. . .the secret to successful selling.
5. Help you select certain techniques so you can fit them into your personal selling style.
6. "It's not telling, it's the selling."

SIX STEP SELLING PROCESS

1. **Pre-introduction**
   - "Positioning phase"
   - Letters, phone calls, video calls, social media, etc., etc.
2. **Qualification**
   - Grades, video, recommendations, games, club events, etc., etc.
3. **First impressions**
   - Getting their attention and keeping it
   - Exchanging information – <u>wants</u> and <u>needs</u> of prospect
   - Sell emotion. . .not logic
4. **The Body**
   - Prospects interests, convictions, and desires
   - Features and benefits of attending "State U"
   - "Ask questions, answer questions, ask more questions…"
5. **Close**
   - Early and often
6. **Handling objections**
   - Prove your position by reviewing features and benefits
   - Call for action by the prospect despite their objections

Note: Steps five and six are interchangeable in selling sequence

Notes:

✓ First impressions are extremely important-the only thing you do not get a "do over."
✓ They say, "no." You say, "why?"
✓ Selling begins when the prospect says "no"
✓ The worst thing that can happen is they say "no."
✓ Know the difference between an "<u>objection</u>" and "<u>condition</u>." (see later text.)

PRE-INTRODUCTION

1. Develop electronic/hard copy/video materials that set you apart from the competition. Think outside the box.

2. Be positive and up-beat.

3. Beware of information overload.

4. Conversation is in control of the person who is asking the questions

A proposal v. a Presentation, the recruiting "Pro" gives a proposal:

PROPOSAL	VERSUS	PRESENTATION
• Is what we do when we meet w/recruit		- Is a one-way conversation, coaches do all the talking
• Demands an answer		- It becomes an information session.
• We must get good info. Exchange.		
• Recruiting is a proposal		

✓ You don't judge a prospect by his/her questions, but by the answers to your questions.
✓ Prospects must answer questions, that is how we evaluate their interest
✓ <u>The conversation is in control of the person who is asking the questions.</u>
✓ Have other sports evaluate your recruiting materials / cross reference with other sports

Etc. You don't sit in church to become a Christian.
You don't sit in your garage to become a car.
AND you do not sit in front of the TV and become a ball player.

HOW DO YOU QUALIFY A PROSPECT

You ask questions to find out the following:

1. Their personal past. What they have done, tells a lot about what they want to become. When you know where they want to go, you'll have some clues on how to sell them on what they need to reach their goals and how you can help them.
2. Your close rate is 50% or better if you qualify correctly.
3. Qualifying means that you work hard with people who will say "Yes" instead of working equally hard with people who say "No."
4. Find out what they are interested in:

Facilities	**Family ties**	**Tenure of coach**
Opportunity to play	**Education**	**Career aspirations**
Tradition	**Athletics (the pros)**	**Location/geography**
School's prestige	**Social life**	**Size of school**

5. Always have them prioritize this list with the option of adding to list.
6. Who in addition to yourself will make the final decision?
7. When do you want to make a decision – early or late?
8. Bracket in on the strong interests to close out qualifying. Later in the process you will probably need to reinforce their choices – kids are known to develop amnesia.

Qualifying Notes:

✓ "Did you start when you were a freshman/sophomore in H.S. Is starting early in your career important to you? At our school talent trumps experience."
✓ "Who are the influencers? Treat them just like the prospect."
✓ "Buyers are liars, that is because they want to procrastinate."
✓ "There are two answers: 1. the answer they give you. 2. the real one."
✓ "Don't think about answers, think about questions."

- ✓ "Always CLOSE on every call or visit. "Player who wants to play early or start, "When do you think you will be able to start? Do you believe this coaching staff can make you a better player? Are you willing to put in the work and be coachable?"
- ✓ "Coaches must get better at the recruiting process because of the limited time."
- ✓ "We are not recruiters we are detectives, must find out what the prospect is thinking, talk to friends, family, relatives, coaches, teachers, principal, girlfriend." Detectives find out who is in the prospect's world."
- ✓ "Close every day."
- ✓ "Is there anything more I can do for you? Are you ready to go with us."
- ✓ "Questions - not answers, think of questions to ask."
- ✓ "If you say something they can deny it, if they say it you can challenge their answer.
- ✓ "Don't use the policeman's authority figure pose. Stay at the same physical level as the prospect."

SELL THE PROGAM

The bottom line, no matter what your product or service, the object is to get a "YES." Nothing up to that point counts. It's all invested effort with no payoff.

"Selling, it is the intangibles, big crowds, education, NCAA tournament, NCAA Champions, All Conference, travel, NBA/WNBA et.al."

Basics of selling:

1. The difference between a PROPOSAL and a PRESENTATION: A proposal is a two-way conversation, and a presentation is a one-way conversation.
2. The difference between a FEATURE and BENEFIT: a feature is a characteristic about something, and a benefit is what it does for the prospect. Typically buying decisions are made when the prospect hears the right benefit.
3. The single most important issue in selling is closing. Most people who fail in selling do so because they can't close.

4. Remember this – Questions produce answers and answers produce action. The person in control is the person who is doing the asking not the answering.

SELLING IS SIMPLE, IT'S A THREE STAGE PROCESS

1. **Interest and/or attention:**

Information gathering, qualify academically, athletically, character. Get their attention with NCAA allowed communication.

2. **Body:** Present your story using features and benefits: This begins and continues through the signing/unofficial commitment and beyond.

3. **Close**: There are two rules: 1. Close early and often. 2. This step takes place any time with the prospect:

A. indicates interest.
B. agrees with a benefit
C. you overcome a prospects objection. Example of a prospect objection: Prospect: _"Wyoming is a long way from home."_ Coach: _"Is that important to you?"_ Prospect: _"Yes, it is."_ Coach: _"All our games on live TV and live streamed, airplane flights are inexpensive. We always schedule an away game in the hometown of our players so all your friends and parents can see you play. OK are you ready to become a Cowgirl._ Coach waits for an answer.

Etc. One value of statistical measurement: it counters coaching "bias." Facts trump opinion. If you believe a player is poor on defense you will see every his/her def. mistake. Conversely, if you believe a player is a good defender you will remember every defensive stop, help and recover, steal, etc. the player makes. Both are opinion lacking factual evidence. Measurement is what is needed to confirm or confront coaching observations/opinions.

135

LET'S LOOK AT THESE THREE
STAGES IN GREATER DETAIL

STAGE 1
The Attention Step

The point of the attention step is to get the prospect familiar with answering questions in a two-way communication environment.

It has two functions:

1. Create interest / get prospects attention / communicate recruitment interest.
2. Allows coach to qualify prospect based on mutual interest level.

This step would typically be used any time you are initially getting involved with a prospect. It can be accomplished through video communication. Telephone techniques are addressed later.

STAGE 2

The Proposal

The objective of stage two is to maintain their interest and create enough desire to include your school in their decisions.

Some principles to remember:

- **Don't sell logic.** The choice to attend a school over another will typically not be made on logic. In these situations, decisions are made based on emotion. If logic was the "linchpin" that drives decisions, can anyone explain why High School All American and future Hall of Fame player, Diana Taurasi from Glendale, CA would attend UCONN and not STANFORD.

- Be positive no matter how tough it gets. Positive emotions trigger "Yes" answers. Negative emotions produce "No" answers.
- Don't sell what _you_ think or feel. See what they want or feel. How many times have you said, "I just know XYZ Univ. is for you, because I just love it . . . there is a shopping mall right on campus, etc., etc. Just because it is a great place for you (the coach) has very little if any validity for the prospect. The recruiter can only know what is important to the prospect after learning through a 'Prospect Centered Approach' that has flushed out what is important to the prospect in terms of their: 1. Needs 2. Values 3. Objectives and 4. Interests.
- You can learn a lot watching and listening. The real key in selling/recruiting is not telling it's asking and listening. Remember questions demand answers, answers produce action.
- Ask questions, questions and more questions."

HERE ARE IMPORTANT TECHNIQUES
INVOLVED IN THE BODY OF YOUR PROPOSAL

It's about:

1. **Features**
2. **Benefits**
3. **Questions/affirm**
4. **Close**

Features are characteristics about your school or program that make it unique or sets it apart from your competition:

✓ Brainstorm with the coaching staff to create a features list for your school.
✓ Prospects buy benefits when emotion is attached. Every feature has to have a benefit. The key benefits will have pay value to the prospect.

✓ Frequently, coaches will state dozens of features about their school <u>but</u> fail to convert them into benefits. Consequently, the prospect has no reason to go there.

✓ Benefits must be supportable anytime you present a prospect with a benefit be prepared to support it. There are a couple of ways to prove a benefit: 1. Visual – pictures, video productions of athletic and academic facilities. 2. Testimonials from athletic administration, academic professors, former players, etc. (brainstorm.)

THE FEATURE GAME

"feature"	*"benefit to prospect"*
great arena	you will play before big crowds
highly ranked law school	great post grad career possibilities
state of the art wt. room	you will be strong, faster, more explosive
12 to 1 prof to student ratio	you will get ind. assistance in class
small fwd. is a senior	you will be able to quickly work into lineup
talent trumps experience w/us	playing time is based on ability to help team
hd. coach is connected with Pro's	this will help you after college career
etc., etc., etc.	

Every feature needs a benefit, prospects buy benefits that have value to them. Buyers – when they hear the benefits to them - not just the features of the school, such as: close to airport, mall on campus, great academics, etc. Only features that have benefits to the prospect count in convincing the prospect to commit to good old State U.

Create a "yes chain" with the above features/benefits and others. It can almost be a "Features/Benefits game." When the prospect hears the benefit that is important to him/her, that is when the coach closes.

The order of conversation: A. state feature B. state benefit to prospect C. "Is this really important to you?" D. close-when the prospect agrees with you (affirms the benefit.) "OK, are you ready to win the ABC Conference with us. Do you want to call Coach Malarky with your decision?"

If I do not "close" the deal on this visit/conversation. The next time, I assume it is the first time I have met with the prospect.

138

IMPORTANT: Never play defense w/ with your negatives (every school has them) play offense. Bring up the negatives before the prospect hears about them from the competition. Don't hope the recruit will not ask about, weather, distance from home, players at their position, type of offense and defense, student – professor ratio. Regarding NCAA issues you may want a 3rd party i.e. Athletic Director to address the prospect. Once negatives are answered "OK, what else can I help you with?

PRACTICING THE "FEATURE" GAME

Feature: "We have a great strength program."
Benefit: "this program will make you stronger and allow you to play earlier in your career."
Question: "Didn't you say that this is important? How important is it?"
Affirmation by product: "Really important."
Close: "So are you ready to be an LSU Tiger?"

Feature: We have a "Great arena" what this means is you will play in front of "Big Crowds." do you like that idea?" prospect: "Sounds great coach" Coach: "Congratulations sounds like you want to a Cowboy. Let's go and take a look at your locker."
String together 5-6-10 Features – create a "Yes" chain - after every feature, the coach asks prospect, "Do you like that?" After the final "Yes" by the prospect, Coach, closes: Looks like we have a match and you're ready to become a "Fighting Eagle," be quiet and wait for an answer.

- ✓ When I do not get a commitment, the next time I meet with the prospect I assume it's the first time
- ✓ As soon as you have given a "feature" go right to how that feature will "benefit the prospect."
- ✓ The feature-benefit game is a game, "Play it.
- ✓ **"Prospects buy when they hear the benefits. They do not buy features.**

139

The way to tie all this together is to use questions and have the patience to wait for answers. That way you can focus on those features and benefits that have the highest priority and she/he is most interested in.

Here are some question types to ask:

1. Tag on questions: "Didn't you say playing in a big-time program is important.
2. Option questions: There are two answers both favor the recruiter, "Do you want to wear #5 or #42, are you going to fly or drive to campus, is your major going to be business or engineering, live on or off campus, etc."
3. Rebound questions: "When you are stuck for an answer, bounce the question right back to the prospect. "How important is that too you?" This gives you time to formulate and answer or "I am not sure about that, but I will find out and get right back to you."

- ✓ "50 -10 rule" – people tune you out for 50 seconds and with you 10 seconds.
- ✓ "Get the prospect in the habit of saying "Yes"- the importance of the "Yes" chain" is that it can lead to the big "YES."
- ✓ Being in control – means never answering a question, but always throwing the question back to the prospect. Example: "How much will I get to play as a freshman?" Coaches' response, "Is that important to you?" (The prospect, now, has to give additional information regarding her playing aspirations.) Coach: "At XYZ U no amount of experience is going to overcome talent."
- ✓ "The person asking the questions is in control, not the person answering, no exceptions.

WHY DO WE USE QUESTIONS?

1. You use question to gain and maintain control.
2. You ask questions to get minor "Yes" answers that build a "Yes" chain of "Benefits" leading to the final, "Yes."

3. You ask questions to determine the benefits that the prospect sees value in.
4. You ask questions to isolate and answer objections.
5. You ask questions that confirm their agreement on a benefit. Remember: you tell them. . . they can doubt it. . .they say it. . .it's true
6. You ask questions to help the prospect rationalize decisions they want to make.

7. Finally, you ask questions to uncover the broad areas in which the prospect may have interest. Then additional questions to better focus on their particular needs. Ultimately, you will ask enough questions to find an opportunity which you can capitalize upon and "Close." Finally, the prospect is judged by the quality of their answers, not their questions.

STAGE 3
Closing and Handling Objectives

The goal of stage 3 is to get agreement. If stage 1 and 2 have gone well, Stage 3 is easy.

The closing situation involving a coach and prospect will not conclude in one meeting. This is a unique situation, but the principles and techniques are still the same.

Here are some principles about closing:

- When to close is not always obvious. While this is stage 3, it might occur anytime during the recruiting process. Yours' and the prospects questions will help you recognize when the prospect is ready to say "Yes." Be prepared to close anytime.
- Closing is simple. All you do is make it easy to say "Yes" and difficult to say "No".
- Sometimes coaches continue to sell long after a favorable decision has been reached. This is "selling past the close." To help answer that question of when and how to close. Try the following closing techniques.

CLOSE OFTEN – CLOSE EARLY

Close when there are verbal and or non-verbal expressions of interest.
Here are some closing techniques:

1. Be enthusiastic including a few theatrics.
2. When you ask a closing question, wait for the answer. First person who talks, <u>loses.</u>
3. <u>Option Close</u> – give the prospect a choice between two "Yes" answers. This works well when setting up visits and/or the finally "Close."
   - Are you coming alone or with your parents?
   - You want #33 or #23?
   - Are you driving or flying?
   - Which is best for you the 15th or 30th
   - High tops or lows

4. <u>Porcupine Close Throwback Close.</u> (Crash and Burn Close.) The prospect says: "What is your TV schedule next year? The typical coach might say, "Yes, we play a lot on TV." And what does he/she have? Zilch, zippo. The "Pro" coach replies: "Is playing on TV next year important to you?" When the prospect says "yes" – it is time to close him/her out, "Well it looks like you are ready to become a "Spartan" (Cowgirl, Tarheel, etc.) <u>then be quiet.</u>
5. <u>The Benjamin Franklin Close.</u> (Listing pluses and minuses)
   The key here is that you assist the prospect, if on a home visit get the whole family involved in developing a "Yes" list. Let the prospect do his own "No" list.
   <u>The Major-Minor Question Close.</u>
   Pose the major decision with a question and without pausing add another question that requires a minor "Yes." Example: "As I see it, the only decision we have to make today is how soon you will be a "Cardinal," by the way will you be driving or flying up for the first summer session.
6. <u>The Higher Authority Close.</u> The assistant coach calls head coach so prospect can commit to the head coach over the phone.

7. The "My Dear Old Mother Close.
   My dear old mother said, "Silence means consent, was she right?" Then be quiet.

8. The "I'll think it Over" Close.
   "Generally speaking, if you have done a good job, the "I'll think it over close" is where the prospect has lied to you or did not have the guts to tell you the real reasons. Call them back the next day or at an appointed time. Be more aggressive over the phone from the standpoint, "We have talked a lot about this, and I need an answer and I need it soon. There are other prospects I have to get back to."
   - "We want to sleep on it."
   - "We don't jump into things."
   - "Let us mull it over."
   - "We'll run this through the grinder."
   - "Call back tomorrow, next week, etc., and we'll let you know." Break the above line using the following agree with the prospect: Confirm and give the prospect a twist. Ask another question, "As Long as you are going to think it over. Just what is it that you are going to think about?" Now be quiet. Once the prospect answers, break down the objection and close again.
     Use the above response and call the next day: "We've talked this through, I need an answer and I need it soon, we have other people waiting on your decision."

9. The Negative Close

   Do you think you are good enough to play on a team that is going to play in the NCAA Tournament? We think you are – BUT DO YOU?

   In summary, closing is getting a "Yes" through whatever technique or means that works for you with the individual prospect. The key issue is to ask a closing question. Very seldom, if ever, will a prospect greet you at the door with: "It's great to see you. . . I'm coming to Minnesota, have you got

143

a scholarship with you?" If you are met at the door with this greeting, maybe you are at the wrong address.

- ✓ The very worst thing that can happen is that the prospect will say, "No."
- ✓ Closing tag lines – As I see it, "I think we've talked about everything, it's time to make a decision." OR "Looks to me like you are ready to become a "Wildcat."
- ✓ Close the parents, influencers, sometimes the prospect is happy that someone else has made the decision for them.
- ✓ Remember buyers are liars.
- ✓ In breaking it down: a. qualifiy b. features and benefits (create a yes chain) and c. Close.

SOLVING OBJECTIONS

Objections are resistance to what you are proposing. Objections don't mean "No" forever. They mean "No" for now.
What the prospect is really indicating.
1. They want more information.
2. They misunderstood something.

Etc. "Commit – then figure it out."
   Jimmy Chen, Master Mountain Climber

Here are some principles concerning objections:

- The key issues: there are two reasons for every objection. The real one and the one they tell you. In other words, they use excuses to mask the real objections, knowing and recognizing the difference between excuses and objections is critical to handling them.
- **There is a difference between objections and conditions. An objection is a request for more information. A "CONDITION" is a valid reason for not going ahead in the process. Conditions are a total block to an offer and can rarely be overcome**.
- Don't argue. Sometimes a prospect will give you an objection and he/she get into an argument. If you win the argument but lose the recruit, what do you have - nothing.
- Don't attack the prospect, attack the objection. It's hard to reject their objection without bruising their self-esteem.
- Objections are opportunities not barriers.
- There aren't many new objections. Most of them you've heard dozens of times. Learn and practice to handle the standard ones and write down every new one you encounter.

OBJECTION HANDLING TECHNIQUES

1. Hear them out and ask why?
2. Reverse objection. "Would you come to Iowa, if you could live off campus." Or "Would you come to Kansas State if I promised you would start by the time the conference season starts." (Now be quiet.)
3. Delay: if it's a serious concern, delay your answer. "I need to talk to my head coach; I will get back to you later today or tomorrow.
4. Negative Recruiting: A hot item. This has been addressed earlier. "I can't control what other people say. But it is not true that our style of play is too slow, or we have too many players at your position." (Have proof/stats, etc. to verify your answer to destroy the objection.) "Now let's talk about something else."

5. Answer the objection, be honest, sometimes you can't overcome those little soft spots, every program has them.
6. Objection: "How many black students do you have on campus?" Coach: "Paris/Tia is that really important to you?" This gives the recruiter time to think of the best answer, particularly if the Universities team is either predominantly African American or White.
7. Always confirm with the recruit that you have answered the objection. "Does that answer your question about getting home for Christmas." Do not leave the question hanging.

8. **Conditions cannot be broken down, conditions are total blocks in going forward. Condition: "I can't to go to the U. of Utah, my parents both graduated from BYU.**

Etc.: Hubie Brown – NBA coach: "Please stop saying "I"" It is "We." It is "Our" staff. It is "The Team."

"WORKING THE PHONES"

Regardless of advancing technology, effective phone and video conversations remains vital to gaining accurate information to advance the recruiting process in your favor.

- Initial conversations are generally kept brief but orchestrated, 8–10 minutes. "Am I taking you away from something?" Words should generate pictures over the phone. After opening with "small talk;" "I've got some questions for you and then I would like you to ask me some questions?"
- With a long conversation you may think you are building an obligation from the prospect; but too often you'll be "Crushed" when he/she goes someplace else, and you end up with a good friend player for another school.
- At some point, ask the prospect, "Let's play a little game? Rate in importance on a scale from 1 to 5 things important to you in attending and playing college basketball." Include, education, opportunity to play(when), distance, facilities, social life, coaches, playing position, TV games, etc. For a prospect who really gets "into this," have them make their own list. Revisit this exercise on subsequent phone calls and compare the prospects real answers.
- Do the same exercise with the schools that are recruiting the prospect. List the schools and have the recruit rate his/her interest in each school on a rating scale of 1-5. Revisit this exercise on subsequent phone calls. Analyze how teams slide up and down. New Schools and those schools that do not change positions.
- It is the "Little Things that are important," it is hard to get bitten by an elephant because you can get out of the way. But it is the gnats that will eat you up alive.

"THE PRO" – REMINDERS

- Recruit to the prospects needs, just because ABC U is a great place for the coach and his family – the prospect does not care, they have their own:

  1. NEEDS 2. VALUES 3. OBJECTIVES 4. INTERESTS
  This is called a Prospect Centered Approach as opposed to a Recruiter's Self-Centered approach.

- Don't rely on the Magic Bullet Approach; That magic set of words you can use to sell to everyone. Don't tell a recruit how wonderful Duke is, how great the program is and why you should go there. Without, first, knowing what the prospects needs, values, objectives, and interests are.

- Avoid the X – Y theory. The prospect bought "X" and it turned out to be "Y" when it was unwrapped it did not fit, wrong color, size, style, etc. You can sell the prospect on what they do not want, but it ends up being counter-productive and they'll end up transferring.

- What are the prospects "Hot Buttons?"

- Sell individually based on the prospects needs, values, objectives, interests. Do not depend on the Magic Bullet approach that is tossed out to every prospect.

- Kids do not make logical decisions. Decisions are emotion based, if not, Paige Bueckers a Minnesota girl lives 30 minutes from the U. of Minnesota campus would have gone to Minnesota or a BIG10 school and not UCONN.

- Every program has a "soft spot" – this is the "anvil" hanging over every program's head. Do not be defensive, go on offense, attack your soft spots, those "anvils" other recruiters try hit you in the head with, small gym, no airport, big campus, small campus, etc.

- Get kids to affirm(agree): If you said it, they can deny it, if they said it you can challenge them ("didn't you say that being close to home was not important to you?")

- The Stanford Approach: "Not everyone can come to Stanford, graduates make big money, athletics is very important, but you and your future is the real key.

COACHING VI

PROFESSIONAL COACHING IS MANY
THINGS.

TECHNICAL KNOWLEDGE, WISDOM,
TEACHING/LEARNING SKILLS AND
COACHING DEDICATION AND
COMMITMENT.

**THE SERIOUS ATHLETE EXPECTS
NOTHING LESS FROM THEIR
COACHES.**

GENO AURIEMMA
UCONN
"CHAOS" AND WINNING"

Coach Auriemma, gives practical information
on the need for learning to play
in a state of confusion i.e. ("Chaos)

I like to play v. a team that every time they do something, they must check with the coach. In my practices, I am not afraid to have practices that look lousy and that only I can understand what is going on.

The ones who can get a grasp in practice and function in a confused (chaotic) environment will be the ones who will really be good when the game goes wild. It is important that you create that atmosphere of unpredictability in practice.

Etc. Coaches should take from other coaches only what they can teach. Don't try to use everything that seems neat, tricky, or just plain new and exciting.

"WHO ARE THE GREAT COACHES?"

HOW DO YOU IDENTIFY A GREAT COACH?

"ARE THE PLAYERS DOING WHAT THE COACH WANTS THEM TO DO?"

Etc. If we train harder than our opponent – eventually they will let us in

TONY BENNETT
UNIVERSITY OF VIRGINIA
"A PAINFUL GIFT"

The University of Virginia, the #1 seed in the 2018 NCAA tournament made collegiate basketball history by losing to the University of Maryland-Baltimore, judged the worst team in the entire tournament. This was the first time in tournament history such an epic upset happened. A 21st Century sports "David and Goliath". Below is a "behind the curtain" look at UVA and Coach Tony Bennett's account and processing of the "PAINFUL GIFT" that was created because of the1ˢᵗ round tournament loss and moving forward with his team and how the loss to UMBC was the event that set the stage for winning the NCAA Championship the very next year in 2019.

Having to face that event with your players and in many ways becoming the laughingstock of college basketball in America and more than that to be really humbled, was a "Painful Gift" in a strange way. It stripped away what you thought mattered and it made you figure out what was important and what truly mattered and how we had to come together face it and then go on.

Immediately after the UMBC loss, our SID came up and said CBS wanted an interview. Initially I said, "no" we were all "GUTTED" I had nothing left, after about 5 to 10 seconds, I told the SID that I'd do the interview. If you are going to enjoy the good times sports brings us and you are able to handle that well, then you need to take the bad with the good.

I am a man of faith, I just kind of thought, "Lord give me the words to speak." Everyone would be listening and watching, if I could handle this in the right way it would be a unique opportunity. There is a rawness and realness in that moment immediately after a loss like that, it is very difficult to face. I don't really remember what I said, except to the extent the Teddy Roosevelt quote comes to mind (See page 165.) No one except the men I coached on that team, our staff, and those that were with us understand what we went through during the year. No one had experienced losing as the #1 team in the tournament to the last team in the NCAA tournament, in the history of the NCAA. CONT PG 154

The way society and social media is you are forced to deal with it. For example, after the game we got death threats, how serious they were I have no idea, but leaving the arena that night we had police security and left through a service entrance. I remember on the bus ride away from the arena wondering what was going through the player's minds. We had a great season, five day earlier we were cutting down the nets in the ACC tourney in the Barclays center and now we were getting death threats for losing a game. In all of that there was a lot to process, but it was a great opportunity to learn about themselves and me as a coach, father and husband.

In the aftermath of the UMBC loss, I took two underclassmen who I thought were key to helping us move forward. I told them they were coming with me to the post-game required press conference. We were going to face this; we are going to honor our two seniors (I didn't want our two seniors in front of the media.} This was to honor the seniors and what they had done for the program, let's keep them out of it (the press conference questioning.) We are sitting in the holding room waiting to meet the press, I told them, this will be one of the most difficult things you will have to do, but you (we) need to face it. The press is going to come after us, but something wonderful is going to come from this if we persevere and stay faithful. We are going to face it we are going to own it. This is the start of what of can be something different and we are going to grow from this moment. I thought this was a pivotal moment for them and me as we were the "Biggest losers," and not the TV show.

In the aftermath, it forced me to come closer to our guys, one on one meetings, having a "smoothy" together or a team breakfast.

Once we started the next season, we looked at things differently because of the UMBC NCAA loss. I used a quote from my wife's attending a "TED TALK." I showed this "TED TALK" presentation to the team. It is about guy who had a major disability and adversity in his life. There was a line in that talk, **"If you learn to use adversity right it will buy you a ticket to a place you could not have gone any other way." We kind of clung to that, but just because something hard.** CONT PG 155

154

happens, that doesn't guarantee you will be better for it, if you do not do anything with your adversity you might be worse because of experiencing adversity.

I was very intentional in using this. We said, "Face it, own it, grow from it, learn from it, and be better because of it." That was kind of our mantra, if you learn to use it, it will buy you a ticket that you could not have got any other way. I did not know what that meant at the time, but in my mind I kind of thought maybe we could punch a ticket to that final 4 dream. More Important, was to be just as good as we can be.

WHAT HAPPENED?

I saw a work ethic in our players, I don't think I would have seen in any other way. I saw a closeness in our team. I saw relationships being formed. The outside world didn't understand, all they wanted to do was to shame us. I saw some unique things happen in my own life and the life of our players. It actually drew me closer to what was important to me, my relationship with the Lord, my family, and relationship with my wife. Those were the things I kept telling my players about. We are in a world that judges us on how we do. What in your life is unconditional? Until you establish what is unconditional you will never be at your best. For me that is my faith, my family, and friends. I challenged the team to really dig deep into what is unconditional for them.

Praise and blame are the opposite side of the same coin and the team had experienced this at many levels, not many young people have this depth of experience(s.) In the sporting world:

1. #1 seed in the NCAA.
2. Winning the ACC regular season championship.
3. Winning the ACC conference tournament

Being the toast of the town and then five days later, we are getting death threats and being shamed. Processing all of that is challenging; it kind of forced the team to decide what they were going to do; what were our unconditionals.

The gift of that humility (UMBC LOSS) and adversity was probably something I am not sure we could have gotten any other way. It is not the way I would have chosen, it sucked, it really did. CONT PG 156

Now on the backside, some may not understand but I think it prepared our guys. There is much worse that can happen in life. I kept saying, "This feels awful but there are so many worse things, it's how we deal with other things." Our team has a chance to influence others, sisters, moms, etc. If the team could handle this well and with perspective, that ripple would affect the lives of others.

At Virginia we have pillars of behavior that binds our team.
One of these pillars is UNITY. "A house divided cannot stand."
My father, (Dick Bennett) established "Pillars" for his teams. The pillars were based on biblical principles.
He told me that before you win at a high level at Virginia you will have to recruit players and hire staff that you can lose with first before you can win big.
Bottom line: Adversity and losing is a truth serum.
We can sit and talk about how great it is to be winning, but you lose a game, have an injury, some guy is not playing as much as he thinks he should, etc. If you can lose with the guys you have; you are going to grow and glean wisdom from it.
Then you will win at a high level if you apply those lessons.
We lost at the highest level in the NCAA; but I knew I could win with this team because we had just won the ACC and I knew I could lose with them because of losing to UMBC.

OK, this is a new season it is October 2018 after the UMBC March Madness loss. You can't win the NCAA in October.
I got a letter from a coaching friend of my father; it was written by the famous coach Clair Bee. He had sent a letter to Bobby Knight after Indiana lost a "gut wrenching" game in the NCAA tournament when they were undefeated (31 -0) and #1 in the country. The main point of the letter I shared with my team was CONT PG 157

CONT PG 157

about being strengthened by the blow that cut you down; the end of the letter said: "Run to the starting line and be strengthened by the blow that cut you down." We used that, we talked about it, we owned it. We would have to face the UMBC game in every road game, that was going to be the story line of the 2018-19 season. But let's not be afraid.

Moving to the 2019 NCAA Tournament. Again, we were a #1 seed and in the same situation we were in the year before. Our first game was with Gardner-Webb. We got down by 14 points, the biggest deficit of the entire season. This was the most oppressive pressure I have ever experienced as a coach; I could see the pressure growing on our players. In addition, there was a feeling in the arena of a UMBC history repeat was brewing. To an extent it was unbearable, yet it was what it was. We hit a couple of shots to go into the locker room down six points at half-time. Last year v UMBC, I had to do a TV interview on the floor before going to the team room at halftime. Our assistant coaches had charged into the locker room and tore into the players. With about 20 seconds left in the Gardener-Webb first half: one of my assistants tapped me on the leg and said, "Speak light, tell the staff to 'Go Light' at halftime." I told the team, "Promise me one thing (we were in the same position as last year) you will not panic." Last year we unraveled in the 2nd half. You must fight for all your worth, lay it on the line, and keep believing. We went out and had a great second half. I really believe that was the most significant moment in the tournament. I think it was one of the most significant moments in the life for our young men and myself, in a basketball sense. The pressure was on us and to watch our team look the pressure in the eye and go through it – it prepared them for the rest of the NCAA tournament.

QUESTION: How did you prepare for the second game of the first weekend?

V. Oklahoma (a strong well-coached team.) After surviving Gardner-Webb there was a huge exhale. Pressure does strange things, even to the greatest athletes in the world, I've watched pro golfers, with tournaments on the line CONT PG 158

157

Miss a three-foot putt. A great field goal kicker misses a "chippy." These are world-class athletes. Pressure does strange things.

V. Oklahoma, we prepared well, and we felt good about ourselves and played at a very high level probably our most convincing win of the tournament all other games were down to the wire.

The pregame talk was "you have been prepared for this moment to face the pressure no one else had to face in the college game. You overcame it. You are prepared for any pressure or stress that will come your way." After we won the Gardner-Webb game there was still stress and pressure, but because of our experiences we seemed ready for the challenge.

We had so many remarkable games: Purdue (last second win,) Auburn, Texas Tech. But we played free and didn't get our feathers ruffled. We were battle tested and prepared for the moment and we had great play.

QUESTION: The pressure of one and done in the NCAA tournament. What is it like to coach in this situation?

The true test of a great team is consistent play i.e., win your conference. To win in the NCAA you can get "hot," good matchups, health of players, and great luck drives winning in the NCAA. That is one and done reality.

One of the best pieces of advice I got when we qualified for the FINAL FOUR came from Dabo Sweeney, Head Football Coach at Clemson. I had met him at ACC meetings but really did not know him that well. He called and said, "Because you guys failed epically last year and you were true to who you were and you did not lose your way and handled it the right way, you are going to win the national championship. It's done Tony, I have observed your team, but I would give you one piece of advice that I have used with my team. There is so much scrutiny when you go to the Final Four, "Let the light that's in you shine brighter than the light that will be shining on you."

That is really the truth of the matter, what's inside and what you believe in your core. Although this is developed through many years, CONT PG 159

but for us the process of going through our NCAA experience, Dabo's words were perfect. If you get consumed with what is going on, on the outside, the what if's, "What if we lose." "What are they saying about me/us, etc., etc., will just unravel a team. We had a presence of mind, this is who we are, this is our time, and we will live with it, if it does not happen, it does not happen, but we are ready to do this (Win the NCAA tournament.)

OK, now you have won the NCAA National Championship, what was it like with your dad. A great coach in his own right?

My father's dream in coaching was to one day coach in the Final Four. I was a volunteer manager on his team (Wisconsin) that went to the Final Four. When I got into coaching, I wasn't sure if it was the right thing for me. I had seen my father go through the ups and downs of the profession. I saw the roller coaster ride in coaching. And I was not convinced that this was for me. Going into coaching was somewhat of a slow process but the more coaching experiences I had the more I liked it. I was the head coach at Washington State and here at Virginia. I wanted to test myself against the great coaches in the ACC and maybe get the Virginia program to a Final Four like I had observed my dad do.

Winning the Final Four was not part of it. Everybody says put your dreams on the board and go for it. I just wanted to maximize the ability of my team and see how far we can take it. When the dream became a reality and we won it, to see the game clock go to zero, it was special to embrace my father. My first thought I had was. "Lord thank You; I am humbled, I don't deserve this." CONT PG. 160

Etc: If opponent is a shooter, make them put the ball on the floor. If they are dribblers, make them shoot. That does not seem so hard, does if?

A side-bar to the above story:

An exercise we do with our incoming freshmen at Virginia:

We put the freshmen in front of the team in chairs and ask them to respond to three questions:

1. _Who is your greatest hero?_
2. _What was a hardship in your life?_
3. _What was a highlight in your life?_

Then we turned it over to the freshmen and they could ask the team the above questions. When we got to the "Hardship" part, I had the players to talk about the hardship of losing in last year's NCAA. The answers from the freshmen and upper classmen were very informative.

Etc. Question: Why would you take a player out of the game after getting their 2nd foul in the final minutes of the first half and then start that same player in the second half? Players need to learn and can be taught how to play with foul issues. But if they are simply going to give a useless "stick man" performance that must be addressed. However, to be an effective a player It's about concentration, keeping hands up and out so referees can see them and playing position basketball.

SUE BIRD
SEATTLE STORM
"THE DIFFERENCE BETWEEN GOOD AND GREAT"

Ms. Bird is one of the most decorated basketball players in American basketball history and for good reason: 4 WNBA Championships, 4 Olympic Gold Medals, 2 NCAA championships, 4 FIBA World Cups to name few of her many basketball accomplishments. A great player. The information in this transcript is exactly what any serious athlete needs to know. It's a great "Road Map" for achieving performance excellence.

"Being good or great is a matter of little things. Little things I am still learning about:"

1. Nutrition 2. Studying video 3. Playing "moment-to-moment," "not game to game." 4. Forgetting the last play, ignoring what might happen next and just, "Playing Now." 5. Personal Accountability 6. Understanding the transition of moving up to the next level of competition and not being the #1 option. 7. Confidence comes from practice. 8. Confidence cannot come from the coach; it comes from the hard work you do. 9. When I played at UCONN, we practiced so hard and it was so demanding, the games were easy.

The #1 thing is that the players need to understand is the level of energy that goes into a game, so it does not take you by surprise. The second thing is you must be able to do is stay focused on what you need to do on the court, and at some point, and time in this game you are going to have to be able to overcome adversity because everything is not going to go your way. How you respond to those things and play the next play is really important to being consistent, which is important in the game.

Consistency always has been an issue with our team, to be able to play at a high level on a consistent basis in this day and age is critical to success. It doesn't really matter what you did last week. You are only as good as your next play, only as good as your next game.

Etc." We do not remember things we say to kids, but they remember everything we say to them." *Russ Bradburd, Former Assistant Coach at UTEP and presently an English Professor at New Mexico State University and accomplished author.*

TEX WINTER
PHIL JACKSON
TEX WINTER – "SEVEN RULES"
PHIL JACKSON – "SACRED HOOPS"

*Coaches, **Tex Winter and Phil Jackson** were joined at the "hip" for years, winning 11 NBA championships together in Chicago and Los Angeles. Asst. Coach Winter introduced the famous Triangle Offense to Coach Jackson. Formerly known as the Triple Post Offense, Coach Winter developed it in coaching stops at Kansas State, U of Washington, Long Beach State et.al. Coach Jackson grew up in Williston, ND. A great player at the University of North Dakota and played for NY Knicks winning an NBA Championship. Coached in Caribbean and won a championship with the Albany Patroons in the CBA before moving to the Chicago Bulls, first as an assistant and then as the head coach and completing his coaching career with the LA Lakers.*

TEX'S SEVEN RULES

1. On offense, penetrate the defenses perimeter via the dribble and pass.
2. Use the transition game (Fastbreak.)
3. Spacing on the half court – spacing allows for penetration. (See #1.)
4. Movement without the ball. Cutting and passing promotes open shots.
5. Offensive rebounding with defensive balance to prevent opp. Fastbreak.
6. Ball handler must have passing options to all teammates.
7. Players individual skills must be utilized: 1x1, shooting, rebounding

PHIL JACKSON – "SACRED HOOPS"

Basketball is a sport that involves the subtle interweaving of players at full speed to the point where they think and are moving as one.
To achieve this:

1. Learn to trust each other on a deep level.
1. Know instinctively how teammates will respond to pressure.
2. Go down as you live, meaning, don't hold back. Play the way you live.
3. Disconnect from me, so you can connect with your teammates. I don't want players looking at me to see if I approve.
4. Good teams become great teams when the members trust each other enough to surrender the "me" for "we."

PETE CARROLL
SEATTLE SEAHAWKS
A COACHING PHILOSOPHY IN 25 WORDS

A terrific coach and leader. An NCAA coach at U of Southern California and a head coach in the NFL with New York Jets, New England Patriots, and winning the Super Bowl as head coach of the Seattle Seahawks.

"I believe in a fundamentally

strong team that is balanced

defensively and offensively

competes and stays

"IN"

each possession

being hard to

play against."

Etc. A strong case can be made that we "grow" in direct proportion to the amount of chaos we can sustain and dissipate in practice, games, education, employment, and life.

163

URBAN MEYER – JACKSONVILLE JAGUARS
FOOTBALL COACH
"CHECK UNDER THE HOOD"

Urban Meyer, former Head Coach of the NFL's Jacksonville Jaguars and winning coach of National Championships at the U. of Florida and Ohio State. The following are Coach Meyer's comments made on FOX's Saturday Football Show sharing his experience and wisdom, responding to why teams need to "look under the hood."

Human nature is built around making excuses. When you see a team get beat the fans and media blame the players and coaches. It is never more evident than in the NFL. The teams in the NFL are not paying the $$$$ to bad players and bad coaches. Now they may not be playing and/or the coaches coaching well. But to call them bad is not accurate. When I coached, I never allowed an assistant coach tag one of our players a bad player; that's an excuse. We must dig deeper "Look under the hood," and find issues that cause under performance. Every time I had a team struggle it was because on one of three possible reasons:

1. **Trust issues** – players do not trust coaches. Coaches do not trust players and worse players do not trust each other.

2. **Dysfunctional work environment** – Expectations are very high, but the team is not working hard enough. Coach must be very clear with the team, this leads to frustration, anger and disappointment because we want to win a championship. We are not working hard enough, so stop with the expectations, your <u>work ethic must exceed your</u> expectations, in order to create a good team environment.

3. **Selfishness** – if you have a selfish team, you've got real problems. Football is an unselfish sport. That means you have got to do "nasty." I'm a running back, I've got to protect my quarterback, I do not only get to run the ball. Sometimes you must run down on a kickoff at 22 mph and throw yourself at a guy coming at you at 15 mph. That is not a lot of fun, but you do it for the team. As we speak, LSU, Penn State, Michigan combined have a 3-10 combined record. Stop with the bad players and bad coaches. It is time to lift the "Hood" and dig down. It's one of the above three reasons.

"ROUGHRIDER"
PRESIDENT TEDDY ROOSEVELT

The 26th President. Below is from "Citizen in a Republic," a speech delivered on April 23, 1910. At the Sorbonne in Paris. A speech often associated with the spirit of athletic competition.

It is not the critic who counts; not the men who points out how the strong man stumbles, or where the doer of deeds could have done them better. The Credit belongs to the man who is actually in the arena, whose face is marred by dust and sweat and blood; who strives valiantly; who errs; who comes up short again and again and tries again because there is not effort without failure and shortcoming; but who knows great enthusiasms, who spends himself in a worthy cause; who at the best knows in the end the triumph of high achievement, and who at the worst, if he fails, at least fails while daring greatly, so that his place shall never be with those cold and timid souls who neither know victory nor defeat. . . there is little use for the being whose tepid soul knows nothing of great and generous emotion, of the high pride, the stern belief, the lofty enthusiasm, of the men who quell the storm and ride the thunder. Well for these men if they succeed; well also, though not so well, if they fail, given only that they have nobly ventured and have put forth all their heart and strength. It is war-worn hotspur, spent with hard fighting he of the many errors and valiant end, over whose memory we love to linger, not over the memory of the young lord who "for the vile guns would have been a valiant soldier.

The Condensed version:

- It is not the critic who counts.
- The credit belongs to the man who is actually in the arena.
- Who strives valiantly.
- Who errs, who comes short again and again.
- Who knows great enthusiasm.
- Who spends himself in a worthy cause.
- Who at the best knows in the end the triumph of high achievement.
- And who at the worst If he fails, at least fails, while daring greatly.

165

RALPH MILLER - HALL OF FAME (1988)
WICHITA STATE – U OF IOWA – OREGON STATE

Why Ralph Miller? 1. To honor one of the lesser nationally recognized greats of the "Game." 2. To highlight the unique and creative style of one of the truly great coaching minds in the history of basketball. 3. In addition, as a young and eager young coach (the collector/editor) was fortunate to experience "Ralph Miller Basketball" on a close and personal level -while attending a three-day coaching workshop in River Falls WI. Coach Miller had just accepted the head coaching position at Oregon St. and was leaving the University of Iowa. In addition to three days of being "at the foot of a future Hall of Famer", Coach Miller mentioned more than once that he had a snow shovel for sale in Iowa City. Clinics were different back then featuring a headline clinician who was present for the entire clinic as opposed to the cameo appearances of coaches at present day clinics. Many years later as a Div. 1 college assistant I was fortunate to spend two days in Corvallis on a deep dive into Oregon State basketball and have collaborated with the Oregon State staff that included Jim Anderson, Puck Smith, Lanny van Eman, Steve Seidler, and Andy McClousky down through the years. In addition, as a freshman at Moorhead State College (MN.) MSC and Washburn University (KS) made a coach exchange agreement. Coach Larry McLoed went from Moorhead St to Washburn and Washburn's Genn Cafer reciprocated and was the coach at Moorhead State for that season. Coach Cafer was a terrific coach and a Ralph Miller disciple and for that season it was just like having, the Master, Ralph Miller himself as our coach.

THE MIND OF A HALL OF FAMER

- Ralph Miller's total thinking regarding the way to win basketball games was forcing the opponent into an "Uncomfortable 40 minutes of basketball" on both ends of the floor by eliminating all rest periods with pressure that attacked the opponents with offensive and defensive tactics whenever possible using the entire floor. The strategies and their execution are based on sound principles and rules. Gambles and over commitment to obtain possession were cardinal sins. This philosophy is not unlike Nolan Richardson's "40 minutes of Hell" at Arkansas that came later.
- The idea is to eliminate all rest periods in the game. This means in a 120-possession game, 60 for each team, without a fast break or press defense, five seconds elapses on every possession this equals 600 seconds or 10 minutes of rest in a 40-minute game. Miller eliminated these rest periods with the speed game (fast break), halfcourt cutting game and defensively With the full-court pressure both man to man and zone. CONT PG 167

- If pressure defense is necessary when behind late in the game, why would it not bear fruit for the whole game.
- We are opposed to the bounce pass. It is too slow for the kind of game we want to play and when the bounce pass comes off the floor it increases in rotation speed making it harder for the receiver.
- The pass becomes the chief weapon of attack. Nothing in the game travels faster than the pass.
- The pass cannot be defended.
- To eliminate opponent rest periods, apply automatic defensive pressure upon a change of possession by: 1. Guarding the player who guarded you, this allows for immediate pressure on the opponent achieving our goal of eliminating rest periods. 2. With immediate defensive pressure by "guarding the player guarding you" assists in "blunting" opponents fastbreak.
- With the Miller pressure game on defense, the speed game on offense and the game score even at the 36-minute mark, Miller believed he would beat the opponent in the last four minutes because of mental and physical fatigue.
- The speed game includes an emphasis on the "counter break"- the use of the fast break after being scored on. (A light sprinkling of opponent scoring quickly CAN be an asset in the "long game" of speeding up the game's pace.) Therefore, a fast turnaround from defense to offense by counter breaking can put strong pressure on a momentarily relaxed opponent, who has just scored. CONT PG 168

Etc. Seen on license plate frame: Never tell me "the Odds"

THE RALPH MILLER OFFENSIVE AND DEFENSIVE STRATEGIES

DEFENSE: Full court: man to man- 2-1-2, 2-2-1, 3-1-1 full court presses. (Presses convert to man to man on missed baskets.)

OFFENSE: Speed game - Fastbreak; Counter Break -when opponent scores; Half court – 1–4 passing cutting style.

MORE MILLER TIME:

- Skills are merely tools for game execution.
- We like the "jump stop," this allows for either foot to be the pivot foot.
- The mark of a good teacher is to simplify the material for easy communication.
- Simplification is the key to sound teaching, eliminating thinking is achieved by trial and error in scrimmage.
- Repetition is tested in scrimmage. This is the best way to learn to play because it is an exact duplicate of how the game is played.
- Every player on the floor is a "Playmaker" when he or she has the ball. Example: low post player becomes a "Playmaker" and must "feel" his/her best play. All players must think "Playmaker," making plays possible for themselves and more likely for teammates.
- The key to winning is understanding the simplicity of basketball.
- A coach can teach anything they want if they stay with it long enough.
- Coaches need to teach the skills of the game that will allow your offense to function. If dribble, shoot, pass, pivot, screen, cut, etc. have not been taught, there is no offense known that will be able to function efficiently.
- Coach Miller. "There has been nothing new invented in the game since the 1930's. when he learned the game." Interpretation: Coaches are teaching a lot of "fluff" and need to stick to the fundamentals. CONT PG 169

THE RALPH MILLER FIVE SKILL DEVELOPMENT DRILLS

#1 Body Position Drill – this is a mentally and physically challenging drill

Players are spaced on the court facing the coach in a defensive stance – low, one hand above head – one hand down. A. All players slide the signal of the coach. B. Players must have one hand up at all times – this is very difficult to maintain. C. First week of practice players work up to 10 min. w/o stopping. D. Second week of practice players work up to 20 minutes w/o break. This is extremely physically demanding but even tougher mentally.

Drill #2 and #3 are run without defense - drills are run by counting consecutive makes. These drills are run at a high pace. Practice will not go forward until the consecutive number of makes are completed. For instance, the team is assigned to make 35 consecutive layups without a miss – it could be any number. If there is a miss before reaching the assigned number, the count starts over. **What this does is put tremendous peer pressure on every team member to "do their job" and not be the one to let the team down particularly, if this is the 2nd or 3rd try to reach the "number" goal.** It is interesting to notice the team as they get close to the goal and the pressure starts to build – team members start counting to see who is going to have to make the last shot. This simple approach creates reliance and accountability on each team member to perform and contribute. A great skill and team building drill.

#2 Layup drill. This is a simple two-line drill with a shooting and rebound line. A full speed drill.

#3 Three-man Rush/Weave drill. This is a down and back drill - three trips - six consecutive makes. If there is a miss. 1. On a miss, an extra trip down and back making both shots or the threesome starts over. Option: every three-man team must make three trips without a miss. On a 15-person squad that would end up being 30 consecutive made layups. CONT PG 170

#4 drill 3x3, 4x4. Full court. This is a basic teaching drill. 3x3 or 4x4 drill is usually run "down and back" twice (the more "trips" the closer we get to game conditions.) Offensive rebounds are put back up. If team does not secure def. rebound that team stays on defense and goes again v. a new group. Action can start a. Free throw attempt. b. midcourt. c. side out of bounds. d. baseline out of bounds with defense playing in a full court press. "Hockey rule:" ball must be dribbled across mid court line; this adds a level of control.

 #5 drill 5x5 Scrimmage. This and Drill #4 are the full court drills that won over 600 games for Hall of Fame coach Miller. Coaching points: coach on the run, do not stop the action, do your coaching during team rotations.

Drills #2 through #5 are high intensity drills with coaches working hard to create and maintain player effort.

Drill #1 Players are lined up as shown in a defensive stance: 1. low in sitting in a chair position. 2. Back straight. 3. One hand up other hand low. 4. Team slides per signal from the coach (Black #5.)

SEE PAGES 177 – 187 FOR DIAGRMS OF RALPH MILLER'S FIVE DEV. DRILLS

Etc.: The respect theory: Want to be respected by your teammates? 1. Say little. 2. Let your teammates see your work ethic.

Dear Dick:

Enclosed please find information that you requested. Please return the
video tape as soon as possible. Maybe your school can make a dub and that
way you can have one for your convenience.

If there are any questions please feel
free to call.

Sincerely,

Steve Seidler
Assistant
Basketball
Coach

SSjah

"THEN AND NOW"
(This is a copy of a letter from <u>Oregon State</u>
Assistant Steve Seidler, sent on July 2, 1984.) It
is a sample of how the coaching fraternity shared
and communicated in another era, before the age of
"Synergy," and other technology advances.
Also, on a recruiting home visits, it was common to
travel with a 28 minute highlight reel of film and a
25 lb. 16mm projector. We Did not bring a "screen."
Thankfully, the recruit provided a wall for the
screen.

171

THE POWER OF THE CONTESTED SHOT...

The team with the highest shooting % wins 80% of the time, that may not be much of a revelation, but the one thing that affects shooting percentage negatively is the Contested Shot. When do you contest shots? Contest every shot where-ever you are – jump as high as possible, it will have an effect on the shot. This is regardless of distance from the shooter. The defender must "jump" and extend – every contested shot this will have negative on the shooter's percentage.

THE POWER OF THE CONTESTED SHOT

An NBA Study of playoff games:

1. "Zero" contested field goal % = 68%

2. "Strong" contested field goal% = 36% (a difference of 32%)

3. Even more dramatic: NBA players make uncontested layups at a 95% rate. But when layups are contested the make rate falls to 49%.

The above statistical information screams loudly, Contest Opponents Field Goal Attempts – lower opponents shooting % improve your chances of having a better shooting % than opponents and win 80% plus of your games.

- NO CLOSE OUT – if contesting shots is a priority, it is unwise to do the popular closeout. The "stutter step" debilitates contesting shot efforts.
- Run as quickly as possible and go straight up with high hands. NOTE: Players do the same thing on their jump shot with the hard dribble and pop right up in the air. Same skill on defense.
- There will be some blocks, but that is not the purpose. Don't be afraid of contesting shots – if a player is afraid of getting faked out, he/she will not go after the contest. If the defender gets beat, the team aspect comes into play.
- On every level the contested shot is a "Winner." The uncontested shot cannot be allowed.
- Finally, do not foul on/after the shot. This wastes effort and loses games.

COINCIDENCE OR NOT???

IF... (A = 1, B = 2, etc.)

A B C D E F G H I J K L M N O P Q R S T U

1 2 3 4 5 6 7 8 9 10 11 12 13 14 15 16 17 18 19 20 21

V W X Y Z

22 23 24 25 26

THEN...

K N O W L E D G E

11 + 14 + 15 + 23 + 12 + 5 + 4 + 7 + 5 = **96%**

AND...

H A R D W O R K = 98%

8 + 1 + 18 + 4 + 23 + 15 + 18 + 11

BOTH ARE IMPORTANT, BUT FALL JUST SHORT OF 100%

BUT...

A T T I T U D E = 100%
1 + 20 + 20 + 9 + 20 + 21 + 4 + 5

I WISH AN EXPERIENCED COACH
WOULD HAVE TOLD ME . . .

1. Promise less and deliver more.

2. Don't say anything bad about your predecessor even if it is true.

3. There is no such thing as a free lunch. Whenever someone gives you or your program something, they will eventually want to be paid back in some fashion.

4. Get all the good ideas you can possibly get, then <u>choose carefully.</u>

5. Less is more - others jump on the merry-go-round of every shiny new thing, only to find out that its "shelf life" is less than you expected.

6. Most parents or other stakeholders would rather see their child make All-State than the team win the State Championship.

7. You make enemies much faster than you make friends in coaching.

8. Who is working when you are not present i.e., assistant coaches, players.

9. The saddest day of your life will be when you find out the coaching profession no longer wants you.

10. Make the "BIG" where you are.

11. There are a lot of great coaches – they just don't have famous addresses.

12. Have thoughts and notes collected in a journal that is just for you.

13. Never allow yourself, staff, or players to get satisfied.

174

RAMBLINGS

WITH SUE ENQUIST, UCLA HEAD SOFTBALL COACH

- The bottom1/3 of the people you deal with "Suck the life" out of you. No one ever told them to put the filter on.
- The Bottom 1/3 don't know life is a team sport and the world does not revolve around them.
- The middle 1/3 blow with the wind and go back and forth – I love my coach – I love my team- I love our school until something goes wrong then they plummet to the bottom 1/3.
- The Top 1/3 are a special group of kids that give you everything they have. I need them to protect me from the bottom 1/3.
- The bottom 1/3 go home with you no matter what happens, they are still there in the back of your mind.
- The bottom 1/3 question everything you do – don't let that cabal "Suck the Life" out of you.
- The middle 1/3 are changeable
- The Top 1/3 are always with you

We all have strong voices and weak voices when we talk to ourselves. Would you want to be friends with your weak voice? "I suck." "Get me out of here." "I want to quit," I am not good enough." "I am letting everyone down." "I can't make another mistake." "Why did I do that again." "That was stupid." "…I'm disappointed in myself." "I am tired, we can't WIN this thing." "I will never play, she/he is better than me."

We all have a strong and weak voice in our self-talk. The trick is to be around people who will model what it is like to believe in yourself.

There is value in getting control of your internal "Voices." Getting to the top and staying on top is being able to manage your weak voice and capitalize on your strong voice.

Coaches we need to "Stain their brain" by having a PHD in "Being Convincing" – when your language becomes their language – we know we can shape character. Become a convincer – we must convince the players in what they cannot see yet – that is our calling. Great coaches eventually get to the players to believe in the mission – the challenge is becoming an engineer – a builder of belief.

175

"PAPER CLIPS"

✓ "Within the first 20 minutes of watching practice, I will know what your program stands for." Jim Calhoun, UCONN

✓ "Bad thought – bad shot."

✓ "Don't fear the moment."

✓ "In order to win a man to your cause, 1st you must reach their heart, that is the great high road to his reason." A. Lincoln

✓ "An elite shooter should make 80% PLUS unguarded at game speed in practice." And do it day after day; week after week; month after month and on & on.

✓ During first Qtr. Time out: "It's a long game – don't get in a hurry." Coach Popovich, San Antonio Spurs

✓ To WIN: 1. Get a "STOP" 2. Get a "SCORE" 3. Get another "STOP" 4. REPEAT

✓ "Help us win today!"

✓ **The Elite Warrior Mentality:**
1. **The Mission**
2. **Preparation for the Mission**
3. **WIN**
4. **Learn from Success**
5. **Next Mission**

✓ Temporary discomfort leads to permanent improvement"

✓ "We were 0 – 18 last year; we weren't really that good.

THE FIVE RALPH MILLER SKILL DEV. DRILLS

1x1 BODY POSITION DRILL

1st purpose

1.Physically develop players footwork, hand work and body position. Players slide in defensive stance on coach's hand signal.

2. Players are in a "Chair position" back straight, low body position, feet - body width apart, one hand up other in a low position at knee level.

3. Players react to coach's hand signal.

2nd Purpose is to increase / highlight the emotional grit expected of each player and team collectively. This is a kind of "Boot Camp" drill to prepare the team for basketball combat.

The first week of practice the drill is worked up to 10 minutes of non-stop defensive sliding staying in a stance. The second week the drill works up to 20 minutes of non-stop defensive sliding.

This is a mentally and physically very challenging drill. It is a staple of the Ralph Miller approach a "Right of Passage" i.e. once a player has achieved 20 minutes of non-stop defensive sliding – they have the emotional and mental toughness qualities to be an Oregon State basketball player.

Some players will get so fatigued that they need to hold the "Up" hand above their head with their other hand. A Tough drill, but the shared experience of successfully completing something challenging will serve the team going forward.

1X1 BODY POSITION DRILL DIAGRAM ON PG 178

1x1 Body Position Drill
RALPH MILLER OREGON STATE

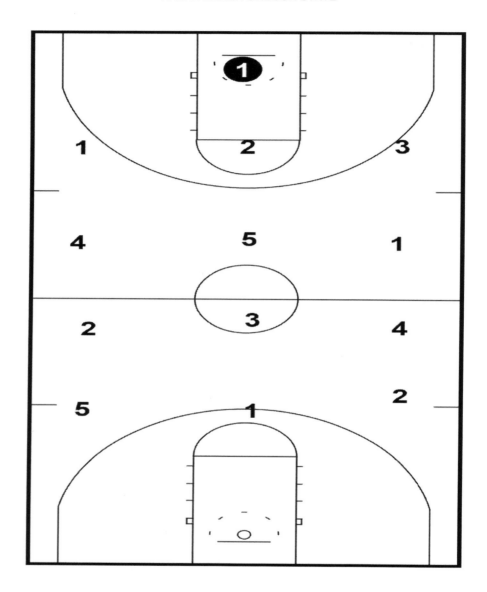

"FAMILY"

The Hurley coaching brothers (Bobby Jr. and Dan) whose father Bob Hurley (Sr) the legendary Hall of Fame Basketball Coach at St. Anthony's HS in New Jersey
were asked if they would ever want to play their father:
"The only way we would ever play our father
is if we knew there was no chance to win."

#2 LAY UP DRILL (SPIT THE POST)
RALPH MILLER OREGON STATE

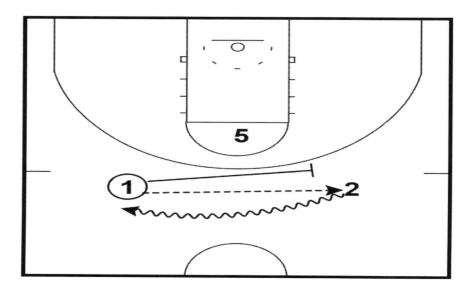

#2 LAY UP DRILL (SPIT THE POST)
RALPH MILLER OREGON STATE

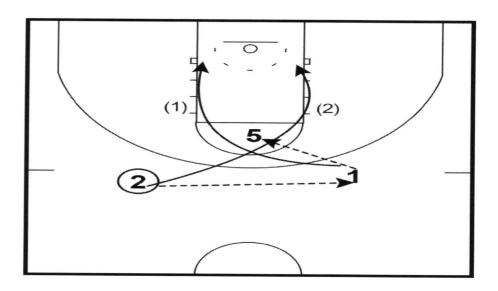

FIVE RALPH MILLER SKILL DEV. DRILLS
DRILL #2 LAYUP DRILL

TOP DIAGRAM:
1. #1 Passes to #2 – follows pass and comes to jump stop
2. #2 dribbles as shown jump stops pivots and passes to #1
3. #1 passes to #5 and is the first cutter.
4. #2 cuts off #1's tail.

BOTTOM DIAGRAM:
SEQUENCE OF ACTIONS:
1. #5 hands ball off to either cutter.
2. #5 takes turnaround jumper.
3. #5 wheels and takes ball to basket.
RECEIVER ACTIONS:
1. Makes Layup
2. jump stops and shoots "Baby" jumper off glass.
3. makes a "touch" pass to other cutter who scores

Alternate Layup drill - two-line layups one shooting line and one rebound line. Make a designated number of consecutive layups. For example, 35 in a row – miss one and go back to "zero." **The personal dynamics are interesting when team gets close to "35" players will be counting to see who will be the player that has to make the last shot. There is strong peer pressure on each player not to let the "team" down.** *Practice will not continue until team makes 35 consecutive – this is a speed drill.*

181

#3 3 MAN RUSH (WIDE THREE MAN WEAVE

RALPH MILLER OREGON STATE

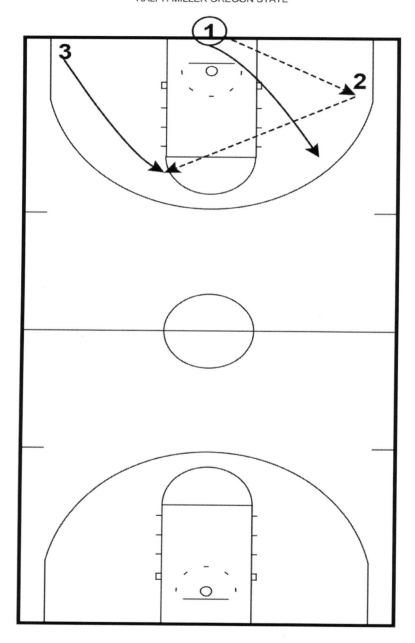

THE FIVE RALPH MILLER SKILL DEV. DRILLS

DRILL #3 – 3 MAN RUSH

1. This is a down and back drill

2. Three player groups make 3 down and back trips – must make six consecutive layups

Coaching points:

1. wide – touch sideline

2. this is a speed drill

3. Ball does not touch floor – ball touching floor - team makes an extra "down and back."

4. missed layup: a. make extra trip b. start over and make all six shots.

Etc. Efficiency is more important than pace of play

Drill #4 3x3 / 4x4 FULLCOURT
RALPH MILLER OREGON STATE

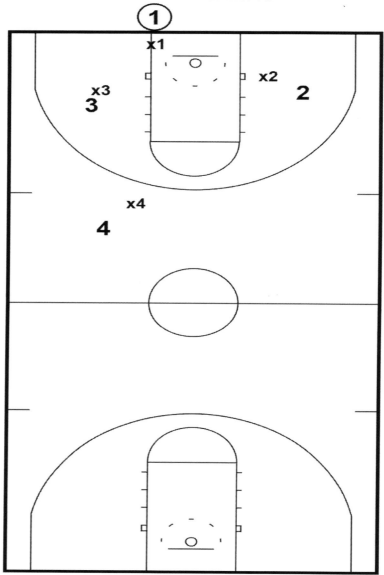

184

THE FIVE RALPH MILLER SKILL DEV. DRILLS

3X3 /4X4 FULLCOURT

This is a core drill for teaching the game.

1. A group 3x3 /4x4 make one trip down and back and rotate from defense to offense. More trips "Down and Back" maybe used, the more trips the closer we get to "Game conditions."

2. Offensive rebounds are put back up.

3. If defensive team does not get rebound, they stay on the floor for the next rotation.

Coaching notes:

1. "Hockey" Rule Option - Player dribbling ball must be first offensive player to cross mid court line. This adds control and eliminates "cherry picking."

2. "Guard the player who is guarding you." This creates immediate defensive pressure.

Etc.: Before you freak out and go ballistic about what just happened, ask,

"COMPARED TO WHAT???"

DRILL #5 5X5 FULLCOURT
RALPH MILLER OREGON STATE

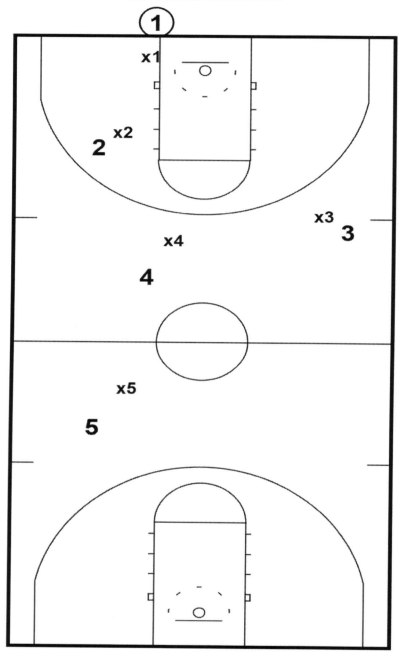

186

THE FIVE RALPH MILLER SKILL DEV. DRILLS

5X5 FULLCOURT

1. Drill is set up like the 3x3 /4x4.

Coaching Points:

1. Coach on the "run" – coach'em up during team rotations.

2. Coaches, "Coach alertness" – players need to be alert and "see" with awareness and vision of all that is happening on the floor –this is a special player. A team that simply "sees" is a special team. "20-20 vision does not guarantee seeing what is going on around you on the floor."

3. Being alert is the first cousin to hustle and effort.

Drill Options:

a. Keep Score

b. Shoot free Throws

c. Each team gets certain number of possessions – keep score.

d. Use Time and score.

e. start ball at half-court.

"COACHING IS ALL I KNOW"
JERRY TARKANIAN, UNLV

Jerry Tarkanian won the NCAA National Championship in 1990 with a 103 – 73 win over Duke and won 79.5% games in his career. A great coach. The editor/collector of this book witnessed several UNLV practices. The first thing that jumps out is the incredible intensity from the beginning whistle until the final conditioning drill. In addition, Wyoming played UNLV in the 1987 Sweet Sixteen. It was a competitive hard-fought game. The UNLV defensive intensity and athleticism was suffocating. UNLV would win in a high-level game and go on to the FINAL FOUR before losing to Indiana University.

Coaching is all I know how to do. I have no other skills. I don't believe I could sell. I'm not a salesman. I can't pound a nail in a wall. I hate yardwork. When I was coaching in high school and at the junior college level, I had to teach P.E. classes and I didn't even like P.E. classes.

All I enjoy is coaching. I enjoy the practices, the competition, my relationship with other coaches and the players. I don't even have any hobbies. I don't play golf. I don't go fishing. I don't go camping. None of my coaches play golf. I go to all the Celebrity Golf Tournaments in Las Vegas, and ride around in the cart and drink beer, but I don't play. In fact, we go so far as to not hire an assistant who owns a set of golf clubs. We just coach.

And we're not into X's and O's as much as we are into technique. We're not into plays. I don't think the plays are important. We try to teach proper technique of getting into a stance and how to move your feet and where we want your hands, and we drill those things constantly and try to stress a habit and a reaction instead of plays.

But off the court we like to have a warm atmosphere. You don't just sit down and motivate someone: It's a relationship you develop from the first time you meet a player, and it's the rapport you have with him off the court. We expect the players to work as hard as they can work and when they don't, we get all over them. The only way you can do that is if you have a strong feeling for them off the court. If you turn your back on them off the court, you're never going to be able to get a maximum effort on the court. CONT PG 189

THE MIND OF JERRY TARKANIAN:

"Game Time:"

1. I don't like our team being "loose."
2. I like tension in the locker-room.
3. Whispering creates tension.
4. Assistant coaches pace floor.
5. A lot of staring in the locker room.
6. At exactly 7:25 I come into the locker room and go directly to the bathroom – comeback and stare some more.
7. I want the team to assume they are going to war.
8. We don't allow music in the locker room to keep us loose.
    Music / Game metaphor: a guy calls the house at 4 pm and says at 8:00 pm he's coming over to your house and kick your butt in front of your family. What are you going to do – play music to get loose?
9. The more your players "Think" the slower their feet become.

-   **IF YOU WANT TO PLAY:** at the next level as an individual or team – the ability to concentrate will be as important as making your jump shots.
-   **WITH OUR GREAT UNLV TEAMS:** we spent 60% to 70% of our time on defense – we knew were going to score off our defense.
-   **SHOOTING IS CONFIDENCE:** a coach can "screw" up a kid anytime he wants by his/her words, body language, lack of communication, etc. in every area, but particularly in shooting the ball. Coaches need to be communicating what they want. Interpretation by players can be tricky.
-   **STRETCHING:** – the worst players are our best stretchers – A kid can stretch as much as he wants until practice starts.
-   **WE DON'T ADD NEW THINGS:** during the season – instead we perfect what we do.
-   **THE ONLY GOAL:** At UNLV, be prepared physically, mentally, emotionally to play as hard as we can.
-   **SCOUTING:** give me 3 drills that our opponents do that we can drill live. It can't be done 5X5. CONT PG 190

- **TEACHING:** don't tell them what to do – you have to drill'em.
- **GUARDING THE DRIBBLER:** the toughest thing to guard is a guy who can dribble. Once you get beat off the dribble the entire defense is in various states of chaos.
- **THE MORE YOU PUT:** in a players head the slower his feet become.
- **DO ONE THING:** and do it well – we don't try to trick anybody.
- **PLAYING HARD:** We want to play harder than anybody we play, more aggressive, and tougher basketball. Be prepared to play emotionally, mentally, and physically as hard as you can.
- **ANYTIME WE DO NOT WIN:** – it's because we don't have <u>patience</u> according to my assistants - what about all those games we won by not being patient. Patience sometimes is exaggerated.
- **TALENT: -** we are not able to control the talent on our squad.
  CONDITIONING: can be controlled by the coach.
- **If YOU CAN KEEP BALL ON ONE SIDE OF FLOOR:** and not allow ball reversal you will have a good defense.
- **POISE:** and loafing, being cool are out – at UNLV we want to play with a frenzy.
- **PLAYERS:** – rarely if ever motivate themselves.
- **"WE ARE NOT GOING TO CRUSH MICHIGAN":** - no, that is BS. we just want to "play hard."
- **TAKING A CHARGE:** – it's because of coaching – kids just don't take charges unless they are trained in the technique.
- **IF YOU DON'T:** pressure the passer you are a TRAITOR.
- **MENTAL TOUGHNESS: -** only comes from working hard.
- **LATE SEASON PRACTICE: –** UNLV does things nobody does regarding length of practice and conditioning. We keep our conditioning up and the length of practice is longer than what other coaches do.
- **THE PERFECT POINT GUARD: -** "A guy who makes all his shots but doesn't like to shoot." CONT PG 191

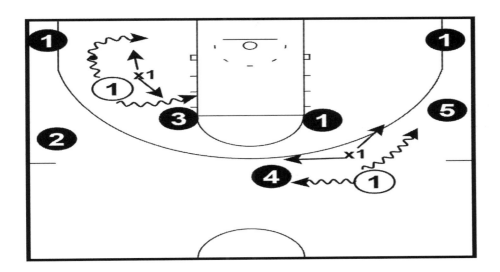

UNLV 1x1 defensive philosophy was not to "fan" or "funnel" the ball to baseline or middle of the floor. Coach Tarkanian felt that by fanning/funneling quick accomplished ball handlers would make it extremely difficult for the defensive player to keep up and control the driver.

In diagram: There are seven "Push Points" shown in w/ black dots.

1. The defender assumes a squared stance

2. The defensive objective is to force ball to a "Push Point" either right or left of the defender.

Left side of diagram shows X1 failing to push the ball to a push point #1 or #3.

Right side of diagram shows X1 successfully pushing ball to push point #4 or #5.

GEORGE LEHMANN, THE SHOOTING EXPERT

A long time ago the editor/collector of this publication attended a Pro Keds Coaching Clinic. Anyone remember the old "Pro Keds" sneakers? George Lehmann was a pro's-pro, as a professional basketball shooter. In his clinic demonstration, his ability to make shots was incredible from all distances and angles while describing what he was doing. It was like a carnival exhibition. His clinic presentation centered on four principles that if properly learned allow players to self-teach and self-correct in order to become better shooters.

As I travel through the country on assignments for PRO KED's, I am constantly asked what is takes to become a better player and how can I improve my shooting? 1. **Attitude** is basic, an attitude of wanting to do the work to become a better player and shooter. A natural outgrowth of attitude is spending extra time and effort. Extra time and effort develop shooting confidence.

2. **Confidence** is necessary and can only be gained through the development of skills. As for shooting, it is the most practiced skill, out in the driveway against the barn or at the local youth center. So why aren't there more expert shooters? Simply stated, most players never learned the successful way to shoot... and outstanding shooters are made through repetition. They are not born. Which leads to the conclusion that too few players have a clear, simple, easily learned idea of what makes a good shooter. Following are the basic steps in shooting ... if taught and used consistently day in and day out they will improve any players shooting ability and confidence.

The basic steps to better shooting. . . building the muscle memory reflex.

1. **BALANCE**- straight up and down, land on the same spot. Any type of drift is the same as shooting at a target that is moving. Shooting is a muscle-memory reflex. The more you do something correctly, the more natural and successful it becomes. This is "muscle memory." CONT PG 193

2. **EYES ON TARGET**- Vision is on the target. The target may be either the front or back rim; never visually follow the ball. <u>Shooting vision tip:</u> Wherever you are on the floor you will see three prongs that hold the net. The shooting target should be just over the middle prong that is directly in front of the shooter.

3. **ELBOW IN AND STRAIGHT**- <u>This is an important step</u>. Elbow is in close to the body, even grazing the side of the shooter's jersey during shooting motion. Elbow <u>IN</u> forces the ball to be shot directly over the shooting shoulder. A common fault is the shooters (particularly younger/beginning shooters) elbow sticking out away from the body which brings the ball to the front of shooters face. The shooter should make sure the ball does not get in front of the shooters face on the shot.

4. **FOLLOW THROUGH** - Every time a shot is taken made or missed a smooth follow-through is necessary. "Stick your hand in the basket." <u>The guide hand/ non-shooting hand's only purpose is to steady the ball.</u> The ball is shot out of the guide hand (This is the non-shooting hand.) The shooting hand follows through to the basket. The non-shooting hand must be coached carefully to not to interfere with the actual physical shooting of the ball – it is only placed on the ball allow the shot to be taken.

5. **DELIBERATE PRACTICE** - Put everything together with deliberate practice, game shots, game spots, game speed. Deliberate practice is an important concept it does not mean mindless throwing up of shots simply to build up great shot volume to brag about to friends and family with little thought to the importance of making shots<u>. Deliberate practice on the other hand includes the mental concentration involved in trying hard to make each and every shot. This is the only way to develop muscle memory and make more baskets.</u>

ANSON DORRANCE
WOMEN'S SOCCER COACH
UNIVERSITY OF NORTH CAROLINA
CORE VALUES

Anson Dorrance coaching record is 1043 wins 140 losses 63 ties. At the University of North Carolina only 13 times in 40 years have the Tarheels lost more than two games in a season.

We have several elements that we believe are critical for developing a championship environment. These are the Core Values of our team:

1. **We do not whine.** "The true joy in life is to be a force of fortune instead of a feverish, selfish little clod of ailments and grievances complaining that the world will not devote itself to making you happy." George Bernard Shaw.

2. **We work hard.** The difference between one person and another, between the weak and the powerful, the great and the insignificant, is energy. . . this quality will do anything that has to be done. . .nothing will make you a great person without it (hard work.)

3. **The truly extraordinary does something every day.** This individual has self-discipline, does the summer workouts from beginning to the end without omission or substitution and every day has a plan to do something to get better.

4. **We choose to be positive.** Nothing can depress or upset this powerful and positive life force, no mood swings, not even negative circumstances affect this "rock."

5. **We don't freak out over ridiculous issues to create crises where none should exist.** Be the best example of someone who is steady and resilient.

6. **We treat everyone with respect.** This is that classy individual who goes out of their way to never separate themselves from anyone or make anyone feel beneath them. CONT PG 195

7. **We play for each other.** People don't care how much you know until they know how much you care. This is the kind of player that works themselves to death covering for all their teammates in the toughest games. Their effort and verbal encouragement make them a pleasure to play with and their selflessness on and off the field helps everyone around them.

8. **We care about each other as teammates and human beings.** This is that non-judgmental caring and inclusive friend that never says a negative thing about anyone and embraces everyone understanding and recognizing differences are part of our humanity.

9. **When we do not play as much as we would like we are still noble and support the team and its mission.** This remarkable self-sacrificing generous human being always has a place on the team.

10. **We are well led.** This is a verbal leader on the court that is less concerned about their popularity and more concerned about holding everyone to their best standards and driving teammates to their potential. This inspirational person competes all the time and demands that everyone else do the same.

MORE COACH DORRANCE

I Prefer Roses to Championship Trophies. Roses are ephemeral in that they are temporary, they die quickly and become a reminder, "let's get back to work." Therefore, I prefer flowers, especially in athletics.

If you want this championship to be a part of who you are and what this program is about. Celebrate the Championship feeling. Celebrate it for a few days, watch the roses die – let it be a reminder, to do this again, we've got to get back to work.

BRUCE PEARL
AUBURN HEAD COACH

Bruce Pearl guided the Auburn Tigers to the NCAA Final Four in 2019. A successful assistant coach for the outstanding Tom Davis at the U of Iowa. Won the NCAA Div. 2 Championship at Southern Indiana University. Coach Pearl, also, was the head coach at UW-Milwaukee and the University of Tennessee. Pearl was second only to University of Kansas' Roy Williams as the fastest NCAA coach to reach 300 wins. Below is Coach Pearl's ideas on substitutions. Pearl's teams are known for their full court pressure defense and Fastbreak style of play.

SUBSTITUTION THEORY

1. Starters control their minutes. However, head coach pre-determines the number of minutes. Players minutes are even 20 each half. Good play will increase minutes to 30. Poor play reduces time to 10 minutes.
2. Starter takes himself out and puts himself back in game.
3. If coach takes player out it is because: a. he's tired. b. he's "dogging it" I assume he's tired.
4. This allows me to coach without having substitutions on my mind.

TAKING A NEW JOB

1. Raise the level of players in program. There is a reason the job was open when you got it. Expectations: Players need to have a clear understanding of what your "OK's" and "NOT Oks" are.
2. Focus on what is good about the program and the players strengths.
3. Build confidence: getting players to work hard builds confidence faster than anything. Working hard will guarantee you success and the converse is also true.
4. Raise your players goals higher:
   a. Academic goals
   b. Strength development goals
   c. Work ethic goals.

196

THE THREE POINT SHOT – "IT'S MAKES – IT'S MISSES."

More and more coaches believe the three-point shot is a way to win and it's effectiveness cannot be disputed.

A team that shoots 36% from "3" would have to shoot 54% from two-point range to equal three-point production; 36% and 54% are very good shooting percentages.

By shooting 36% from 3-point range, still translates into 64% missed shots which means a lot of defensive rebounds many are long rebounds that fuel the opponents fastbreak– and through experienced antidotal observation the defense will get 80% of those misses that give way to defensive rebounds, which statistically are the 2nd highest scoring possession in the game, the Fastbreak at .92-.95 points per possession (PPP.)

Now shooting a lot of 3's cannot be linked to winning or losing, but the number of missed 3's and their effect is something that coaches should be aware of when evaluating the three-point field goal.

Etc. Losing the "Big" game, is a "Big" deal and causes all kinds of crises that can affect coaches, players, families, schools, communities, whole states and occasionally entire countries. However, we need to remind ourselves during these times that: "1.393 billion Chinese didn't even know there was a game."

THE GREAT AND THE NOT SO GREAT... WHY?

It seems there is little difference between the really great players and a next level player. Is it because of weaker defenses?

In the classroom, make the test easier, and the test scores go higher. Does this analogy also apply to the defenses in basketball at all levels? The poorer the defenses the more lesser offensive players are elevated.

Make the (test) defense tougher and it will separate the great player from the others.

Just like the more difficult test in the classroom will separate the good from the better students.

Is it poor defensive resistance that allows the average player to be thought of as better?

Etc.: "Everyone in this game has a lot of talent, but that doesn't make a winner. It's a mental thing. A lot of guys become comfortable losing if they don't look bad. A winner doesn't want to lose no matter how he looks."

Joe Morgan, 2nd Baseman, for Cincinnati's
Two-time World Series Champions.
Inducted into baseball's Hall of Fame – 1990
Joe Morgan died in 2020 at the age of 77

"BEST DEFENSE - WHAT IS IT?"
RON EKKER – COLLEGE / NBA COACH

Coach Ekker is a career basketball coach who has had a lifetime of success in the game he loves. He has had success at every level of competition. High school, small college, major college, NBA and internationally in China representing the NBA as a coaching consultant and leadership role in the development of China youth basketball. In addition, Coach Ekker is an author of several basketball books. He is the creator of the "Basketball Talk Pro" UTUBE videos that provides basketball people with over 160 basketball and coaching development videos. Also, Coach Ekker was a pioneer in the statistical measurement area long before it became chic to know some insignificant statistic that can be passed around but has no usefulness in winning games. In contrast, Coach Ekker's deep dive into the value of statistical measurement was done for one reason, to win games. Coach Ekker is a creative and energized coach who continues to help the game and the coaches who coach it.

To be a good defensive team there is a strong offensive connection. An effective defense needs attention to the following:

1. **MADE BASKETS**
2. **MADE FREE THROWS**
3. **ELIMINATE STEALS**

The above three phases of offense provide the <u>defense</u> with the three poorest ways to get the ball. By studying the above three areas and coaching to maximize them in your game plan will help your team.

Do not underestimate the value of possessions. There are only two possessions (defensive rebounds are steals) that have offensive advantage because the ball does not have to be taken out of bounds.

Putting together an offense that will help your defense.

1. Need good shot selection including offensive rebounds.
2. Making free throws is an integral part of your offensive plans.
3. To cut down on steals – team ball handling skill development – including passing and catching skills. Design actions that give passer multiple receivers.

199

QUESTIONS THAT NEED ANSWERS

Practice sessions are the life blood of developing the team. There is little time, none actually, set aside for things not directly meant to maximize team development.

Coaches cannot get hung up on non-productive activity and/or non-productive people. The Coach needs specific answers to the following questions from ANY team member whose body language and /or behavior is screaming to the coach, "I'm not OK."

1. "Are you sick?"

2. "Are you injured?"

If neither, "I am going to give you two minutes to get yourself straightened out and join your teammates or we are going to have a fantastic practice WITHOUT you."

Etc.: Practice Etiquette: 1. Be on time. 2. Pay attention.
3. Empty your" bucket." (Effort.)

GARY COLSON
VALDOSTA STATE, PEPPERDINE, U OF NEW MEXICO
FRESNO
"GONE, LIKE A FIVE CENT COKE!"

In 1958 a Coke was five cents. Gary Colson was hired as the Head Coach at Valdosta State. For 10 years, Coach Colson's job description included:

1. Taping ankles.
2. Driving the team bus.
3. Called the newspaper after away games-
4. Ordered all the equipment – then fund raised to pay for his purchases.
5. Taught classes.
6. Raising money for recruiting and uniforms.
7. Did not have an assistant coach.
8. AND he coached the team to a 176-73 record.

In 1968 a Coke cost 25 cents. Gary Colson was named Head Coach at Pepperdine College.

1. By this time, he found himself with one assistant, to help him do all the duties Coach Colson has done by himself at Valdosta.
2. An upgrade.
3. Coach Colson's record at Pepperdine was 153-137.

In 1986 a Coke cost 50 cents. And Coach Colson accepted the head coaching position at the University of New Mexico playing in the historic 18,000 seat arena known affectionately as the "PIT." The site of the 1983 NCAA tournament championship won by Jim Valvano's NC State Wolfpack over the "Phi Slama Jama" U of Houston.

As the Lobo coach, Coach Colson seemed to hit the jackpot. CONT PG 202

1. He inherited an associate head coach.
2. Fulltime assistants.
3. A nearly full-time volunteer (paid with non-university funds.)
4. Two graduate assistant coaches.
5. Coach Colson's record at UNM was 146 – 106.

Coach Colson went on to have a successful "run" at Fresno State **As the price of Coke** has continued to escalate.

The price of Coke apparently has gone up again, this time at the U of Oregon. The men's basketball media guide includes 17 staff members.

MORE FROM COACH COLSON

TWO ON-ONE OFF
PRACTICE THEORY

We made a decision two years ago to begin official Fall practice by working out two consecutive days then rest a day. We worked hard for two days and then took one day off. We used this practice plan two on and one off. Until we got to the first game of the season. We liked it and our team liked it. They seemed to really work their tails off for two straight days knowing they would get a day off. They also seemed mentally simulated and were eager to go after that day off. I realize this may be very controversial to the hard-nosed everyday routine, but I felt with this team having six seniors, it was ideal. Try it, you might like it.

NOTE: Jud Heathcote, Magic Johnson's coach at Michigan State used a similar practice plan method with the NCAA Champion Spartans. CONT PG 203

MINI SCRIMMAGES

In our practice sessions, we use a lot of mini scrimmages, in which we divide the team into two – six-man teams, which gives us one substitute. We now set up situations for the teams to attack. For instance, team A will play Team B six possessions and Team B will be in a one-three-one half-court trap. We will keep score and swap the situations so that there will be a total of twelve possessions. We substitute after every possession. Sometimes we will let the defense convert before we blow the whistle. We will punish the losers or reward the winners. After we do six or twelve possessions, we will change the situation and change the teams. As you can see there are a hundred situations that can be set up and made very realistic through the mini scrimmage plan.

Etc. In tournament play, winning the first game is <u>everything</u>, <u>don't look past it</u> - after that "Momentum" takes over. Paul Westhead, Div. 1 and NBA Championship Coach

"THAT'S OUTSIDE MY BOAT"

Charlie Jones, the famed NFL, MLB announcer was assigned to cover the '96 Atlanta Olympic rowing competition. Rowing was a sport he knew very little about. Being a professional, he set out to learn about the intricacies of the sport. To learn the sport, he went to the athletes to teach him what goes into being an Olympic class rowing athlete. What he found out turned into a book. Titled:

"THAT'S OUTSIDE MY BOAT."

"What is in my Boat, is what I Control"

- Attitude
- Purpose
- Grit
- Preparation
- In the moment
- Body language

"Letting Go of What is Outside My Boat?"

- Broken Oars
- Lane Assignments
- Rain
- Sun
- Wind

QUESTION: "What is in your boat?" "Are you in your boat?" "Be in your boat and row." Don't spend time worrying about what's outside the boat.

VIC SCHAEFER
UNIVERSITY OF TEXAS
CORE VALUES

Vic Schaefer is one of the most successful basketball coaches in the country. A defensive genius, who was in charge of Gary Blair's defense in the 2012 Texas A&M National Championship team. Head Coach at Mississippi State where he racked up a 78%-win percentage including a 2018 NCAA Final Four runner up. In the Spring of 2020 Coach Schaefer came home to the state of Texas, being named the head coach at the University of Texas.

RECRUIT TALENT – A Recruit based talent program will always go farther than a skill developed based program.

QUALITY COACHING - Quality talent is always looking for coaches who can make them better players.

CULTURE – Attitude – players have a certain written / unwritten code of behavior expectations.

TEAMWORK – The synergy of the group is greater than the individual talent.

LUNCH BUCKET – Work ethic.

GET DEGREE

Etc. Ric Majerus, University of Utah, Final 4 coach: "Guards need a "tight (no mistake) game."

DAN FITZGERALD – FORMER HEAD COACH
GONZAGA UNIVERSITY
"LET'S GET SERIOUS ABOUT SHOOTING THE BASKETBALL"

Coach Fitzgerald, a respected and excellent basketball coach could be considered the "Godfather" of the Gonzaga basketball juggernaut. "Fitz" coached at Gonzaga for 15 years and had a 60%-win total, recruited NBA, Hall of fame, Gold Medal winner, John Stockton to Gonzaga. Became Gonzaga Athletic Director and hired Mark Few as his head coach. A real basketball man who was well liked and respected in the profession. Coach Fitzgerald died in 2010. This is an article that needs to be seriously considered by coaches who want better shooting from their team.

Shooting is the most important skill in the game, we believe you can improve shooting:
  a. Practice sessions must have time blocks in practice for shooting.
  b. **Shooting is generally the most poorly organized part of practice.**
  c. **SHOOTING DRILLS SHOULD BE THE TOUGHEST THING WE DO IN PRACTICE IN TERMS OF CONCENTRATION, INTENSITY AND ACCOUNTABILITY OF PERFORMANCE.**

Shot Selection Factors:
  a. Range (making 8 of 10 shots in practice / game shots / game spots / game speed.)
  b. Time to shoot (open shots – shooting shots in rhythm.)
  c. Selfish shots - must be addressed immediately.
  d. Hard shots – we talk about. (use "Hard" terminology as opposed to "Bad" shot)
  e. Each player takes the right shot for him/her.
  f. Your shooters must shoot the ball – they must pull the trigger.
  g. Good shooters taking questionable shots – not that bad.
  h. Bad shooters taking good shots – is questionable and can be a problem.

206

THE MODERN GAME (NBA)

The Nets, Steve Nash, and Rockets Shane Battier at the Sloan Analytics SAAC conference, 2018. The Sloan Analytics Conference conducts an analytics sports performance several day convention held annually at MIT. It focuses on sports science issues in various sports with a strong emphasis on basketball's present and future trends. This was a round table type discussion regarding how the game is played at the highest level and how the game is changing and the pace of that change. The participants were former NBA players, Shane Battier, a solid NBA player recognized as having a strong interest in the study of analytics and their on-floor application and Steve Nash an outstanding NBA point guard.

This resource is highlighting several ongoing trends in the game. Coaching techniques and how the overall direction of the game flows downward from the NBA to the colleges, high schools, etc. This article can give coaches an opportunity to explore some ideas that can help win games.

Steve Nash is currently the Head Coach of the NBA Brooklyn Nets. Shane Battier is currently in the Los Angeles Lakers front office. Nash and Battier's "back and forth" is recorded in the following transcript.

Don Nelson, former NBA coach offensively played elbow to elbow using the 2-man game, spacing the other 3 players and emphasized the Fastbreak.

Mike D'Antoni, NBA on the half court promotes the Pick and Roll (PNR) style with spacing. He guided the PNR development without dictating play for the players. Everything centers around spacing, PNR, the fastbreak and a high pace of play producing a shot within 7 seconds of possession with an increased number of 3-point shots.

Pick and Roll Defense v. the PHX Suns (Middle Pick and Roll)
1. Maintain physical contract with Amari (Stoudamire) the screener & roll man.
2. Be able to "bluff" Steve Nash, who is coming off of Stoudamire's pick so Nash does not turn the corner and get to the basket.
3. And the corner defenders must be able to help and still get to their men and contest the corner jump shot. CONT PG 208

Defending the pick and roll 30 plus times a game is hard to do. You need everyone to know the game plan and be able to execute it. If one guy is not spaced correctly on defense, if the defender's position is off by 12 inches, that is all a good middle PNR team needs to take advantage.

D'Antoni with the Rockets had an offensive system that worked. Stretching the defense vertically (three-point shot) and horizontally (corner jump shots) is an important part of the D'Antoni system. The Rockets did not let Battier a #3 man go to the offensive boards, Battier had to get back and help the defense get set and stop the fast-paced offensive styles of play. Steve Nash agrees, "one thing that helps to create pace with the Fast break is when the defense is not set."

Vs. the great offense the defense must maintain discipline in defensive spacing. You must be in correct position to begin with and out of defensive scramble. Great offenses stretch you out and will expose you, all a good offense needs is one misstep to take advantage of the defense. Disciplined positioning is a key.

D'Antoni thought the pressure to win an NBA championship got to the Suns team. "We knew we could win with Pick and Roll basketball, but because we were the only ones in the league doing it, everyone was always chipping away at our style and as a result we kind of drifted away from our values."

Steve Nash on winning but being denied the NBA championship ring, "It hurts, yes, I have regrets AND no regrets, you move on, life is good."
Great shooters must be judged on shooting % that includes shot difficulty. 38% from being open in the dead corner is different than a 3-point shooting % of 38% off the dribble v Defense.
Battier - on opponent play calls; "Whenever a coach / player called a play, I called the play to our team like I knew the play when I had no idea, but our opponent did not know I didn't know."
Defense - When you play against a team that plays open, fast and free, defense is about concepts not guarding plays or schemes. And getting back on defense fast enough so you can defend the drag Pick and Roll by a very good post shooters on the perimeter. You learn to think quick and process what the offensive
CONT PG 209

possibilities are: an example is transition wing drag screen that creates a middle drive and/or a dribble lob dunk; so defensively, I may take a chance on the corner "3" shooter and plug the middle – allowing the screener's man to prevent the lob dunk off penetration.   In addition, Battier via analytics knew an offensive player goes to his right 20% more than to his left, making it possible to get to my correct position defending the corner. I had to process this information from a defensive point of view.

Defenses in Today's NBA must be quick and active w/o being physical like the old arm bar shiver. Today's game must defend farther out and needs a lot of versatile defenders that can switch. Defenses have developed to utilize the switch furthering the need for versatile defenders. Pace demands quick decisions.

Blackjack – You need to play a mental basketball "Blackjack" game by knowing the odds/tendencies; defenses need to pick the smallest dose of poison. Playing "blackjack" needs a higher rate of knowledge to allow decision making Battier a more effective defender through video study and statistical analysis.

"The 7 Second or Less Season," a book by Jack McCallum. The book stated, the Suns put up 2097 – 3 point shots the most of any season at that time – **today that would rank 19th or 20th in the NBA. Pace of play has exploded since the 90's.**

CONT PG 210

Etc. Your role may change on the team, but your status will always remain the same.

The next challenge to the NBA player:
1. What will the players do with all their sudden financial wealth?
2. Do they understand being good in college does not necessarily translate to the NBA.
3. Are their habits and work ethic improving at the same rate as their bank account?

Nash on player development. I was a slow developer. I was a good player, but because of where I went to school (Santa Clara) being from Canada and looking like an unlikely NBA player. I did not get much attention. But I had passion, discipline and resilience. These things need to have a measurement. We need to be able to forecast the personality aspect beyond athleticism.

Battier: "There is never a bad day in the NBA. For me it was really about the work and the journey, it was the game, it was the struggle, the bus rides, it was about being doubted, it was about the work you put in. The NBA out shined my expectations every day. That is what made me appreciate the successes and failures. I would do it all again knowing how tough it could be.

Etc. The West Point Mission: 1. Educate. 2. Train. 3. Inspire.

SECTION VII

<u>STATISTICAL MEASUREMENT</u>

"IF YOU DON'T MEASURE IT
YOU CAN'T MANAGE IT."
Peter Drucker

DEAN SMITH
UNIVERSITY OF NORTH CAROLINA
PIONEER IN STATISTICAL MEASUREMENT

Dean Smith coached at the University of North Carolina for 36 years winning 78% of his games.

In 1988, Dean Oliver, the godfather of basketball statistics, believed he had published a groundbreaking paper offering that it was <u>not</u> the number of points scored that determined winning; it was the points scored per each possession (PPP) that determined winning. Shortly after Mr. Oliver discovered his innovative approach had existed and used for decades.

In the 1950's, a similar idea existed and was revealed in a basketball book authored by North Carolina coach Frank McGuire. The chapters in McGuire's book that dealt with the subject of Points Per Possession (PPP) were written by Coach McGuire's young assistant, a mathematics major who would eventually ascend to the highest level of basketball, Dean Smith.

Coach Smith was a masterful basketball coach in many areas. The "Carolina Way," evolved under his leadership including multiple defenses and offenses/a blistering transition game/ requiring acknowledgement of all assist passes/the bench standing for players coming out of the game. The famous "4 corners" offense that was virtually indefensible in protecting late game leads and spurred the addition of the shot clock to the game before the 1985-86 season.

Dean Smith coached in an era without computers before the current statistical wave swept through the game and made metrics like Points Per Possession (PPP) common among the stat geeks. Coach Smith was one of the first to embrace statistics. He was tracking his teams' Point Per Possession (PPP) in the 1950's. Dean Oliver's final analysis of the Smith effect, "We're standing on the shoulders of a giant. He helped pave the way." CONT. PG 214

And yet, perhaps his most meaningful and longest lasting contributions came during the turbulent racial tensions of the 1960's as a revered and hugely successful coach in a state that loved its basketball, he recruited the first black player to ever play at North Carolina, and almost single-handedly dismissed segregation of the time by entering a segregated restaurant with a black student and an assistant coach. Shortly after, schools were integrated. In 1981, Smith is quoted as saying, "You should never be proud of doing what's right. You should just do what's right." In 2013 Dean Smith was awarded the "Presidential Medal of Freedom" the nation's highest civilian honor for his basketball career and vocal support for social issues by President Barack Obama. After a long illness, Coach Smith died in 2015.

Etc.: A lot of statistical things are cute and cool to know and fun to pass along to boosters, fellow coaches, media, etc. However, the coach's real task is to filter through these things to discover what is really important to winning games.

THE FALLACY OF PERCEPTION

If you do <u>not</u> think a player can rebound, you will see every rebound he/she does not get. If you believe a player is a <u>good</u> rebounder, you will see every rebound he/she gets. Only measurement can verify or expose a coach's perceptions. What is the first country directly south of Detroit? If you said Brazil or any South S. American country your perception is correct, it is obvious that a South American country must be the first country straight South of Detroit. However, regardless of your perception, the fact is the first country straight South of Detroit is Canada. **PERCEPTION IS A MIRROR OF WHAT YOU WANT TO SEE – IT'S NOT A "FACT.**

"Cold" is a perception thing, "Ya know."

- At 65 degrees, Arizonians turn on the heat, People in Minnesota plant gardens.
- At 60 degrees, Californians shiver uncontrollably, Minnesotan's sunbath.
- At 50 degrees, Italian & English cars won't start, Minnesotans drive with their windows down.
- 40 degrees, Georgians get coats, thermal underwear, gloves, wool hats. Minnesotans throw on a flannel shirt.
- At 35 degree, New York landlords finally turn up the heat, Minnesotans have the last cookout before it gets cold.
- At 20 degree, people in Miami all die, Minnesotans close their windows.
- At ZERO, Californians fly to Mexico, Minnesotans get out their winter coats.
- At 10 degrees below Zero, Hollywood disintegrates, in Minnesota, the girl scouts are going door to door selling cookies.
- At 20 degrees below zero, Washington DC runs out of hot air (Ya think, nah.)
- At 30 degrees below zero, Santa Claus abandons the North Pole; Minnesotan's get upset because they can't get the snowmobile started.
- At 40 degrees below zero, all atomic motion stops. People in Minnesota start saying, "Cold enough for ya, eh?"
- at 50 degrees below, hell freezes over. And in Minnesota, Public Schools will open 2 hours Late.

215

THE STATISTICAL "THREAD" TO SUCCESS

Collector/editors comment: There was a time mostly in the last century when coaches had a wavering interest in the statistical measurement side of the game. The prevailing attitude was, "I was at the game." I saw what happened." "I know what happened." "What do you want to know?" Several years ago, a series of videos was produced by Ron Ekker, a former Div. 1 head coach and NBA assistant coach. Coach Ekker, in searching for an "Edge," developed a statistical measurement approach for one purpose and one purpose only; the pressure to win games. Below is a brief overview of the "Thread" of events that lowers opponent FG% and raises your FG%.

1. **Possession (PPP.)** The PPP is a more accurate than total points per game in determining who wins games. This is a number that determines the overall team efficiency. The standard or goal is to get a number of 1.00 or near 1.00 Pt. Per. Possession.

2. **Field Goal Percentage wins games.** The single-most important factor in winning games is the team that has the highest field goal percentage wins 80% of their games. Other statistical measurements i.e., rebounding, turnovers, 3-point shooting, etc. are important, but none more important than winning the field goal shooting percentage.

3. **Contesting Shot directly affect field goal percentage.** A strong contesting of shots dramatically reduces opponents shooting percentage. This leads to missed shots – more defensive rebounds and fastbreak/transition scoring. And the thread continues.

4. **Some possessions are better than others.** Many basketball people are unaware of the importance of how the possession is gotten. The two highest value possessions are steals and defensive rebounds.

5. **Measuring effectiveness of Plays.** The effectiveness of set plays, both yours and opponents paints a picture of the efficiency of plays. This information will allow the coach to see which plays are making baskets.

6. **Measuring ball containment.** 1x1 Containing the ball defensively is a tremendous help to the team defense. It keeps the defense out of help and recover; this keeps shot contest people in position to contest, creating misses and defensive rebounds that facilitates a very good scoring possession, the fast break. Record success and failure in this area.

GETTING TO 1.0

What does <u>Getting to "1.0"</u> mean and why do we want our teams to get to 1.0. 1.0 Point Per Possession (PPP) is the "gold standard" of efficient offensive basketball.

In the 2017-2018 NCAA basketball season 25 out of the 353 Men's Divivion1 basketball teams operated at 1.0 points per possession (PPP) or higher. That is roughly 7% of all teams.

In Division 1 Women's Basket two of the 351 teams, UConn and the U of Oregon were the only teams operating above 1.0 (PPP.) To achieve the top 7% on the women's side a team would have to play at a .912 PPP or higher.

DEFENSE

The caveat is that the highest PPP always wins. This does not have to be a high PPP, just higher than your opponent. A .80 PPP trumps a .78 PPP. A Coach can decide to use defense to hold opponents to lower, percentages therefore not having to achieve UConn or Oregon type numbers to win.

<u>**See Oregon State on page 218**</u>

Etc.: Analytics continues to struggle in measurement of individual players, otherwise Draymond Green would not have been drafted #35 falling to the second round of the NBA Draft

THE POWER OF POINTS PER POSSESSION:

Big 5 Conference Point Per Possession:

- **Conf. Champion**: Offensive PPP = .94   Defensive PPP = .78 Diff (-.16)
- **Median Team:** Offensive PPP = .86   Defensive PPP = .76 Diff (-.10)
- **Last Place:** Conf Team PPP = .73   Defensive PPP = .82 Diff (+.09)

In 2015-16 Oregon State University won the PAC 12 Championship. They won with Defense:

- ✓ OSU's Offensive PPP of (.85) was very, very average
- ✓ OSU's Defensive PPP of (.67) was very, very strong.
- ✓ A PPP differential of (-.18) is championship caliber – comparing OSU's minus .18 with the Big 5 Conference champions above. What this means is that a team can win with Offense or Defense.
- ✓ The real strength of a team is in the difference between their offensive (PPP) and the defensive (PPP.) This is how OSU won the PAC 12.

Etc.: What a coach thinks is a perception and may or may not be accurate. Analytics/measurement can help eliminate a coach's bias for players who: 1. have "attitudes." 2. Quiet personalities. 3. Players who are statistically getting too much playing time or 4. Players who are statistically not getting enough playing time.

WIN 80% OF YOUR GAMES
RON EKKER
HIGH SCHOOL, DIV. 1, NBA COACH

It is hard to imagine another person in the coaching fraternity, with more claim to the title, "Coach." A lifetime of coaching, an author, a mentor, producer of "Basketball Talk Pro" online videos, NBA assistant coach and was sponsored by the NBA as a basketball consultant and ambassador to China. In addition, a pioneer in the statistical measurement area that he initially became interested in as an Assistant coach at the University of Minnesota in the 1970's. The collector/editor of this book's interest was heightened in this subject when Coach Ekker explained the beginning of his involvement in statistics happened in the daily search for ways to "Win Games."

Win 8 of 10 games by controlling the following three game elements.

1. **Field Goal %** - Your field goal percentage just needs to be higher than the opponents. Your team shoots 35% and the opponent shoots 32% you will win 80% of the time. Conversely, you can shoot 55% and give up 58% to your opponent and you will lose 80% of the time.

2. **Contesting the shot** – <u>An important question: "Is it the shooter that determines field goal percentage OR is it the shot?"</u> There is no data readily available that says if you are better at contesting shots gives you a better chance of winning. But anecdotal evidence invariably points to when you contest 70% -74% shots of our opponents' shots – you win. When we do this usually our opponents are contesting less than 70% of OUR shots – BECAUSE contested shots create a lower shooting % AND more defensive rebound possessions. This is one area where there is incomplete data – but the belief is that it works 80% of the time.

3. **Defensive Rebounds plus Steals** – If you have more combined defensive rebounds plus steals than your opponent you will win 79% of the time. Almost the same as Field Goal %.

These three areas are unified. Do not look at contested shots, higher field goal % and defensive rebounds/steals as being three separate parts. They must be recognized as a continuum. They are interdependent, they depend on each other if you control these three elements, they will give you an 80%-win ratio.

CONT PG 220

It is simple, <u>field goal %</u> you get from the box score. <u>Defensive rebounds and</u> <u>steals</u> are also in the box score. And you can trust, contesting a higher percentage of opponent shots leads to an 80% winning statistic. Statistically, control these three areas: <u>contesting shots</u>, <u>field goal %</u>, <u>defensive rebounding and</u> <u>steals</u>. You will win.

All three elements work together. Contesting shots is the best way to lower opponent field goal %. A lower opponent field goal shooting percentage is a huge advantage for your offense. It allows your team to have a lower field goal % and still win. Contesting shots is a critical part of what the field goal percentages are for both you and your opponent.

Defensive rebounding and steals, when you have the majority, you get more uncontested shots IF YOU UTILIZE THE FASTBREAK/TRANSITION STYLE OF OFFENSE IN THESE POSSESSIONS. The converse is also true, if you get fewer DR + ST than your opponent; your opponent will get more uncontested shots.

This can be proven, the best place to get uncontested shots is from defensive rebounds and steals. Statistically, a defensive rebound that fast breaks is worth .92-.95 points per possession and a steal possession is worth .96 points. <u>NOTE: coach should coach deflections as opposed to players hunting the classic steal/uncontested layup (dunk). Deflections also break up offensive play. Statistically 10 deflections will produce four plus steals. We call defensive rebounds and steals POP's (Positive Offensive Possessions). These two possessions are the highest scoring possessions in the game.</u>

By cutting down on uncontested shots and not giving up a lot of defensive rebounds and steals will lower the opponents field goal % making it easier to win. <u>Everything connects like a thread or continuum; field Goal%, defensive rebounds and uncontested shots. Take these three elements of the game and through study develop specific drills, team offenses and defenses to improve each area and you will have success.</u> CONT. PG 221

All practice sessions should relate to achieving winning percentages i.e., more contested shots, more steals and defensive rebounds will lead to a higher field goal percentage.
This is a simple approach based on statistical information, facts. Work hard on these three things every day and your team will be on its way to winning more games

Etc.: You can acquire talent and still not win! Take a look at the programs that have winning cultures. Mimic those coaches and programs and do what they are doing.

IT'S A POSSESSION GAME
POINTS PER GAME IS A FALSE POSITIVE

Using 1.0 PPP as a standard. The Points Per Possession (PPP) is the most accurate measurement in describing the strength of a team's offense. Also, the most accurate measurement of a team's total strength is the differential between a team's offensive Points Per Possession (PPP) and the points they give up in their Defensive Points Per Possession (PPP.) This is opposed to using total points per game as a measurement to offensive and defensive efficiency.

 As an example, a recent conference champion team had a PPP of .90 and defensive PPP of .65. This is a differential of .25, this is very strong. On the flip side the last place team in the same conference had an offense that produced a .67 Point Per Possession number and a defensive Point Per Possession of .83 this is a minus .16 difference. This demonstrates the power of points per possession. The NBA calculates by using 100 possessions to measure PPP. In the above example, the Conference champion would score 90 points and defensively give up 65 point and the last place team would score 67 points and give up 83 points per game.

Basketball is a possession game. Points Per Possession (PPP) are important. Pace, a fast or slow does not win or lose games. Points Per Possession wins or loses games.

To predict a team's future performance don't look at a team's win%, look at their Offensive and Defensive Pt. Per Possession margins.

POSSESSIONS (P) = FGA – O. REB + TO + (FTA X .44)
OF GAMES PLAYED, IF MORE THAN ONE GAME

Once the number of possessions has been calculated the offensive and defensive PPP calculations are straight forward.

Off. PPP =   Points scored   **Def. PPP =   Points Given Up**
Total game poss.   **Total game poss.**

I'VE GOT A LOUSY TEAM, WHAT CAN I DO?"

What good are analytics if the team can't shoot. OK, what can we do can when facing the challenge of a superior team and / or schedule.

The coach is a model to the players. They will respond to every visual and verbal signal the coach presents to his team. Be careful in what the team is seeing, hearing and feeling from their coaches.

1. **Three points is more than two.** But be careful, there will be more misses than makes, these misses lead to defensive rebounds (many of them long.) These rebounds lead to opponent's fast break which is the second-best scoring possession .92-.95 points per possession. Too many missed 3's fuel a faster paced game. A high possession game works in the favor of the better team.

2. **More layups/close in shots** are always a goal. Every layup is statistically worth over 1 point. How do we get more layups (close in shots?) 1. Offensive rebounds. 2. Live ball turnovers i.e., steals /deflections that lead to fastbreak baskets. These are two possessions that help your offense and also help your defense.

3. **Strong Contesting of opponent's field goal attempts.** A strong contest has a dramatic effect on shooting percentages, lowering it by as much as 32 percentage points. All these misses are either defensive rebounds or offensive rebounds. It is critical that 70% - 74% of missed shots be defensively rebounded allowing as noted in #2 above. Defensive rebounds from these misses should be taken advantage of by advancing the ball with pace (fast break/transition.)

4. **Free throws are a high scoring possession.** If a team was fouled on every possession and made one free throw on each possession. The points per possession would be 1.00 and the free throw shooting team would win a lot of games. This illustration will never happen; however, it does point out the value of getting fouled. The late Dean Smith said that he was not in favor
CONT PG 224

of the speed dribble and quick shot. He wanted to give the defense time to foul. Coaches need to brainstorm strategies to get fouled: a. Strong offensive rebounding. b. ball reversal and drive gaps. c. a side benefit of the dribble drive is the "inside out pass" to a set 3-point shooter.

5. **Shot Fakes.** Shot fakes both on the interior and perimeter that actually look like shots are rich with fouling potential by the defense. Shot fakes neutralize opponent's athleticism.

6. **Know the value of your possessions.** There are seven ways to get possession, each possession has a different scoring value. For our purposes steals and defensive rebounds are the only "live" possessions. All others are require taking the ball out of bounds. All defensive rebounds and steal possessions should be "pushed" hard to take an advantage of an unsettled defense.

7. **Defensive Effort.** Competing defensively is a requirement when playing against a superior team. The three pillars of defense must be part of every practice plan: 1. Defensive rebounding 2. Contesting opponent's shots (this should be a very aggressive action that approaches a hostile act. 3. Ball containment 1x1, without help is the ideal. This will help eliminate "blow bys," help and recover, rotations and make it easier to contest shots.

8. **Pace of Play.** Is very important. This is knowing: a. the number of possessions a superior team averages (use possession formula) and use the above strategies to control the pace of play or depending on the data speed up the pace of play to disrupt the pace of opponents play. b. a key is the difference between the superior teams offensive PPP and their defensive PPP (Pts. Per Possession opponent gives up.) The greater the difference the stronger the team. c. strong gritty defensive play slows the offensive pace of play. d. The pace of play either faster or slower needs to be controlled v. a strong opponent.

9. **A caveat** is playing a strong team like Virginia that thrives on a high Point Per Possession (PPP) by using a lower number of possessions or pace of play. Slowing a team like this with fewer possessions plays right into their game plan. **Evaluate the facts and combine with coaching experience and the team's talent to give your team the best chance to win.**

UNDERSTANDING TURNOVER PERCENTAGE

This is not a statistical category that is paid much attention to; but can be important in communicating awareness and team accountability. Teams will turn the ball over 25% of their possessions and not even realize it. An accurate turnover % is a simple calculation of dividing the # of turnovers by the number of possessions (To calculation possessions see possessions formula pg. 222) A goal of 80% plus of error free possessions is acceptable. Turnovers can be deceptive. For example, you think 15 turnovers is a good number while 20 turnovers are poor. Study this illustration: 15 turnovers in a 50 possession game equals 30% turnover rate. Meanwhile, 20 turnovers divided by 100 possessions equals 20% turnover rate. Therefore, turnover percentage efficiency cannot be evaluated until we know the number of possessions. **The team needs to know the acceptable number of turnovers and likewise needs to be held accountable for the team's turnovers. Providing facts will help the coach.**

Etc.: In a post-game interview, John McCay the great U. of Southern California football coach was asked: "Coach, what do you think of your team's execution," Coach McCay immediately replied, "I'm all for it."

TWO IGNORED THINGS THAT WILL HELP YOU

(THIS IS A DEEP LOOK AT DEFENSIVE REBOUNDS AND STEALS)

The Wall Street Journal, "People that perform the best do things very simply. They say, "No to clutter and remain focused on the important things."

As Coaches we need to do that. It will make a big difference in your career. Perfection is finally attained <u>not</u> when there is no longer anything to add, but when there is no longer anything to take away. As coaches we begin with this huge briefcase of things we need to do. The longer we coach the more we realize that less is more. By not having clutter you will know what to do.

Two things that will help you:
  1.   Defensive Rebounds and 2. steals
Statistical data reveals, if you can win these two areas you will win 79% of your games. Coaches can have nice careers with more the def. rebounds & steals

1. **Defensive Rebounds:**
    The 2nd highest scoring possession at .92-.95 PPP if you Fastbreak off the Defensive rebound. You are much better off in the Fastbreak /transition. Set plays yield a mere .54 PPP
    Why is it that these possessions are so much better? This is simple. It is contested shots that drastically lower shooting percentages; this provides additional defensive rebounds which provides a higher field goal shooting percentage when combining the rebound with the fast break. Also, by the defense giving up the offensive rebound you get the same result, a high field goal percentage by your opponent. You are looking to dominate the rebounding of missed shots on the defensively end.
    Missed shots by your opponent are highly valuable to you and conversely; opponent offensive rebounding is destructive to your offense. To excel in defensive rebounding, the defensive rebound percentage should be in the 70% to 74% range.
    The defense helps the offense i.e., missed shots creating defensive rebounding and the potential fastbreak transition/opportunities. The offense helps the defense i.e., when they make shots. CONT PG 227

2. **Steals:**

How do we get steals? Steals are the highest scoring possession .96 PPP. The defense needs steals.
Our thoughts on steals are not very exciting, but they are productive.

- Steals are interesting, "Deflections" is a key function in the stealing process. Statistical analysis tells us that every 10 deflections end up being 4 to 5 steals.
- Emphasis on intercepting passes weakens the rest of the defense when you do not get the ball, which is most of the time.
- The intercepted pass from point to wing is dynamic, but what we are talking about are steals that come from a different way.
- A deflection is knocking and digging the ball loose from the dribbler.
- Active hands and awareness help in deflections and steals and by digging make it hard to pass the ball into the lane and other scoring areas.
- A bounce pass opposed to an "air" pass is more likely to get deflected and / or stolen particularly on perimeter passes.

Drill: **Three player "Cat and Mouse" deflection drill.** This is a well-known and commonly used drill. It is not the drill, it is how you coach the drill, it is the coaching points.

1. Two players on offense 12 feet apart, with a defender between them.
2. The defender plays normal 1x1 defense, up on ball with active hands, and being aggressive – but always maintain defensive stance and balance.
3. Offense cannot throw lob passes to each other. May allow offense one dribble to create a passing lane – defense slides and defends.
4. On pass the defender follows the ball.
5. Offensive player receiving the ball waits until defender assumes defensive position.
6. Any deflection stops the drill and defensive player rotates out of middle. This drill creates player deflection awareness. This is a good drill, but it must be coached hard and correctly.
7. Keep in mind the value of steals/deflections. Steals gives the offense a .96 Point Per Possession, the best scoring possession in the game. Work at getting more steals/deflections in every game. Spend time practicing this drill and emphasizing the value of steals.

BRIAN OSTERMANN

KANSAS STATE UNIVERISTY
ASSOCIATE HEAD COACH
"PLUS – MINUS PLAYER EVALUATION"

A member of the Western Missouri University Hall of Fame. Coach O is a master basketball coach who is highly respected in the coaching profession as a basketball strategist and teacher of the game. A long-time head and assistant coach. Coach Ostermann has been an Associate Head Coach at TCU and Kansas State University since 2008.

The plus – minus technique is a simple measurement that can be kept on the bench in real time. This a straight-forward method of communicating to players why they <u>are</u> or <u>are not</u> getting "their minutes."

"IF YOU ARE ON THE FLOOR:" On defense and opponents score you receive a minus (-.) When on offense and the Wildcats score you receive a plus (+.)

Etc. The Coaching Game. "At the end of the year we have five good players Instead of five good plays." Don Meyer, Northern State Hd. Coach

MIKE NEIGHBORS
UNIVERSITY OF ARKANSAS
HEAD COACH
"ANALYTICS AT ARKANSAS"

Mike Neighbors has coached in high school, Assistant College Coach and a head coach at the University of Washington where he led the Lady Huskies to the NCAA Final Four and then went home to Arkansas to lead the University of Arkansas. Coach Neighbors is one of the outstanding coaches in college basketball. An unconventional thinker who not only coaches the game, he loves the game.
he "Lives" the game of basketball. Coach Neighbors took the University of Washington to the NCAA FINAL FOUR and has his Razorback program on the right pathway to being one of elite programs in the game.

Analytics is one tool to help win games, but it is not the only technique to use. At Arkansas we will always have the five out on the floor that play well together, sometimes that is not your best five players.

You do not need a lot of algorithms. Coaches are dismissive of analytics because they either do not want to see the numbers or more likely do not understand the meaning of the numbers (facts.)
For us at Arkansas, it is just simple math. What was the score when you went into the game and what was the score when you came out of the game? Did your time in the game produce a plus or minus differential on the scoreboard?

Etc. Training must translate into improvement, visual, and statistical results."

SECTION VIII

WHAT'S A "GRINDER?"

American Heritage Dictionary

1. A person thought to work excessively
2. To devote ones-self to study or work
3. Slang: a hero sandwich; to move hips

Grinders "are essential workers."

Grinders "get things done."

Grinders "weeds the garden."

Grinders "do what others won't do or can't do."

Grinders say "Ok"

Grinders say, "I'll do it."

Grinders say, "We can do it."

Grinders say, "Let's get started."

Grinders "Are winners".

Grinders "Don't know enough to give up."

Grinders "Are OK with starting over."

Grinders "have a "get it done" approach."

Grinders "are patient and anxious."

Grinders "are not good at telling time."

Grinders "solve problems before they become problems."

Grinders "are sleuths, detectives working behind the scenes."

Grinders "true grinders do not change."

Grinders "not everyone wants to be a grinder."

Grinders "The world needs more grinders."

GRINDERS WE KNOW

Tom Izzo. Head Coach Michigan State University. It was the 1981–82 season. Tom Izzo was on Coach Glenn Brown's staff at Northern Michigan in Michigan's Upper Peninsula. The collector of this book was an assistant with Dave Buss at Green Bay. Northern Michigan had won at 57–50 in Green Bay. The Phoenix won 57-56 in Marquette. Coach Izzo was young and aggressive, a firebrand type on the UNM bench; actually, very similar to Hall of Fame Coach we have seen on the Michigan State University bench for over 20 years. After Northern Michigan, Coach Izzo's "Grind" moved from Marquette, MI to E. Lansing to work for Jud Heathcote at Michigan State as a "gofer", "gofer this, gofer that." Then came 3rd Assistant, 2nd Assistant, 1st Assistant and the "Grind" finally paid off; Tom Izzo became the great Jud Heathcote's hand-picked successor to be the Spartan's head coach in 1995. From "Gofer" to National Champs and the Hall of Fame. "Grinders don't know enough to give up."

Frank Vogel, Head Coach, Los Angeles Lakers emerged from the video darkroom, to scouting, assistant coaching, to being the head coach of the NBA champions. Frank Vogel's college playing career started at Div. 3 Juniata College (PA.) Vogel transferred to Kentucky and participated on the Wildcat's JV team. Another film room gig in Boston to assistant coaching positions with Boston, Indiana, and Philadelphia. Head Coaching stints at Indiana and Orlando, then unemployment AND then to the World Championship as the head coach of the LA Lakers. "Grinders are all right with starting over."

*Etc. Every program is improved when **FINISHING** becomes a non-negotiable: Finishing practice strong - Finishing conditioning drills – Finishing individual workouts and finishing the fourth quarter.*

... MORE GRINDERS WE KNOW

Eric Spoelstra, **Head Coach, Miami Heat**, a point guard at the U. of Portland, played two years in Germany as a player/coach. In 1995, Coach Spoelstra snagged a part-time video Coordinators job. Where do you go from being part-time and spending all day, every day in a video darkroom? But Grinders are positive and willing to work and learn. Work and learn is exactly what Eric Spoelstra did. One NBA championship as an Assistant Coach and two NBA Championships as Head Coach of the Miami Heat. "Stop grinding and you stop."

Buzz Williams, Head Coach, Texas A&M University, Born Brent Langdon Williams. His coaches at Navarro College nicknamed him "Buzz" because of his boundless energy (a classic trait of "Grinders".) Coach Williams Has an enthusiastic "gung-ho" style personality. He possesses the typical "Grinders" coaching resume'. With an insatiable desire to learn the "Game," he was a basketball manager at Navarro CC in Corsicana, TX., A graduate assistant at Oklahoma City University followed by assistant coaching stops in Arlington, TX., Kingsville, TX., Natchitoches, LA., FT. Collins, CO., College Station, TX., and Milwaukee, WI. As a head coach, the "Buzz" coached at U of New Orleans, Marquette University, Va. Tech, and Texas A&M and in the process accumulated a 275- 171. SEC Conference Coach of the Year, eight NCAA appearances. And It is notable that many "Grinders" because of their proven value often return to former coaching assistant coaching stops as the Head Coach. Buzz Williams, a supreme "Grinder.'

Etc. Coaches seem to prefer players who ask, "How do I do this?" As opposed to players who ask, "why are we doing this?"

. . . ANOTHER GRINDER

An anecdotal account of a "Coaching journey."

A High School Teacher and Coach for over nearly two decades. As a first-year teacher taught five classes was an Assistant Football Coach, Head Basketball Coach, and Head Track Coach and maxed out at $5200 per year.

Europe and Belgium Pro Leagues. Siemen Gent, Belgium's 1st Division pro team qualified for the league playoffs. The Americans Bobby Brannen (U of Cincinnati) and Rashad Tucker (Southern Illinois University) both had strong seasons. The team had a terrific season. It was a good hard working, talented team that liked each other was competitive from game one until the final playoff game. However, not unusual in Europe, the Club was unable to fulfill its financial obligations to the team and staff. In desperation the coaches and players hired a good Belgian lawyer. He garnished the game receipts from the Clubs biggest rivalry (Derby) game. Team and coach got back some back pay; it was not near what everyone was owed. Holding that team together and winning without getting paychecks was probably one of the better coaching jobs I had done in a while. These were professional players with families, mortgages, etc.

On to Austria and the Alps. A lasting memory, other than winning the National Championship was the return trip on a slow-moving train ride through the magnificent Austrian Alps with great friends.

A New Gunslinger in Denmark. As a "hired gun" for the **NATIONAL TEAM OF DENMARK,** the Danes won a crucial FIBA **European Qualifying Tournament**. It was critical to win this FIBA championship. The fact that Denmark was the host country added another layer of pressure to win. When you are a hired "Gun" you are expected to win. The "Great Danes" lost an unexpected tournament game to Georgia (the country, not the state.) As the tournament played out it came down to Denmark v. Romania for the championship. The Danes came through down the stretch with great pressure play for a tremendous Championship win. A lasting post game memory was the wild celebration including nonstop guzzling of Pilsner from the Championship Cup. CONT PG 235

It's Hot in the Desert. Immediately, knew this coaching experience was going to be like no other. Jeddah, Saudi Arabia a beautiful city on the East coast on the Red Sea with a gorgeous corniche stretching 30 miles along the coast. The Club had just opened a state-of-the art YMCA type club. It was a shrine in marble, a beautiful complex that supported every sport imaginable. Basketball had its own practice and competition arena. What was immediately noticed was that the nets to all the basketball courts had been installed upside down. On a made shot the ball would bounce around on the tightly stretched upside down nets and finally come to rest and had to be retrieved with a broom. In some ways this was a metaphor for the general state of Saudi basketball.

The Kingdom Second Act. 15 years later, returned to the Kingdom, this time at the request of Abal Abdullah Aziz ("Triple A") a personal friend to this day. Hired as the Head Coach of the Saudi Arabian National Team. The National Team traveled to tournaments in Tehran, Iran, Tripoli, Libya and Kuwait City, Kuwait in the summer before 9/11. In Iran there was another American team participating. It was nice to see how the Iranian youth enthusiastically cheered for the American team. The impression was this was a subtle way of showing their displeasure with the lifestyles they lived under. On 9/ 11, the day of the attack on the towers in New York the Saudi National team was in Kuwait competing in the Gulf Championships. Even though, there were few personal issues, I eventually left the Kingdom. All of our competitions were cancelled because of post 9/11 security concerns in the region.

Winning's not Easy. 21–4 an 84%win percentage is a nice record, but it can still be a hard season. Appointed to the head coaching position at Anoka – Ramsey Community College in June with one player on the roster. With no athletic recruiting budget or scholarships. All the recruiting was done on my own "dime" in the summer months. Chicago, Milwaukee, Minneapolis, Casper (WY) Junior College transfers, and Div. 1 transfers made up the bulk of the squad. There were a lot of wins and a lot of them were away games in an eight-passenger van. During the season, I removed a Big 10 transfer point guard from the team for disciplinary reasons, and eventually allowed him back on the squad. The team really didn't need him, but he needed the team for a variety of reasons. The result was we were on the cusp of nailing down a big win in the National Junior College Regional tournament. With a two-point lead and 15 seconds remaining and running out the

235

clock when our "guy" dribbles the baseline going under the basket and comes out wide open. Rather than do the right thing, he pulls up for an easy in rhythm 12-footer and misses. The rest is history, the game was lost in overtime and the winner went to Hutchinson KS. In allowing the point guard to return to the team violated a "the team comes first" coaching pillar. Not a pleasant memory even 40 years later.

Big Ten Time. Kevin McHale, Trent Tucker, Randy Breuer, Ben Coleman, et.al and the University of Minnesota. All of the above players were in the NBA and Kevin McHale was inducted into the Naismith Hall of Fame. This was a great team at a time when the Big 10 was at its zenith. Michigan State, Indiana, Michigan, Iowa either had won NCAA champions or had Final 4 appearances during this era. Not to mention Purdue and Illinois being powerhouse programs. And the coaching was a series of Sports Illustrated covers. Bob Knight, Indiana Jud Heathcote, Michigan State Jim Dutcher, Minnesota; Lute Olson, Iowa; Lou Henson, Illinois; Johnny Orr, Michigan; Gene Keady, Purdue and others. Because of the NCAA designated restricted earnings for my position, I pocketed $3000, took money out of my teacher retirement account, got an insurance license in order to keep enough food on the table for a family of five. It was a great year for me personally and the team got to the NIT championship game losing in the last seconds to Ralph Sampson and Virginia (This was the era when only the Conference Champion was assured of an invitation to the NCAA tournament.) That years' experience would lead to an assistant coaching position at Green Bay.

Head Coach Div. 1 Probably the three years as head coach of the Green Bay Phoenix were some of the more fun times of my career. All the fun ended with my staff and I getting "run." We just could not win enough games. Day in and day out we happily battled every obstacle to success and there were many. I still claim in private that our staff was responsible for saving the Div. 2 to Div. 1 transition. We were faced with overwhelming financial hurdles that affected every aspect of the program – recruiting, scheduling, travel, scholarships, equipment, Div. 1 amenities, and support staff, et.al. For example, in May with no money to finish recruiting, I made a trip of mercy to the Fort Howard Paper Co President to basically plead for $1000 to finish recruiting. CONT. PG 237

The Wild West. For the second time I accepted a $3000 stipend and joined the University of Wyoming Cowboys. When I told my wife, Loretta. Her first question of course was how much are "we" making. A told her $3000, she said, "Not bad." I am not going to share the conversation that followed once she learned the $3000 was the annual salary. But Wyoming was a "hot number" on the basketball stage. They had just come off a great season and finished the season in New York City as an NIT Finalist. Had the whole team returning. Also, we had been in Laramie before, my cousin had received his doctorate at the U of Wyoming. I liked everything about the University and the state. It just felt "right." Loretta got a job as a teacher's aide and we received 4 or 5, three and four figure checks from an insurance company merger from the insurance company I worked for while at the U of Minnesota. This mystery money was as welcome as it was unexpected. The teams at Wyoming won two WAC tournament championships and advanced to the NCAA Sweet sixteen beating perennial heavyweights Virginia and UCLA. It was the greatest run in Wyoming basketball history, and it was exciting to be a Cowboy and a part of that history.

Southern Methodist University. Dallas a great city, great people, great university, great place to live, but a long year. SMU was operating under the burden of the NCAA "Death Penalty." And literally were signing players to athletic scholarship if they were all-conference players and worse players who had "lettered" in high school as long as they met the "Death Penalty sky high athletic academic standards.

At the **University of Houston** there were outstanding coaches and people to work with, state of the art support facilities, liked the urban university setting, a recruiting hotbed and U of Houston had good teams.

Back to Front Range. Colorado State University was my first experience on the women's side. The experience was great, beyond what I could have imagined. CSU recruited four international players in addition to attracting high quality Colorado prospects. In the course of the next four seasons this core of players did a really nice job of going from a two-win season to a new era in women's basketball at Colorado State University. CONT. 238

Continuing to Coach on the Women's Side. There was head coaching in the Czech Republic, assistant positions at Drury U and Missouri S&T. A trip to the Div. 2 NCAA tournament in Erie, PA. And working with the University of Tennessee as their Advance Scout Statistical Analyst. All with their own stories and memories, the journey continues.

Etc.: ***STAYING THE COURSE – QUIT AT YOUR OWN PERIL.*** *Pablo Casals was considered the greatest musician of the twentieth century. He is from Spain but spent most of his life in exile because he did not believe in the dictatorial government of Francisco Franco that controlled the country. Early in his life he developed the habit of practicing his instrument – the cello – for three hours every day. Very late in his life he was approached by friends who asked him why he continued to practice three hours every day. He replied, "I am beginning to see some improvement."*

THE CULTURE OF ENTITLEMENT

1. DON'T REWARD MERE PARTICIPATION – **participation** should not demand a trophy.

2. DON'T REWARD ATHLETES WITH THINGS THEY HAVE NOT EARNED – nothing screams entitlement more than giving out rewards for routine things that for the most part is expected.

3. DON'T CODDLE YOUR ATHLETES – this produces lazy, fragile and excuse making

4. DON'T ALLOW DOUBLE STANDARDS – Nothing is more distasteful to the team when they believe or even have the impression that team standards are not for everyone.

5. DON'T LET THEM LIVE IN A BUBBLE – Entitlement leads to athletes thinking the world should cater to them. Real life experiences, community service, visit hospitals, volunteer at food shelters, etc.

6. DON'T ALLOW UNGRATEFULNESS – Watch for it, address it sooner rather than later. Foster a we are grateful for everything, expect nothing and we must earn all that we achieve culture.

Etc.: This could only come from one person, Jerry Tarkanian, the great UNLV Coach. "In a marriage, only one person can be happy, and it better be you.".

SECTION IX

"THE PLAYBOOK"

1. THE 1-4

2. Coach Rupp's Kentucky 1-3-1 H.C. Zone Def.

3. Lin Dunn's 5 Def. Pick and Roll Schemes.

4. Finishing Drills

5. The Three Pillars of Defense

HALL OF FAME COACH
RALPH MILLER
WICHITA ST., U OF IOWA, OREGON ST.
HIGH 1-4

An historically successful way to play offensive basketball made famous by the coaching genius of Coach Ralph Miller. The 1-4 produced Steve Johnson an "All American" who shot an NCAA record high 74.6% shooting percentage from the field; that field goal % record stood for 36 years. Johnson had a ten-year All-Star career in the NBA.

In this section, the basic 1-4 is explained and diagrammed. This is a proven offense with 1-4 elements scattered throughout the present-day basketball landscape for that very reason – it is a "Proven way to successfully play."

Also, included is the concept of "positionless" offensive basketball is discussed in the 2.0 and 3.0 versions of the basic diagrammed 1-4 (1.0 Version.) This is a tiered approach, learning/perfecting each version before moving on. It will take significant practice time to arrive at the needed level of execution of the 2.0 and 3.0. 1-4 versions.

I live by three general principles:
1. *The difference between success and failure is so small it is imperceivable by most people.*
2. *Man must accomplish to live. It is the winner who is truly alive.*
3. *And the four-letter word: W- O -R -K.*
   George Allen, the eccentric, but great NFL coach. A winner of 88% of games With Rams and Redskins. Lost Super Bowl 7 to Dolphins.

COACHING THE 1-4

The 1-4 is not revolutionary. Over the years many coaches have employed the 1-4 or different versions of the 1-4 alignment – elements of the Ralph Miller 1-4 are still in vogue.

Why the 1-4?

1. Great spacing: a. Driving lanes are available. b. Contains a low post component as well as a high- low game. d. players being interchangeable advances unpredictability of the offense.
2. "Free flowing" movement with an element of structure.
3. Possibly the most important element that promotes a "Free Flow" offense is the timing of the cutting action takes preference over the cutter "setting up" (waiting) for the screen. This waiting slows down the offense. Example: The cutter makes his/her cut when the ball is ready to be passed regardless of the timing in the screen OR the cutter makes the cut upon receiving the screen regardless of the readiness of the passer.

KEY TERMS:

"Ball Centered" – Ball when "Centered" between the free throw lane lines Wing or Post option are both in play with the centered ball having four passing options.
"Long Screen" – a perimeter player screening low post player.
"Lob" – with three interchangeable perimeter players / the bigger players are the best "lob" players – when ball is centered to the small forward – that's a "bingo" call for the lob action.
"Swing and in" – reverse ball and look to go inside.
"High-Low" – There always is a high low component after 1ˢᵗ pass
"High and Wide"- This is a constant reminder to four non-ball handlers to keep coming high and wide when ball is "centered"– players tend to linger near the baseline as the game goes on. Classic game "slippage."
"Speed Cuts"- the general pace of play on the half court. CONT. PG 244

"Back Cut / Back Door" – Invite defensive overplay - don't fight denial defense welcome it – walk it higher and back cut/" backdoor" v. pressure. Movement with purpose breaks down defensive pressure.

1-4 version 1.0 (Learning 1.0 is the key to moving forward w/ free-lance integration)
The core of the 1-4 is a continuity of play that meshes the stability of structured play (1-4) with improvisation a hybrid form of free-lance/motion type play. An example would be: The offense initiated in the 1-4 alignment with either the Wing or Post option - during the execution of the play if any event causes a breakdown of the 1-4; for example, during a 1-4 option the ball is fumbled in the lane recovered by the offense passed out and "Centered." At this point the defense is in its weakest form, "scramble," **The player with the ball centered - passes to the first open receiver**. The remaining four players react to that pass, regardless of where they are on the floor to either a Wing or Post option. The offense does not need or want to get in a "set" 1-4. On the first pass, the offense is in either Wing or Post. Do not wait for the play to "set up" For instance, on a point to wing pass the point player makes the "lob" cut regardless of whether the screen from the post is in position or not. This may look chaotic, but all the offensive players have an edge in knowing what to do on the first pass. The purpose is to create a continuous attack taking advantage of a defense in its weakest form being scramble and not able to get "set" because the offense is not allowing a defensive re-set. Without a re-set the offense is always in quick attack mode

"DIVERGENT BASKETBALL" & THE 1 – 4

The following titled VERSION 2.0 and VERSION 3.0 are developing offensive ideas – similar to an experimental "concept" car – it's still a car but because of divergent thinking (see pages 39-40 of this book.) it's "different." V-2.0 / V3.0 are not new creations, but they are different because of the "divergent" thinking process that produces different offensive ideas based on a familiar foundation.
1-4 Version 2.0 (This is the 2nd step in the development of the 1 -4.)
CONT. PG 245

In the 1-4 (1.0) sequence of events on the offensive end of the floor v ½ court defense: a. wing or post option b. there is not a shot; poor execution or good defense. c. ball is "centered" and offense quick attacks v a scrambled defense.

2.0 goes to the next level. The offense can be initiated from any of the 1-4 Wing or Post floor positions. At this point the other four players react to the position of the ball and run either the wing or post options. DO NOT wait for sequence of the set play. This is not a set play it IS knowing where you are on the floor: wing, post, or point and reacting to the position of the ball. Again, the purpose is too "quick" attack an unsettled defense with a second wave of the 1-4 attack. Only visible to the trained professional, However, difficult to defend by players on the floor. 2.0 does not look or act like 1-4 1.0 but it still provides a level of structure with improvisational and instinctive play.

<u>1-4 Version 3.0</u> **(This is the final level of integrating structure with free-lance.) This is like the 1.0 and 2.0 except it adds the dimension of all five positions being interchangeable.** This may place big players on the perimeter and perimeter players in the 4 and 5 positions.

The final point is that 1-4; 1.0, 2.0. 3.0 is purposed to create a continuing attacking offense without re-setting the offense or allowing a weakened defense to re-set IMPORTANT: keep players working high off the baseline – left to their "own," players will tend to "cheat" the offense and not come off the baseline.

Different from free-lance or motion offense, the 1.0, 2.0, 3.0 is the execution is a hybrid that contains both structure and an element of free-lance i.e., improvisation and instinctive play. Therein lies the conundrum of what do we teach in those times when the offense is probing v. the unorganized or scrambled defense. Or a bigger question, do we teach <u>anything</u>? Every "Do this" rule leads to structured play which in this system leads to pattern play. The object of the 1-4 is to get a hybrid of free-lance and the 1-4 wing / post action.

The ability of a team to get efficient at the 2.0 and/or 3.0 level is a process and dependent on: A. The experience level of the team and B. the quantity of deliberate practice involved in 2.0, 3.0 advanced level of play.

THE ICONIC 1-4 ALIGNMENT
RALPH MILLER OREGON STATE

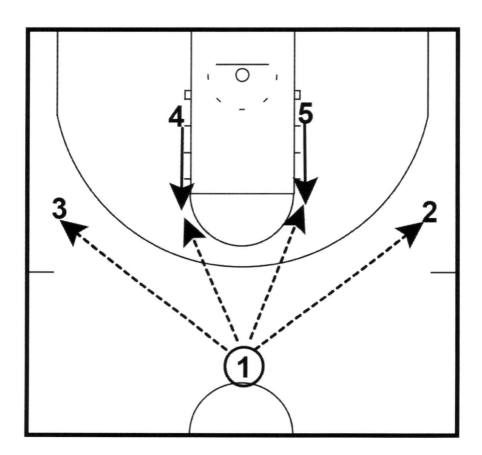

Great spacing
1. Four "Ready" pressure releases
2. Cutting and driving lanes and available with the basket area open.
3. Positions are interchangeable
4. The basket area is the least guarded area on the floor.

THE HIGH 1-4

1. Initial alignment of the 1 – 4

2. All players should <u>always</u> work themselves away from baseline when ball is "centered."

3. #1 should work between the lane line rails. This gives #1 – 4 passing lanes

4. Important that wings alignment is at the top of the free throw circle extended as shown.

5. #4 and #5 are interchangeable. #1, #2, #3 are all interchangeable.

6. Spacing is important "High and Wide" as shown.

7. The offensive goal: is to advance to versions #2 and #3 of the offense, where all five positions are interchangeable. Visualize the ball being centered to the biggest player on the team, and the #5 player running a wing option "lob." This is an example of the kind of play we are interested in developing.

Etc.: "Your job is to touch everyone and get to their soul. Every morning you are in your office, you are useless." Jack Welch, Chairman & CEO of General Electric

1 -4 WING OPTION
BEAVERS OSU

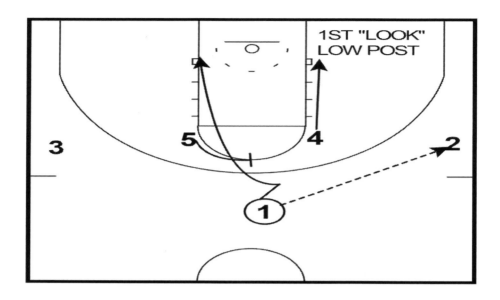

1 -4 WING OPTION
BEAVERS OSU

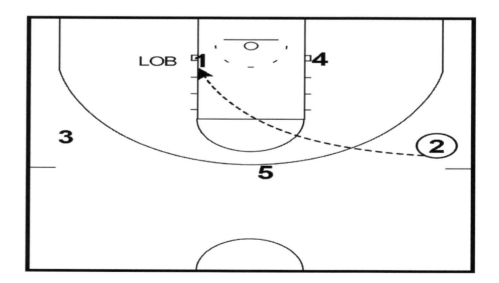

248

1-4 WING OPTION

TOP DIAGRAM / BOTTOM DIAGRAM

Actions in Top and Bottom happen simultaneously:
On #1 to #2 pass - #4 drops to block: #2 "scans" #4 in process of reversing ball.

1. #1 does not wait on cuts off #5's high screen.
2. #2's lob is to the front of the rim.
3. #1's cut is in the lane (do not belly wide) and go to the block.

Coaching Points: Top and Bottom Diagrams.

1. #5 sets screen on a line between baskets and straddling the top of the free throw circle.
2. #2 needs to see both #4 and #1 as their cuts are simultaneous.
3. General Rule: Offensive players do not wait for screens, etc. All players should know what to do based on where they are on the floor and the position of the ball. Movement is more important than waiting for whatever you expect to happen.
4. If you need to wait for a screen, it is too late – just make your cut.
The 1-4 values movement in the form of concise cutting actions.
Waiting for actions to materialize slows down movement
and pace which is valued in this offensive concept.

1-4 WING OPTION CONT.
BEAVERS OSU

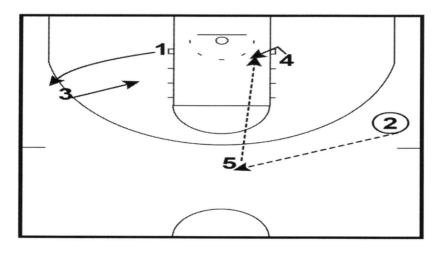

1-4 WING OPTION CONT.
BEAVERS OSU

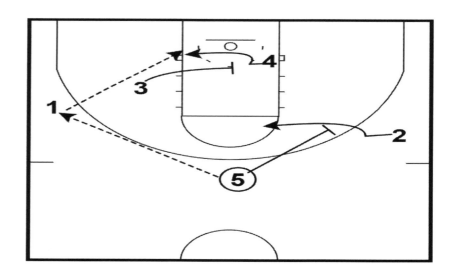

WING OPTION CONT.

TOP DIAGRAM:

1. This is a continuation of previous page diagrams of Lob and Low post diagram.
2. #2 Reverses ball to #5 who "scans" the Hi to Lo pass to #4 - Do Not Wait for #4 to open up for potential Hi-Lo feed. If open, make play – but do not wait/search for #4 – there is something else coming.

Bottom Diagram:

1. 5# reversed ball to #1
2. #3 head hunts #4 and "lays the wood" to #4's def. player – this is referred to as the "Long Screen." This #1 to #4 pass is a "Bell Cow" option in the offense.
3. #5 Screens away on a defensive sagging defender guarding #2 – this is a good option. The #1 to #2 pass is #1's – 2nd "look, this is a good jump shooting option that is simple – this option is good because #4 can "bury" a sagging defender on #2.
4. #2 coming off #5's screen – if they do not get a scoring opportunity - #2 is centered and hits the first open player either a post or perimeter player and play continues. There is no re-set.

Etc.: Less is More.

1-4 POST OPTION - FIRST CUTTER
BEAVERS OSU

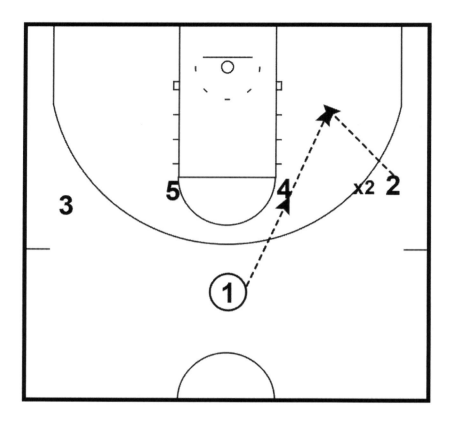

Etc.: Two the sweetest words in coaching:
"OK COACH."

POST OPTION – "FIRST CUTTER"

1. The high 1-4 "dream" is when the defense plays denial defense as shown in the diagram.
2. Wings Do not fake and juke to get open – they walk the defense as high as they will come in a denial / semi-denial position.
3. Ball is entered to High Post player #4 who makes a bounce pass to the speed cutting #2
4. #4 coaching point on the pass is to make the pass with back to baseline the ball is a bounce pass to the corner.
5. If timing is correct the cutter #2 will run into the ball – where shown on the diagram.

Etc. "In the competitive world there are no entitlements; do not fall into this trap of feeling like you are a victim. You are not, get over it and get on with it. And "YES" most things are more rewarding when you break a sweat to get them."
Matthew McConaughey, actor
U of Houston Graduation Speech

1-4 POST OPTION - 2ND CUTTER
BEAVERS OSU

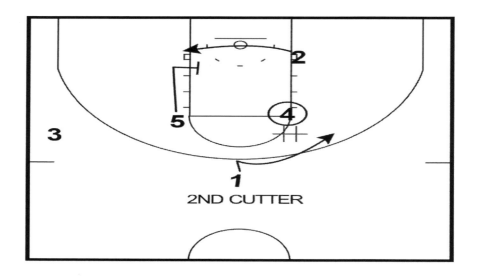

2ND CUTTER

1-4 POST OPTION - 2ND CUTTER
BEAVERS OSU

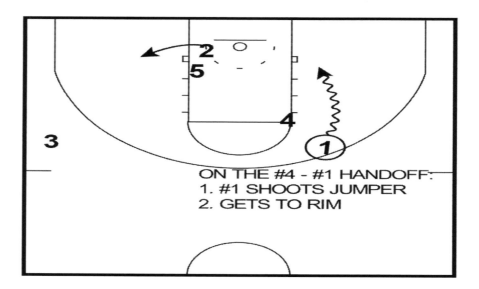

ON THE #4 - #1 HANDOFF:
1. #1 SHOOTS JUMPER
2. GETS TO RIM

POST OPTION – 2ND CUTTER

TOP DIAGRAM:

1. #4 has checked #2 the first cutter. The backdoor cut the diagram shows #2 in route off #5's screen.
2. #1 makes a quick jab step and cuts off #4 on the cleared right side of the court.

BOTTOM DIAGRAM:

1. In diagram, #4 is handing off ball to #1 - #1's objective is to get to the rim.

2. If #1 cannot get to the rim or take the jump shot on the handoff. #1 flattens the dribble and looks for #4 dropping to the block and / or has option to pick and roll with #1 – who needs to keep his dribble. **(See Bottom Diagram on page 260)**

(See Bottom Diagram on page 260)

Etc. It is not about whether
You win or lose
It is about
Do you accept
The Challenge?
<u>African Mali - Lore</u>

1-4 POST OPTION 3RD CUTTER
BEAVERS OSU

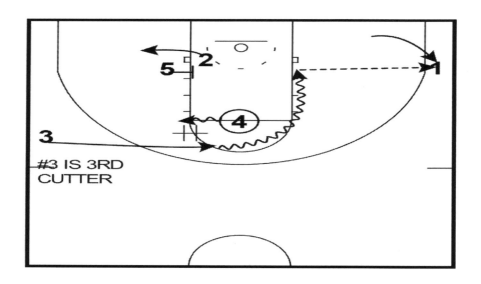

#3 IS 3RD
CUTTER

1-4 POST OPTION 3RD CUTTER
BEAVERS OSU

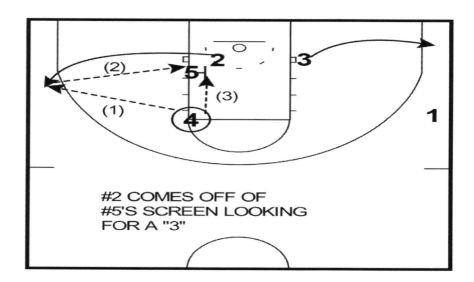

#2 COMES OFF OF
#5'S SCREEN LOOKING
FOR A "3"

OPTION – 3RD CUTTER (SWING)

This is a continuation of previous POST OPTION DIAGRAM.

TOP DIAGRAM:

1. #4 uses a "crab" type dribble to cross the basket-to-basket midline as shown. As #4 starts "crab" dribble . . .

2. #3's cut is quick this is a scoring cut for: 1. Jump shot using #4 as a screen.

3. If #3 does not shoot the ball over #4 – #3 the drives to the rim - this is a strong scoring option with the option of kicking the ball to spotted up corner jump shooter #1.

BOTTOM DIAGRAM:

1. #4 - not handing ball off to #3 makes the (1) pass in diagram to

#2 coming off of #5's screen.

2. #2's options are: a. shoot perimeter shot b. look to go inside to a posting #5. (The #2 pass in diagram.)

3. If #4 does not pass to #2 – #2 look inside to #5 (The #3 pass in diagram)

4. Important: If there is no shot – ball is "centered" to the closest player, this would probably #1 coming to the top and the other four scatter to 1-4 positions ball is passed to first open player post or wing and "away we go."

2nd & 3rd time through the offense is what breaks down the defense.

Etc.: Does anyone have an offense drawn out
that works if you can't Pass and catch?

1-4 WING DRIBBLE
BEAVERS OSU

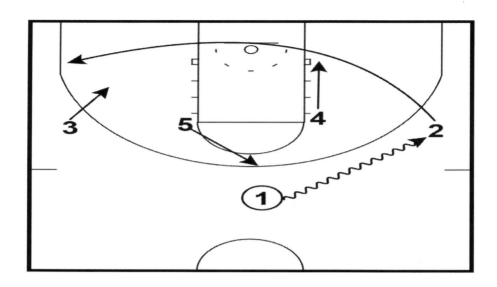

1-4 WING DRIBBLE
BEAVERS OSU

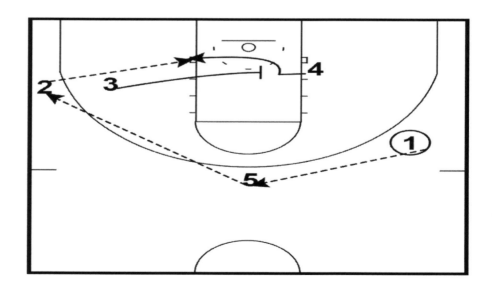

WING DRIBBLE OPTION

The offense does not subscribe to many options, rather a few variations that can be imbedded in the offense and not thought of as "options." Its nature is more instinctive and/or improvisational. AND, thought of as part of the offense.

Top Diagram:

1. #1 dribbles out #2 as shown - #2 runs to get an open "3."

2. #1 should "see" the high post drop

3. #1 can turn the corner and get to the basket. If not "turning the corner" #1 should not get below the free throw line extended – this facilitates the reversal pass to #5 who has popped to the top.

Bottom Diagram:

#5 steps out and reverses ball to #1

#3 sets the "long screen" on #4

Note: This is run with pace - #2 has to be sprinting

Etc.: Knowledge equals Confidence and Confidence equals PLAYING FAST!"

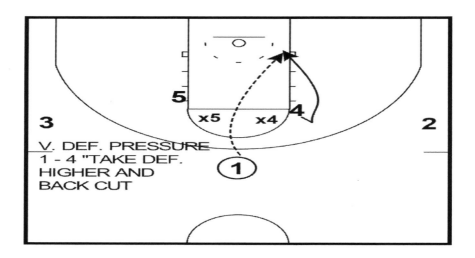

V. DEF. PRESSURE
1 - 4 "TAKE DEF.
HIGHER AND
BACK CUT

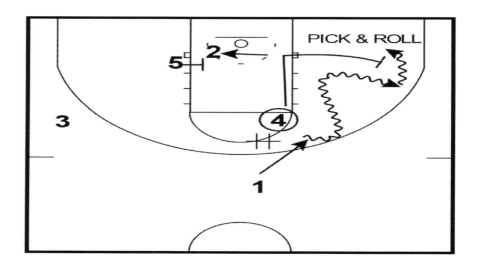

260

1 – 4 PRESSURE RELEASE / POST LOB

PICK AND ROLL (PNR)

TOP DIAGRAM:

1. With hard denial or pressure on passing lanes.

2. NOT SHOWN: is the hard dribble at the wing and backdoor

3. The "Lob" to the high post player.

Important: This a tricky concept, that can only go from concept to effective action through practice. The concept in the back door and the lob pass is an action that requires both the passer and the cutter be aware of each other's intention. The concept of "Seeing" what is going on around the players and on the court is important in "On time and on target" execution.

BOTTOM DIAGRAM:

In diagram – the play is picked up after the back cut by #2 on the point to post pass (See bottom diagram on page 254)

1. This is the post option 2nd cut and handoff to #1 who flattens the dribble and #4 sets a PNR screen

2. This side is cleared giving #1 and #4 space.

Etc.: I will form good habits and become their "slave."

1 -4 WING OPTION "QUICKIE"
BEAVERS OSU

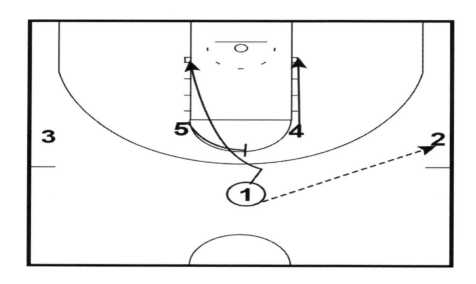

1 -4 WING OPTION "QUICKIE"
BEAVERS OSU

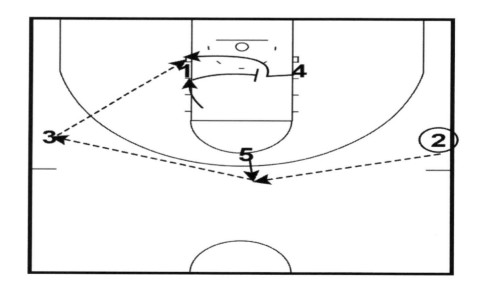

WING OPTION (QUICKIE)

Top Diagram:

1. Wing option lob – sell this cut make defender guard the lob action

This is "Quickie" for a reason, it is a quick hitter and it

eliminates the possibility of a switch on the "Long Screen."

Bottom Diagram

1. #1 the lob cutter turns and "head hunts" (screens) for #4

2. Ball is reversed through the high post.

3. #3 looks to go inside to #4

*Etc. If you practice like the next game is the most important game -
then when it REALLY IS – you will know what to do.*

COACH RUPP'S KENTUCKY

1-3-1 HALF COURT ZONE PRESS

ADOLPH RUPP, the Kentucky basketball BARON, throughout his 28 Southeastern Conference Championships, his 82% win % and 876 career wins; was achieved with a hard-nosed man to man defensive approach. But because of the innovative "spread" offenses he relented to using the 1-3-1 half court zone. Coach Rupp liked the 1-3-1 for two reasons:

1. *It was an attacking defense, which had the same philosophy of pressuring the ball and denying the passing lanes that his man-to man defense employed.*
2. *Important to Coach Rupp was that this 1-3-1 had specific rules and responsibilities whereby he could pin-down individual player breakdowns.*

TEN TEAM RULES FOR THE 1-3-1 HALF COURT ZONE

A. Always see the ball – watching passer's eyes.

B. Adjust to players in your area. BUT never move more than one arms-length from your "Home" rule.

C. Move quickly on the flight of the ball.

D. Disregard ball fakes.

E. When ball is passed – convert quickly to your position in relationship to the ball.

F. Anticipate screens, especially on the baseline.

G. Back men "ALERT" teammates of screens and weakside flash cutters.

H. Play for DEFLECTIONS – not steals.

I. Stay in passing lanes – inhibit perimeter passing – force lob and bounce passes.

J. Be aggressive-mentally alert physically and keep hands up and alive.

1-3-1 POSITIONING
File Cabinet

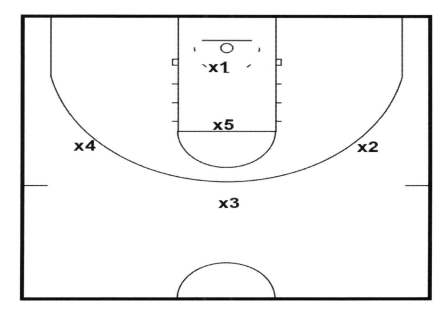

NOTE: The ½ court 1-3-1 zone is an attacking aggressive defense-

 there is no time to rest.

X3 = athletic small forward or guard. (By changing this position to a big guard or point guard will change the look / personality of the press.)
X1 = a guard must be tough and cover corner to corner. Front any post player.
X2 = big guard in diagram but could be another player with some size.
X4 = usually a big forward – this is a rebounding position
X5 = Center - between ball and basket by rule fronts low post.

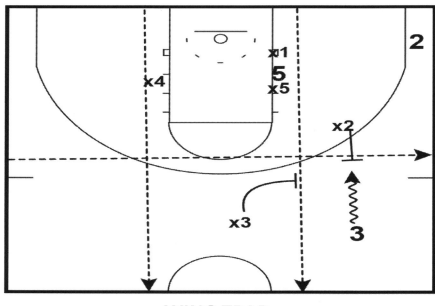

WING TRAP

VERTICAL "RAILS" identify X5 middle player & X3 (point) boundaries
HORIZONTAL dotted lines are boundary "rails" for the wings.

X1 – by rule straddles the low block area. Covers corner (#2) when ball is in the air to corner.

X2 – faces midline and traps at dotted line area.

X4 - by rule is between ball and corner behind him/her

X5 – by rule plays between ball and basket fronting low post.

The defense is designed to create two angle passes lobs or bounce passes; facilitating the defensive covers and keeps the defense from getting out of "Shape"- which can force the defense into a destructive "scramble" mode.

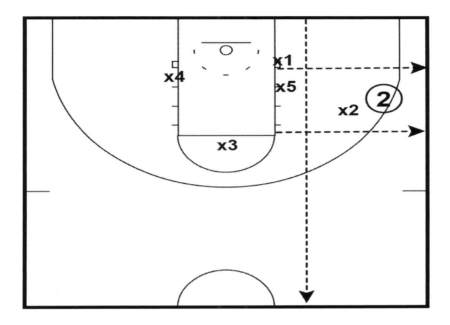

BALL IN 1X1 BOX

a. When ball gets in the 1x1 Box as shown in diagram, X2 plays the ball 1x1 forcing ball to the baseline. If ball is dribbled into the "low or "high" trap areas. The areas below and above the horizontal dotted lines the ball is trapped high with an X3/X2 high trap or an X2/X1 baseline trap.

b. X3 by rule is in the middle of the free throw line, between the ball side corner and the midcourt sideline corner behind him/her. Others play by rule Coaching Point: if the trapping action is too high or too low, outside the "trap areas" it will make it difficult to make covers on passes out of traps – allowing for dribble penetration, open shots and quick passing, all are to the disadvantage of the defense

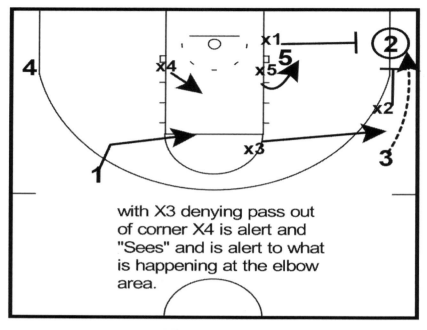

with X3 denying pass out of corner X4 is alert and "Sees" and is alert to what is happening at the elbow area.

CORNER TRAP

X1 By rule stays "Home" straddling the lane line. He/she goes to cover (trap) #2 with ball in the air to #2 in corner.

X2 By rule, traps when ball is in the corner below the 2nd hash mark from baseline.

X3 denies the pass back out to #3

X4 By rule is between the ball and corner behind him   X4 "reads" the "Elbow" area and may have to make that cover as X3 makes interception cut. X4's by rule position – will put him/her in good position to **"see"** (important word) what is happening around /him

X5 by rule, plays between ball and basket

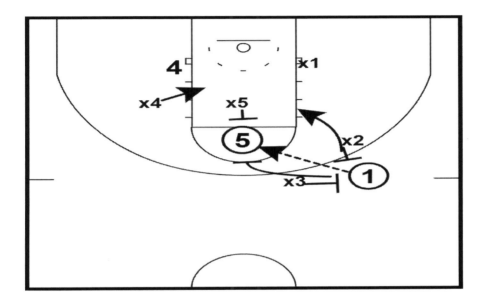

HIGH POST COVERAGE

Ball entered to the high post is an X5 and X3 quick trap on the ball.

a. X4 & X2 dive to rule positions between corners and mid-court line and sideline by Sprinting to their rule Positions X4 & X2 there are interception possibilities to "run" into an errant pass by #5.

b. X1 holds his/her "home" position and is alert/sees any high-low action. In diagram by rule they should be alert for the pass to the low post.

c. Objective is to get ball kicked back out to perimeter and then recover to 1-3-1 positions

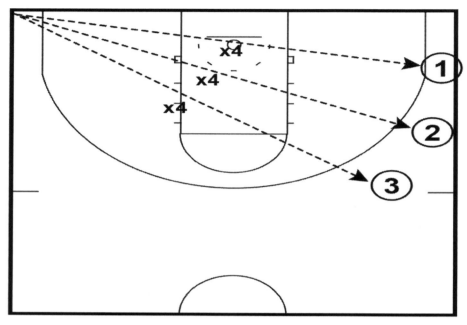

WEAKSIDE COVERAGE

The diagram shows the positioning of **X4** on the weakside of floor with #1, #2, #3 designated as having ball.

a. On the weakside, the **Position Rule** - play between the ball and the corner behind you and adjust one "arms-length" to the offensive player in area.

b. The weakside defenders need alertness and concentration.

c. The **positioning by rule and adjustment of one arm's length** should be followed - not following positioning rules will stretch the defense out of shape and allow gap penetration and quickly throw the defense into scramble.

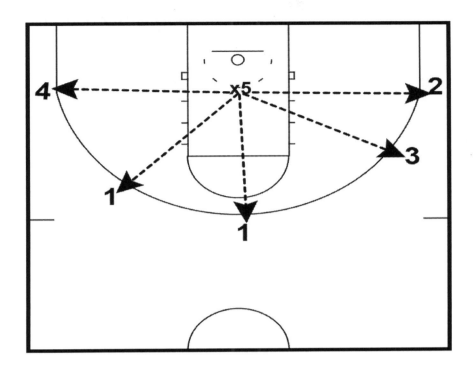

POSITION RULE MIDDLE PLAYER

a. Play between the ball and the basket.
b. Dotted line marks area of coverage for X5
c. Front the low post. There are times when <u>not</u> fronting the low post is appropriate. Example: playing behind the post player will do 3 things: 1. Help the post defender in rebounding. 2. The offensive post player will have to score over the defender and 3. Not fronting the low post will take pressure off the weakside wing to defend the lob.

"OUT" CALL

X1 With ball in the air – X1 Sprints to cover #2 on reception of #3 to #2 pass.

X2 Faces baseline and plays the pass back out to a receiver behind X2 forcing a slow lob pass out of the corner – X2 does not trap corner in "Out" call.

X3 the point drops to the critical elbow area playing any player at the elbow area. Also, X3 can be in a "wide" position helping to keep ball from going into the low post below X3.

X4 plays rule between ball and corner behind him/her. On a diagonal pass out of the corner "first man cover" (first player to ball makes cover.)

X5 Play rule fronts low post. Unless strategically instructed to play differently.

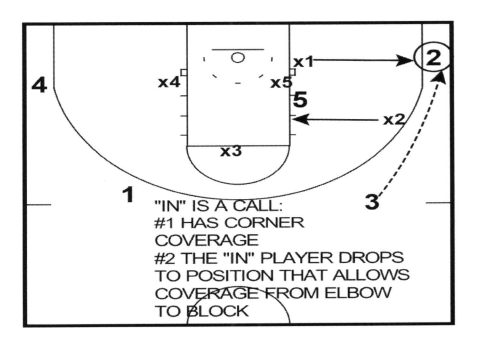

"IN" IS A CALL:
#1 HAS CORNER
COVERAGE
#2 THE "IN" PLAYER DROPS
TO POSITION THAT ALLOWS
COVERAGE FROM ELBOW
TO BLOCK

"IN" CALL

X1 By rule, ON PASS sprints to cover #2. This is 1x1.

X2 covers lane as shown to a position that he/she can get a hand front on low post player and with good hand work still be able retard passes to the elbow.

X3 different from "OUT" call gets to the middle of the free throw lane – this is X3's by rule position between ball and the corner behind him/her – this is the sideline/midcourt

X4 by rule between ball and corner behind him/her.

X5 by rule between ball and basket.

NOTE: The "IN CALL" is effective in defending diagonal passes out of corner to primarily #1. It puts X3 by rule in a better position to play the diagonal pass.

273

LIN DUNN
NCAA/WNBA HEAD COACH

"FIVE DEFENSIVE SCHEMES V.

THE PICK AND ROLL"

Coach Dunn coached the Purdue Boilermakers in two consecutive NCAA Final Four's amassing 447 wins on the Div. 1 collegiate level. Professionally she won 409 games including the WNBA title with the Indiana Fever. An inductee into the Women's Hall of Fame in 2014. After a brief retirement, Coach Dunn was announced as a special assistant to the Women's Basketball Coach at the University of Kentucky. Coach Dunn is recognized as an outstanding basketball tactician and personality in the game.

Our Defensive identity: "Disruption."
1.   Keep opponent out of the paint
2.   Stop ball reversal
3.   Keep an unknown/surprise defensive strategy ready

The two-man game is executed on:
1.   Side (free throw line extended.)
2.   Corner
3.   Elbow
4.   Top

Every team needs defensive schemes v. the five two-man game strategies.
1.   Trap the – on ball screen
2.   Switch the - on ball screen
3.   Show vertically and get over- on ball screen
4.   "Ice" force ball away from screen – on ball screen
5.   "Ice-red" – double team before screener gets to the screen Everything starts on the ball side – but the game is won on the weakside. Doing the little things makes the big things possible.

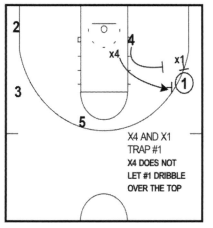

X4 AND X1
TRAP #1
X4 DOES NOT
LET #1 DRIBBLE
OVER THE TOP

TRAPPING THE "ON BALL" SCREEN

LEFT DIAGRAM

X4 makes sure #1 does not get over his/her top leg and get into the middle.

RIGHT DIAGRAM:

On trap deny one pass away - **X5** denies one pass away – this defends the Hi – Lo from #5

to #4 Which is a mis-match with #2's rotation

X2 rotates and fronts #4

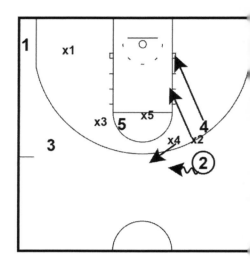

SWITCHING

LEFT DIAGRAM:

On the switch **X2** must get over the top of the screen – otherwise **X2** will get "rolled" and buried on the basket cut by #4 – if **X2** goes under the screen

RIGHT DIAGRAM

On **X4** switch – important that the bigger **X4** does not allow #2 split the between **X4** and **X2**.

OFFENSIVE NOTE: On Offense - if switch is a mismatch as this diagram shows - spread the floor and let #2 beat the bigger **X4**.

Assistant Coaches:
1. Take care of your family and your health
2. Take care of your players, academics, social, spiritual, family
3. Recruit every day
4. Be an expert at your position coaching responsibilities
5. Be passionate about coaching.

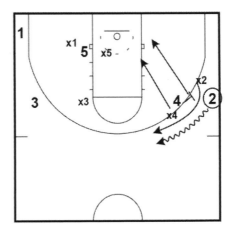

VERTICAL "SHOW" AND "OVER"

LEFT DIAGRAM:

X2 seals the side opposite the screen being set by #4.

X4 rides hip of **4** – at point of screen **X4** vertically steps aggressively one or two strides towards the midcourt line as shown. Forcing ball handler high.

RIGHT DIAGRAM:

X4's action allows X2 an "alley" to get over the top of and guard #2"s middle dribble.

X2 <u>must</u> get over the top of the screen by #4 so as not to get "rolled" into the post by #4.

X4 takes #4 on roll to the basket with **X5** in a good help position.

277

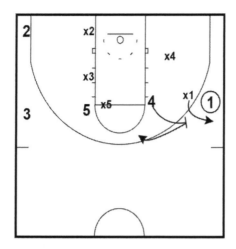

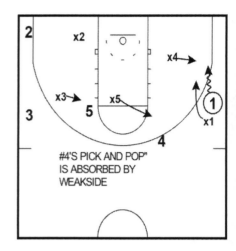

#4'S PICK AND POP"
IS ABSORBED BY
WEAKSIDE

"ICE" PICK AND ROLL

LEFT DIAGRAM: X1 gets high and forces #1 away from screen – do not allow #1 to use screen. If #4 is a perimeter shooting threat **X5**, the next man must rotate.

X4 plays as shown giving baseline support.

RIGHT DIAGRAM:

X1 forces #1 away from the screen – DOES NOT ALLOW #1 TO USE SCREEN.

If X1 does a good job. **X4** will be in position to help/trap on drive toward baseline.

If #4 is a "Pop and shoot" type player – in diagram, #5 would rotate.

278

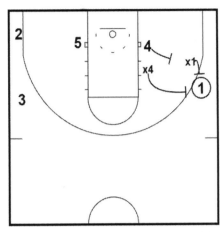
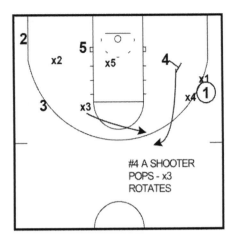

#4 A SHOOTER
POPS - x3
ROTATES

"ICE RED" PICK AND ROLL

LEFT DIAGRAM:

#4 goes to set screen on **X1, X4** beats #4 to ball setting hard trap with **X1**

RIGHT DIAGRAM:

If #4 is a shooter, a <u>pick and pop player</u>, weakside rotates in RIGHT DIAGRAM this would be **X3**

Etc.: Overheard player saying to teammate during the pre-game National Anthem:
"I never play well when I hear that song."

ONE ON ONE FINISHING DRILLS

This is a time saving way to work on both offensive and defensive techniques that are game like.

The creative coach can take the following drill examples and expand them to meet their specific defensive and offensive objectives.

IMPORTANT: <u>At the point of the screen – the screener becomes the defender – defender allows the pass to be completed.</u>

Use any screening/cutting that fits your offense or any screen/cut you anticipate playing against.

<u>Coach sometimes passes to the screener.</u>

Play to a defensive rebound or play to a score by either the offensive or defensive player – rebounder goes on offense. This adds a degree of "grit" to the drill.

Etc.: At age 29, Pat Riley told me I could become a head coach in the NBA. Pat told me to remember four things and I could lead anyone:

> *1. Be competent – know your stuff.*
> *2. Be Sincere – strive to understand.*
> *3. Be reliable – do what you say you are going to do.*
> *4. Be Trustworthy – being authentic and consistent.*
> *Jeff van Gundy, Former Hd. coach: NY Knicks, Houston Rockets*

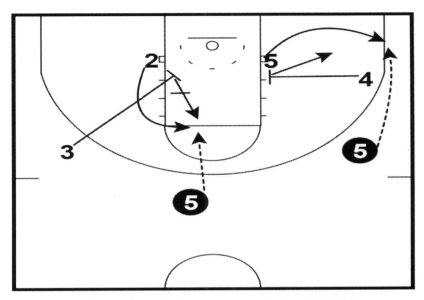

DOWN SCREEN - CURL   FLAT SCREEN

RIGHT SIDE DIAGRAM – FLAT SCREEN ACTION

A.   #4 sets screen on #5
B.   #5 cuts when screen is set
C.   #4 converts to defense when He/she is even on #5's cut
D.   Action plays out in 1X1.

LEFT SIDE DIAGRAM – CURL ACTION

A.   #3 sets pin down screen on #2
B.   #2 makes cut - #2 can back cut, pop, etc.
C.   #3 converts to defense when #3 is even with #2's cut.
D.   Action plays out in 1X1.-

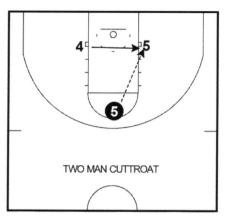

TWO MAN CUTTROAT

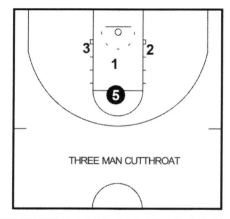

THREE MAN CUTTHROAT

TWO MAN CUTTHROAT   THREE MAN CUTTHROAT

TWO MAN CUTTHROAT BLACK = COACH

   a.   Coach passes to either player

   b.   NO dribble - receiver takes Ball to the basket – go through the defense.

   c.   Player that rebounds the Ball goes back up without dribble - Defender is body on body with high hands = go up with the Offensive player.

   d.   Coach may control drill by not allowing blocked shots.

THREE MAN CUTTHROAT

   a. Players line up as shown in diagrams #2 and #3 are above low block.

   b. Coach puts up a soft on the rim

   c. All three players go after ball; the player that gets Ball goes up to basket – DO NOT ALLOW FADE AWAY SHOTS – NO DRIBBLE.

   d. TWO players not getting ball immediately attack player with ball.

   e. If ball gets loose – ball goes to coach who puts ball in play – This is an "in the paint drill."

   f. Play continues until there is a score– coach decides number of makes needed for rotation of new players. NOTE: 1. Do not allow players to play their side of the basket – every rebound must be contested by two non-rebounding players. 2. Coach may want to play a "No blocked shot" game. 3. No tipping – pull ball With two hands and take ball back up to the basket.

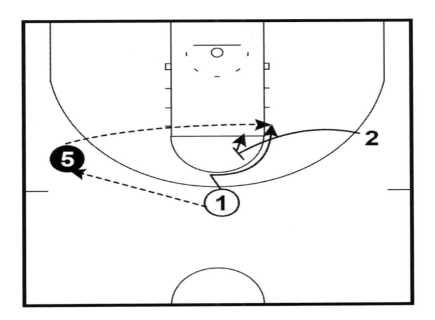

FLAIR

COACHES CAN USE ALL SCORING ACTIONS IN THEIR OFFENSE AS A FINISHING DRILL.

1. #1 passes to coach #5 and makes flair cut.
2. #2 sets the flair screen and converts to defense when #2 is even with #1
3. Drill concludes with a defensive rebound or score.
4. Coach can control when they pass the ball allowing #1 to make a secondary cut before passing – this adds another dimension to the drill – Defense must play position relative to ball and offensive player #2.
5. Defensive fouling delegitimizes hustle.

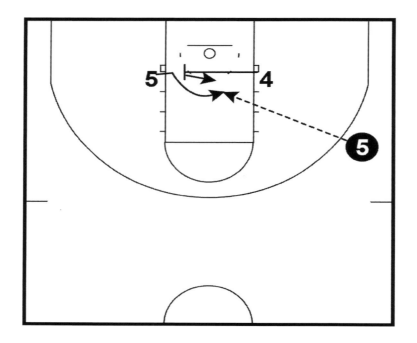

CROSS PICK

Coach signals the #4 to cross-pick

1 #5 makes cut either high or low relative to 4's screening action.

2. #4 changes from screener to defending #5 when #5 is even with #4.

3. At this point it is a 1x1 drill.

4. By moving #5 lower to "block" and below and eliminating the dribble forcing #5 to go through #4 to score.

5. By moving #5 higher – to above the block positions up the lane (even as high As the as the elbow) adds the dribble move to the drill.

THE THREE PILLARS OF DEFENSE

1. **BALL CONTAINMENT –** The ability to control the ball in 1x1 situation requiring little or no team support.
2. **CONTESTING FIELD GOAL ATTEMPTS** – Being in position to contest field goal attempts has a dramatic effect on lowering the offenses shooting percentages.
3. **DEFENSIVE REBOUNDING** – The conclusion to a successful defensive possession makes defensive rebounding vital to the defensive effort.

Following the defensive "Thread" to success.

The "Thread" of defensive success begins with guarding the ball i.e., **Ball Containment (1x1 Defense)** this leads to fewer help and recover or defensive rotations, AND keeps the defense <u>set</u> and out of "scramble" allowing for better positioning versus the FG att. and Def. Reb.

<u>Contesting shots</u> lowers the shooting percentage this cannot be denied. No player shoots better when well-guarded; begging the answer to the question, <u>"Is it the shot or is it the shooter?"</u>

Continuing to follow the "Thread" of defensive effectiveness ends by retrieving a greater number of missed shots caused by increasing the number of contested shots causing more **Defensive Rebounds.**

COACHING EMPHASIS AND SPECIFIC TRAINING IN THE THREE PILLARS OF DEFENSE WILL MAXIMIZE THE EFFECTIVENESS OF <u>ANY</u> DEFENSIVE SCHEME OR PHILOSOPHY – THAT IS WHY THEY ARE REFERRED TO AS "PILLARS."

Etc.: Good teams have good players – great teams have great teammates

DEFENSIVE PILLAR #1

BALL CONTAINMENT (1X1)

When the offense can penetrate the defense, it creates defensive 'scramble," when the defense in scrambled it is at its weakest – forcing rotations that lead to mismatches and open shooters, due to lengthened rotations, etc.; all a result of the offensive "scrambling" the defense. Good 1X1 defensive play will be Important to playing winning team defense.

By guarding in a 1x1 environment the defender will learn all the required game skills: stance, defensive slides, footwork, handwork, anticipation, including toughness in winning the 1x1 battle. One notation regarding handwork, active handwork is required, but not the "reach" type that gets a defender to give up defensive balance.

When guarding a dribbler, "If you are even with the offensive player, you are behind." To re-gain proper position the defender turns and sprints to keep the ball from "turning the corner," re-establishing a "head on the ball i.e.," positioning between head on a line between the ball and basket.

"Handwork v. the Dribble: Inside hand is the "dribble" hand should be in a position close enough to the dribbler to prevent a change of direction in front of the defender. Other hand is up in the "passing lane" interfering with dribbler's passing angles. Coaching Point: The "UP" hand should be at ear level.

1x1 containment is not easy. However, it becomes easier with concentrated physical practice and developing attitudes of toughness and pride in being "able to guard my yard, with an "I don't need any help, don't want any," attitude. CONT PG 287

Etc. It's not pressure defense – until they "Feel" your pressure.

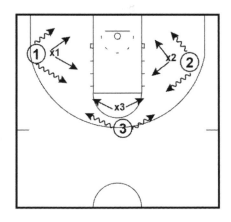
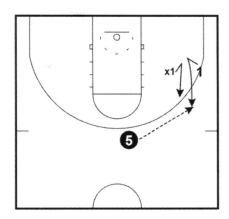

1x1 CONTAINMENT

RIGHT DIAGRAM – 1X1 WING CONTEST

a. Offensive player works to get open – defensive player is closer to passer than #1:

    a. Defensive player contests/denies ball to the 3 pt arc. Allows ball to be received outside the 3 PT. ARC. X1 readjusts position to force to middle-statistical justification: Lane area is well guarded and these become low percentage shots.

    b. Offense is not allowed to shoot 3-point shots. Offense puts ball on floor tries to get ball into the lane – defense works to keep dribbler from turning corner into the lane.

    c. Offense has a 5 second time limit to get off shot – both players rebound.

LEFT DIAGRAM – 1X1 CONTAINMENT

    a. #1, #2, #3 have ball – guarded by X's – Offense is in a triple threat position, Defense in position: 1. Close enough to touch offensive player. 2. Feet alive. 3. Active hand work. 4. **Disregard speed and quickness differences in practice– adjustments are for games – this is practice, defenders must challenge themselves & offense.**

    b. Offensive Players: Sequence, practice each one until coach is satisfied: 1. **Fake shot (no dribble)** 2. **Fake, pivot, shoot**. Defense contests shot hard BUT does not block or foul shooter. 3. **Fake, pivot, drive ball with 1, 2 or 3 dribbles and shoot**. Defender goes UP with the shooter – does not block offensive players shot.

    DEFENDER: controlled reactions to offensive actions – do not over-react to offensive fakes - be close enough to touch offensive player – but do not allow offensive player to touch defender – this is important. LIVE 1x1 is final step. Do Not Allow Shot Blocking in Above Drills.

287

DEFENSIVE PILLAR #2

CONTESTING THE FIELD GOAL ATTEMPT
THE POWER OF THE CONTESTED SHOT. . .

The team with the highest shooting % wins 80% plus of the time and the one thing that affects shooting % more than any other measurement is contesting shots. Is there anything more important than contesting shots? "NO." A team that contests 70% + shots will win a lot of games. When do you contest? Contest every shot, jump as high as possible, it will have an effect on the shot. This is regardless of distance from the shooter; the defender must "jump" and extend, every contested shot has a positive effect on lowering the shooting percentage.

NBA STUDY OF THE CONTESTED SHOT:

1. Zero contest field goal % = 68% makes
2. Strong contest field goal % = 36%

The best players in the NBA make 91% of their in close shots. However, any kind of "Contest" action lowers the made in close shots to 49%. <u>This is the power of the contested shot.</u>

"**No Close out.**" If contesting shots is a priority, then it is unwise and bordering on delusional to promote and teach the wildly popular "stutter" step approach. When approaching the ball, do so with the idea the shooter is <u>always</u> going to shoot.

With the contested shot being the focus, the "stutter step" is counter-productive, forget the "stutter step" and come running out at a strong pace and <u>go straight up with the shooter and as high as possible</u>. NOTE: an offensive player does the same thing on his/her jump shot coming off a hard dribble and popping up for the jumper. Same skill as the shot contest.

You may get some blocks but that is not the purpose. Don't be afraid to contest shots, being afraid of getting faked out and the defender will not go after the contest. If the defender gets beat on a shot fake drive action, then the team aspect of help comes into play. The key is to practice contesting shots.CONT.289

The defensive player needs to go "UP" with the shooter, not after the shooter leaves the floor and conversely the defender does not over-react to shot fakes.

At every level of play the uncontested shot needs to be made at a high level. Uncontested shots just cannot be allowed.

The ball is approached with the mindset that he/she is always going to shoot and that shot must be contested.

IMPORTANT NOTE: The above "shot contest" discussion should include contest decisions that are based on statistical/scouting information on the capabilities of opponent's "shooters" in game competition. **Conversely, maximum learning of this skill can only take place when in practice a strong contest is always coached. Contest adjustments are for games, not in practice.**

Etc.: If you make a commitment –
remember sacrifices are
built into your decision.
Decide carefully.

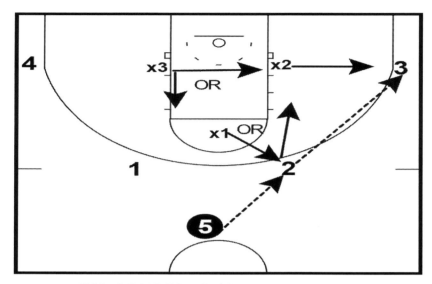

4X3 CONTEST SHOT DRILL

DEFENSE (THREE DEFENSIVE PLAYERS V FOUR OFFENSIVE SHOOTERS.)

A. Defensive player on ball cannot follow the pass

B. On pass, the on-ball defender (X1) drops back to the uncovered lane area. So, this position is always covered.

C. Defensive players play their positions – do not anticipate.

D. NO CLOSE OUT – sprint to contest – go up with the shooter – <u>fouling shooter is a sinful act that cannot be tolerated.</u>

E. Rebounding 4X3 can be added when coach is satisfied with the effort and technique of the "shot contest."

OFFENSE No shot fake – this drill is specific to a strong contest of the shot - Shoot when open Pass ball quickly- use skip pass

.

THINGS TO PONDER

The primal instinct is to freak out and try and do things that players are not trained to do when faced with tremendous amount of adversity. They need to be mindful of taking a deep breath and just focus on the next thing.

Players are prone to reverting to a behavior of comfort and just cruise through the day, going through the motions is an easy thing to do.

The master knows the details, but coaches with simple instructions.

The master understands every word in the playbook but concentrates on the central ideas. Explaining complicated things with clarity is a mark of mastery.

Unfortunately, the ones who have mastered the least are the ones that talk the most.

Simplicity makes things easy. Coaching with clarity is earned by confronting the complex, breaking it down and presenting in understandable parts.

We ask them (players) to play a little overt their head – 2% on every possession.

Doing your job: execute the play-pressure the ball- be in your gap – rebound all the misses, that's doing your job.

Etc.: No one is perfect – when things go bad and they will, it's a long practice, it's a long game, It's a long season – having a boxing match with yourself doesn't do anybody any good.

DEFENSIVE PILLAR #3

THE ART OF REBOUNDING – ANOTHER WAY

Differing from the traditional method of defensive rebounding – this is another way.

- ✓ **John Wooden's** teams did not block out. The UCLA teams would cross in front of the offensive player in a moving screen type action. The UCLA teams were very mobile in their rebound effort.
- ✓ **Charles Barkley** said his college coach Sonny Smith at Auburn told him to forget about blocking out and go after the ball. he never blocked out after that in his college or NBA career, where he averaged 11. 7 rebounds for his entire career.
- ✓ **Dennis Rodman** never blocked out, if he was near the basket and the offense tried to push him under the basket, he was quick to push back.
- ✓ **Bill Russell** was the same way, he played behind the offensive post man and "blocked out" only if the offensive postman tried to push him under.

You do not get anything from blocking out or keeping your man from getting a rebound. It is getting the ball you need to get - not the block out that you need to do.

On the shot attempt you have one maybe two seconds max to:

1. **Follow the flight of the ball, this will tell/<u>feel</u> where the ball will go, don't get into a debate with your mind.**
2. **Screen (not block out) your man by crossing in front of his direct line to the ball.**
3. **Position: when in the "charge/block arc area" Don't get pushed under basket, this will look like you are "blocking out."**
4. **Most important, the mindset and physical effort is all about "Getting the ball," in the rebound game.**
5. **Rebounding is done away from the rim – playing "deep," like a baseball shortstop allows the rebounder to cover a larger area.**

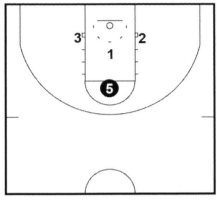

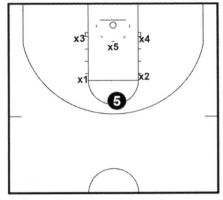

LEFT DIAG.-3X0 "GET BALL"　　**RIGHT. DIAG. 5X0 "GET BALL"**

REBOUNDING

RIGHT DIAGRAM 5X0 REBOUNDING "GET BALL"

a.   Coach puts up a soft shot on the rim

b.   All five players visually track ball holding position momentarily until they determine where ball is going.
"Get Ball" – Period.

c.   No court boundaries all five players compete for ball – This is all out and aggressive – do not allow grabbing or holding or other non-basketball actions.

LEFT DIAGRAM 3X0 REBOUNDING "GET BALL"

a.   Coach puts up a soft shot on the rim.

  a.   THE DRILL IS EXACTLY LIKE THE 5X0 DRILL

Etc.: "By forcing the ball to the middle or to the baseline – defenders are unable to guard a great Player, at UNLV we square up shoulder to shoulder." Jerry Tarkanian, UNLV.

293

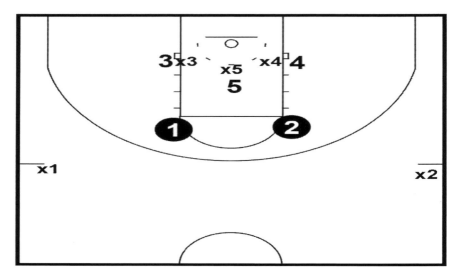

3X3 TWO BALL REBOUNDING CHAOS DRILL

This is an excellent drill that creates game continuous effort under chaotic conditions.

 BLACK #1 & #2 = COACHES EACH WITH BALL. Coaches #1 and #2 each have a ball. X1 and X2 outlet players are deep as shown.

a.   Drill begins with one coach putting up a soft shot. The two teams, X's on defense and #'s 3-4-5 on offense compete for the rebound – no tipping of ball, pull ball with two hands **on defense** outlet to X1 or X2 – **on offense** rebound and score.

b.   ON A SCORE OR A DEFENSIVE REBOUND THE 2ND COACH SHOOTS THE 2ND BALL **IMMEDIATELY** AND THE DRILL PROCEEDS AS BEFORE. ONCE BOTH BALLS HAVE BEEN DEF. REBOUNDED AND SUCCESSFULLY OUTLETED. THE DRILL IS RESET. COACH MAY WANT TO HAVE A 3RD OR 4TH SHOT PUT UP BY COACHES TO CREATE ADDITIONAL CHAOS. CHAOS = IS WHAT WILL BE EXPERIENCED IN "LIVE "GAME ACTION – MOST LIKELY IMMEDIATELY AFTER THE JUMP BALL IS SECURED.

5X5 HALFCOURT CHAOS
(Drill not diagrammed)

This is an excellent half court drill. It is particularly good the day before a game when keeping players fresh is factored into practice or any time for that matter. Drill develops playing with control in confusion (chaos.) The action develops concentration and quick changes from offense to defense. Coaches need to coach this hard early to create intensity. Penalize losers.

a. 5x5 make it – take it.
b. Drill starts at halfcourt.
c. On score, the scoring team (make it-take it) immediately gets ball beyond the 3-point arc and attacks again without setting up. Offense attempts to attack defense before defense can get set. Getting the ball back in play quickly after "centering" beyond the 3-point arc is an important drill objective.
d. On a defensive rebound, that team passes or dribbles ball "out" beyond "arc" and attacks - do not set up offense. Immediate offensive attack v. an unsettled defense is a drill objective.
e. On a turnover, bad pass, the ball does not have to be taken beyond the 3-point arc. The opposing team takes ball and immediately converts to offense/attacks.
f. Keep score – free throws may be shot, or points awarded on fouls to keep play at a fast pace.
g. Short games – 7 points or less will keep play focused.
h. Offensive goal is to attack offensively while defense is in "scramble."
i. Defensive goal is to communicate and get the defense organized and out of "scramble" and into a 5 on 5 defensive posture.
j. This is fast moving high intensity drill.

Etc. A great drop back defense is a key in winning – you can press and still play good drop back defense – players must be trained to know they can catch the offense from behind.

SECTION X

"IT'S IN THE
BOTTOM DRAWER"

RUTGERS BASKETBALL

DEFENDING THE LOW POST

DUKE – ON THE CATCH

Everyone's butt to the baseline. We dig on the catch. Always seeing the ball AND your man.

DUKE – ON THE DRIBBLE

Everyone's butt to baseline. We dig on the post player's dribble.

NOVA

Closest man doubles post and we rotate as a team.
Double down man will rotate to weak side.

MONSTER (PLAYS PLAYER NAME)

Whoever's name gets called, sprint for every double team.
Example – "Monster Jordan."

BRUIN

Double off of opposite big man.

FRONT

Front the post.

NETS Double off 2nd man or middleman

"DON'T WAIT"

DENVER POST – DEC. 31,2011

KC-DEN WINNER ADVANCES IN
NFL PLAYOFFS

Champ Bailey, All Pro Defensive Back and 2019 elected to HALL OF FAME. Bailey is widely considered one of the greatest cornerbacks in NFL history

". . . all week I have been telling the guys, 'When you're young, you think you are always going to have a chance to go to the playoffs, always have a chance to go to the Super Bowl. But when you're older, you learn, if you let things pass you by, they don't always come back.

I still think about (2005). We didn't show up against Pittsburg in the game to go to the Super Bowl. I have been in the NFL for 13 years and I am still trying to get to the Super Bowl."

That's the message: **"DON'T WAIT!"** The time is **NOW**!

Etc.: Enthusiasm is contagious, if you don't have today, fake it and it will spread.

"A DOZEN THINGS"

1. Colorado Rockies, Charlie Blackmon. What do you do when you are in a hitting slump? **"I shut off my brain and trust the training of my body."**
2. On an NBA telecast, Hubie Brown's frustration with a player's weak defensive effort: "If you are not on the offensive boards and you are not back on defense, WHERE ARE YOU."
3. The Concentration corollary: a high level of concentration, naturally increases alertness with the by-product being a more aggressive player. An alert player is in an "Act First" state of mind.
4. What I look for in hiring: Virek Randive, Owner, Sacramento Kings:
   - The smartest guy in the room.
   - Who is the hungriest?
   - Who is the most passionate?

5. YOU RUN to get layups and YOU RUN to prevent layups.
6. TIME: A year from now you may wish you had started Today.
7. Playoffs/tournament play is a single possession game for 40 minutes – plan and play accordingly.
8. Move the defense before you put the ball on the floor: "Shot Fake," "Pass Fake."
9. **Three Questions, players want answers from coaches**: 1. "Coach, can I trust you?" 2. "Coach, can you make me a better player?" 3. "Coach, do you care about me?"

10. **Three Questions, coaches want answers from players:** 1. "Can I trust you?" 2. "Are you coachable?" 3. "Do you care about your team and coaches?"
11. Some people want the air conditioner on in the gym, so they won't sweat. I wear my beanie in July so I will.

12. **Defending the modern-day Offense**: The first 6 to 8 seconds are critical – being able to defend this time frame makes it possible to get the defense settled five on five.

KEYS TO MOTIVATION
LEE CORSO

The most famous personality on College Football's "Game Day," Coach Corso has been on the Saturday show since its inception in 1987. And he was a very good college football coach with coaching assignments at U of Louisville, Indiana University, and Northern Illinois, winning the 1979 Holiday Bowl as the head coach at Indiana.

This information by the 'Ole ball' coach has some key elements that coaches of all sports can use to help their players reach a higher level of play.

1. Recognition – The more important you are in the eyes of another person – the more important your statements are to that person. (Coach: being seen as trustworthy, dependable, and having a sincere interest – the players will listen to you.)
2. Rewards - Are a vital part of motivating people to peak performance.
3. Reinforcement – What gets reinforced gets repeated. The flip side of this is if behavior is not rewarded, recognized, or praised, the behavior may simply stop being repeated.

Strive for excellence in all that you do in your life, success is a by-product. Excellence is doing the right thing repeatedly under extreme pressure from your competition trying to make you do the wrong thing.

The coaches who have this as a philosophy – never coach against the other team. They coach against perfection. They never coach against the scoreboard. They do not care about the other team.

Your goal is to be the best you can possibly be and don't care about what the other guy does.

"THE BOYS IN THE BOAT"

By Daniel James Brown

"Nine Americans and their Epic Quest for Gold at the 1936 Berlin Olympics

The following is from the book, "The Boys in the Boat."
This is a story about the U of Washington crew that earned their way to the 1936
Olympics in Berlin. It is a story of life during the great depression of the '30's: the
struggles of families during the time. It is a story about Nazi Germany and the
build up to WW2. And it is a sports story about rowing & beating the odds.
Finally, it is about coaching and what goes into "coaching'em" up.
"<u>A successful quest for Olympic Gold would require finding nine young men of</u>
<u>exceptional strength, grace, endurance, and most of all mental toughness.</u>"
That brings us to JOE RANTZ, Coach Ulbrickson had been studying Joe for a year.
Asst. Coach Bolles had first warned Coach Ulbrickson that the boy was touchy and
uneven, that there were days when he could row like quicksilver---so smooth and
fluid and powerful that he seemed a part of the boat and his oar and the water
were all one---and there were days when he was downright lousy. Since then,
Coach Ulbrickson had tried everything---he had scolded Joe, encouraged Joe, he'd
demoted him, he'd promoted him. (Coach, sound familiar.)
But he was not any closer to understanding the mystery of Joe Rantz. Joe had a
hard scrabble life growing up. A poor family, a father moving the family as he
changed from job to job. When Joe's mother died Joe was given the responsibility
of looking out for his younger siblings. Now Coach Ulbrickson turned to George
Pocock, a team confidant\world renowned builder of racing boats for some help.
He told George to take a look at Rantz --- "talk to him, try and figure out and fix
him if possible." It helped that Joe spent summers earning tuition money for
school working as a logger. This gave him an interest in Mr. Pocock and his work
with wood and the builder of world class racing shells. Mr. Pocock's workshop was
located on the upper floor of the rowing team's club house.
Pocock quietly and casually creating an interest from Joe in his building of the best
racing shells in the rowing world. Finally, Mr. Pocock got around to showing Joe
CONT. PG 303

the secret of building the perfect racing shell: from bow to stern was a line of 62 feet and on that line, Pocock's standard was not to have a variance of more than one centimeter from being online for the entire 62 feet of the racing shell. And then, Pocock emphasized to Joe that in the end this trueness and exactness could only come from the builder, from the care with which he exercised his craft, and from the amount of heart he put into it.

Pocock paused and stepped back from the frame of the shell and put his hands on his hip, carefully studying the work he had done so far. He said for him the craft of building a boat was like a religion. It wasn't enough to master the technical details of it. You had to give yourself up to it spiritually; you had to surrender yourself absolutely to it. When you were done and walked away from the boat, you had to feel that you had left a piece of yourself behind in it forever, a bit of your heart. He turned to Joe. "Rowing is like that, and a lot of life is like that too, the parts that really matter anyway. Do you know what I mean Joe?

Joe a bit nervous, not at all certain nodded tentatively.

Several days later, George Pocock tapped Joe on the shoulder and asked him to come up to the loft (racing shells workshop.) While varnishing a new shell, he, in a fatherly tone told Joe what a fine oarsman he was and then went over a few technical things Joe could do to improve his stroke but that was not what Mr. Pocock really wanted to talk about. He told Joe there were times Joe attacked the water like it seemed he was the only person in the boat, and it was up to him to get the boat across the finish line. When a man takes this approach to row on his own rather than work with the crew and what is worse, he does not allow the crew to help him row. What matters more than how hard you row is how well everything you do in the boat harmonizes with your crewmates. . .it wasn't just the rowing, Mr. Pocock paused and looked up a Joe, <u>"If you don't like some fellow in the boat you must learn to like him. It must matter to you whether he wins the race, not just whether you do. Joe, when you really start trusting those boys you will feel a power at work within you that is far beyond anything you've ever imagined."</u>

In August 1936, the USA nine-man rowing team won the Olympic Medal with Joe Rantz wielding the #2 oar, winning by sixth-tenth of a second over Italy and Germany. CONT. PG 304

George and Joe:

1. George realized Joe had a hard time while growing up poor in the depression years of the '30's. Mr. Pocock, also, recognized Joe had a good heart and he wanted to do the right thing.
2. George's mission was to help Joe understand his great talent could only maximize the team's performance if it was blended with the team's needs.
3. The USA could win gold with Joe or lose with Joe.
4. George talked to Joe in a relaxed way that promoted trust due to their common interests and experiences – this relaxed Joe's initial tentativeness. Mr. Pocock's method of using the building of precise racing shells as a metaphor for Joe's rowing was a way of using an "inanimate object" as a teaching technique, avoiding any defensive reaction from Joe.
5. George did not make any demands of Joe.
6. George reaffirmed Joe's talent, potential and value to the team's goal.
7. George painted a picture for Joe of what his role was and how he could maximize his value to the team by investing in the team and ultimately being one with the team.
8. He left Joe with a vision of not only who he was but what he and the team could become.

*Etc., The Legendary Australian Football, Hall of Fame Coach, **John Kennedy Sr**. was known for his "Fire and passion." In a championship match during a period break he exhorted his troops with that passion and fiery simplicity: **"DO SOMETHING, DON'T HOPE, DON'T THINK, DO, ACT, TRY, AT LEAST WHEN YOU COME OFF THE PITCH KNOWING YOU DID SOMETHING. YOU CAN AT LEAST SAY, I CARRIED ON, I TRIED SOMETHING…"***

THE '84 OLYMIPICS

In 1984 the Cold War between the USA and the Soviet Union was raging. The result was the USSR and 14 other Eastern Bloc countries boycotted the Los Angeles Olympics. Without the Soviet Union, the USA coach, Bob Knight was determined to win in a manner so there would be no question who the best team on the planet was, regardless of who boycotted the "Games." And this was exactly what the US did winning the Gold by going undefeated and averaging 95.4 points per game and giving up 63.3 points per game winning by an average of 32.1 PPP. George Raveling (Head Coach at the University of Iowa at this time) one of Coach Knight's Olympic assistants addressed the team prior to the Gold Medal game.

"How you play in today's

Olympic Gold Medal game

Will determine how

You will be remembered

The rest of your life.

As a basketball player,

Every one of you has

Had someone in

Your background die

For this Country.

The very least you can do

In memory of those

Who gave everything

Is today, give everything."

"LOVE CLINT"

This is interesting on several levels regarding the 2013 National League Pennant race. This piece centers around a series of "Thoughts of the Day" emails Hurdle sent to his team as it struggled to close out a post-season playoff spot. The emails went out to several hundred people, primarily his players, their wives, his player's friends, his friends, et.al. But this is about more than emails. It is the "Ups and Downs" of Clint Hurdle's complicated professional and personal life. And for coaches, the magic of his leadership and working with players. **SEE CLINT HURDLE'S PERSONAL STORY ON PG 310**

On Sept. 9, 2013, 142 games into a renaissance season, the Pittsburgh Pirates manager was on the team bus, typing rapidly into an iPhone. His Pirates had been swept the day before in St. Louis, unmercifully outscored 26-10, and the annual Pittsburgh panic was setting in. There'd been no winning season since 1992. Babies born that year were now old enough to drink. And the Pirates were driving them to do just that.

The Pirates had flown from St. Louis to Texas, where they would face a dominant Yu Darvish and what the team needed most was a message from its calm warhorse manager.

 *So there sat the Pirates' skipper, once the opposite of serene, entering a "Thought of the Day" to his players, his players' wives, his players' friends, his coaching friends, his lifelong buddies, his month-long buddies – all received the following email:

Tim Wrightman, a former All-American UCLA football player, tells a story about how, as a rookie lineman in the National Football League, he was up against the legendary pass rusher Lawrence Taylor, Taylor was not only physically powerful and uncommonly quick, but a master at verbal intimidation.
Looking Tim in the eye, Taylor said, "Sonny, get ready. I'm going left and there's nothing you can do about it."
Wrightman coolly responded, "Sir, is that your left or mine?"
The question froze Taylor long enough to allow Wrightman to throw a perfect block on him. CONT PG 307

"It's amazing what we can accomplish if we refuse to be afraid. Fear, whether it's of pain, failure, or rejection, is a toxic emotion that creates monsters in our mind that consume self-confidence and intimidate us from doing our best or sometimes even trying at all."

Make a difference today.

Love Clint

Sent from my IPhone

*That same night, the Pirates "loved" Clint Hurdle back. They defeated Texas 1-0, for their 82nd win, then hugged their manager for always hugging them. Just knowing that he was always up at night thinking of them, that he was always on his phone typing to them, had helped the 2013 Pirates change one of the losingest cultures in sports. Three weeks later, the team clinched a National League wild card berth, the first playoff spot that might have been won partly because of emails.

***Jumping back to Jan. 16, 2013, one month before spring training, and the beginning of the historic season that was described above. ***

*"When I was 5 years old, my mother always told me that happiness was the key to life. When I went to school, they asked me what I wanted to be when I grew up. I wrote down 'happy.' They told me I didn't understand the assignment. And I told them they didn't understand life." - John Lennon

Make a difference today.

Love Clint

*In the first month of the season Clint wrote: on April 27, 2013 (half-game out of 1st place):

Watch your thoughts; they lead to attitudes.
Watch your attitudes; they lead to words.
Watch your words; they lead to actions.
Watch your actions; they lead to habits.
Watch your habits; they form your character.
Watch your character; it determines your destiny.

  - Unknown

Make a difference today. Love Clint – from my I Phone CONT 308

*It's now the middle of the 2013 season and the Pirates are in the thick of the pennant race 1 ½ games out of 1st place on July 13 Clint writes:

"Failure should be our teacher, not our undertaker. Failure is delay, not defeat. It is a temporary detour, not a dead end."
-   Dennis Waitley
    Make a difference today.
    Love Clint
    Sent from my IPhone

*It's now the "Dog days" of August and the Pirates are in a good position being only one game out of first place.
"You miss 100% of the shots you don't take." - *Wayne Gretsky, Hockey Great*
See, failure isn't missing the shots. Failure is never even trying in the first place. And this brings Clint to another relevant quote:
"I have not failed. I've just found 10,000 ways that won't work."
Thomas Edison
Make a difference today.
Love Clint   Send from my IPhone

*"Its September 13, 2013 (The Pirates are still one game out of first place and 500 people were getting his emails.)
"I never worry about the future. It comes soon enough."
    Albert Einstein
Make a difference today.
Love Clint - Sent from my IPhone

*With two weeks from the end of the 2013 season and the Pirates and St. Louis are dead even after 145 games.
On the next page, is one of the better emails I received in a long time. I hope you take time to share it. CONT PG 309

Through a child's eyes: letters written to God by children:
- ✓ *Dear God, I went to this wedding, and they kissed right in church. Is that okay? Neil*
- ✓ *Dear God, instead of letting people die and having to make new ones, why don't you just keep the ones you got now? Jane*
- ✓ *Dear God, please put another holiday between Christmas and Easter. There is nothing good in there now. Ginny*
- ✓ *Dear God, maybe Cain and Abel would not kill each other so much if they had their own rooms. It works with my brother. Larry*
- ✓ *Dear God, we read Thos. Edison made light. But in Sunday School they said you did it. So, I bet he stole it from you. Donna*
- ✓ *Dear God, thank you for the baby brother. But what I prayed for was a puppy. Robert*
- ✓ *Dear God, I bet it is very hard for you to love everybody in the whole world. There are only 4 people in our family, and I can never do it. Nan*

Make a difference today
Love Clint
Sent from my IPhone

*The Pirates would go on to be the National League Wild Card Champions with a 6-2, win over the Cincinnati Reds on Oct. 1, 2013, for the first Pirate postseason appearance since 1992. A 21-year absence. CONT PG 310

The Clint Hurdle Story

The Sports Illustrated March 11, 1978 cover proclaimed Clint Hurdle "This Year's Phenom." A former high school honor student receiving all A's in high school except for one "B" in driver's ed.; was accepted into Harvard before deciding on baseball. Problem was his batting average would linger in the 250's. His partnership with alcohol would play a somber role in his baseball career. He managed in the minors and always a friend and confidant to the players and always willing to meet them any time after 10 PM in the hotel bar. Two divorces and a life constantly spiraling in directions that ended up leading to Alcoholics Anonymous that allowed him to re-focus his life, and the breaking of old and destructive life-style habits.

A successful marriage, a child challenged with the rare Prader-Willi syndrome, a pennant winning manager, World Series manager in Colorado, a fired manager, and a playoff manager in Pittsburgh (Clint Hurdle managed Pittsburgh for nine seasons; was fired by Pittsburgh in 2010) would all be part of his life.

In the final analysis, Clint Hurdle was a teacher and managed in the minor leagues before managing in the big leagues. The following illustrates the of kind of leader and mentor he was and the essence of the teaching / learning process. **"These are the questions a 17-year-old going into pro ball has about their manager. Can I trust him? Does he trust me? Can he make me better? Does he care about me?" My goal was to get these questions answered under my watch. Because then their skill set will come out. They won't let you coach'em until they trust you." Clint Hurdle "gets it." We can all "get it" by keeping Clint hurdle's wisdom as the center piece of our coaching.**

W.W.U.D.
"WHAT WOULD YOU DO?"

Team building activity: Carefully Follow Instructions:

1. Go to: www://wimp.com/girl falls/
2. This is a video of a college indoor track meet – 600-meter run.
3. **Important:** watch only the first two laps of the race – PAUSE the video as soon as the "Girl falls"
4. Now ponder the following possibilities:
    a. Remain lying on the track in a "Born to Whine" moment.
    b. Remain lying on the track "screaming "at the girl who tripped you."
    c. Get up "limping" (a "losers limp") and get off the track.
    d. Just get off the track beaten.
    e. Get up and slowly jog the last lap just to finish – kind of a hybrid "losers limps."
    f. Get up and finish by giving it the "Old college try." but not really believing in the effort – kind of like in "hoops," leaping into the stands needlessly, after a loose ball that has already gone out of bounds.
    g. Rising from the track and running as hard as possible – because this is who I am and what we do – realizing I cannot "lose," if I try.

5. NOW START THE VIDEO AND WATCH THE LAST LAP OF THE RACE – NOTICE THE FAN REACTION.

6. WWUD and Why? Write a brief on paragraph WWUD?

7. Finally, pick two of the above choices you would <u>not</u> do.

8. Create a lively team "Back and forth" on the dynamics of winning and losing.

WINNING / LOSING AND THE LAST 5 MINUTES

"Garbage time," is the least productive time in a game whether ahead or behind; often players just "jack" up shots and do crazy things. But by creating a new game beginning at the five-minute mark with a new score of 0-0 can re-direct the team to win the "Game within the game." Instead of "garbage time" the team has a purpose and allows the coaching staff to keep coaching.

How It Works

With five minutes remaining in the game, a student assistant or manager starts a new game 5-minute game with 0-0 score and keep score until the finish of the game.

We judge the last five minutes on two levels:

1. With a 7-point advantage either up or down in the regular game. This is a game that can be either won or lost. The execution under pressure will be highlighted in the "Five minute" game within the game.
2. The other situation is in games that have large differential either up or down. "The "five-minute game" keeps the team in focus the final minutes of the game.

Why can this help your team?

1. Players will become aware of importance of last five minutes.
2. This gives the coach an awareness of how to handle the final minutes.
3. The coaching staff must sell the five-minute 0-0 game score to the team. Post standings on the locker room bulletin board, etc. Having a new purpose, builds pride and motivation in the final five minutes. If you have a mediocre record and learn to play well in the final five minutes, it should help with the team's overall record.
4. The last five minutes is an indicator of what the team can do.

FOULING WITH A THREE POINT LEAD

A good 3-point shooter can make 33% plus when guarded. And the "make range" is being extended by longer shots being made.

Five things that **Must** happen successfully in the game if you choose to foul.

1. **Must** make the free throw #1

2. **Must** miss free throw #2 on purpose and legally ball must hit rim. This is not as easy as appears. Practicing missing free throws should be practiced for this specific situation.

3. Shooter's team **Must** rebound the miss.

4. Offensive rebounder **Must** score without committing a violation if trailing by two. If trailing by three, ball is passed out beyond the arc.

5. Finally, a 2- or 3-point shot **Must** be made to tie or win the game.

   Based on the five **Musts** outlined above, it is hard to debate against fouling with a 3-point lead in a last possession situation. The caveat is that the defensive player must not foul with the 3-point shooter in the act of shooting. Just like missing the free throw on purpose, fouling on purpose is unnatural and should be coached to be done when the ball handler is in passing or dribbling action. The last thing the defensive player needs is to foul in the act of shooting.

Etc. Three team non-negotiables: 1. Defense 2. Rebounding 3. Ball protection. Kyle Smith, Washington State University

THE "227" – "NEVER AGAIN"

The 227 Club is dedicated to a band of Women's CSU basketball players who displayed extraordinary perseverance during 2007- 2008 season.

These qualities culminated with this special group being the architects of the greatest upset in Mountain West Conference Tournament basketball history and one of the better upset victories in women's college basketball.

Because of this improbable achievement, the 2007-08; the CSU women's basketball team established a legacy of not quitting, possessing lasting hope, and a fighting spirit.

"WE ARE THE 227"

#2 Bonnie Barbee (Fr)

#3 Amaka Uzomah (Jr)

#4 Sara Hunter (Sr)

#5 Lauren Young (Fr)

#11 Elle Queen (Fr)

#13 Britney Minor (Jr)

#15 Kandy Beemer (Jr)

#21 Emily Neal (So)

#22 Kelly Finley (Sr)

#23 Zoi Simmons (Fr)

#32 Carine Reimink (Jr)

#34 Devran Tanacan (Jr – Redshirt)

#35 Juanise Cornell

This is a team award created to honor the 07-08 CSU Rams, after going 2-27 and defeating the 11th Nationally ranked U of Utah in the MWC in post season play.

EVERETT CASE, HEAD COACH
NORTH CAROINA STATE UNIVERSITY
"IF I COULD START AGAIN"

Known as the "Gray Fox," inducted into the Naismith Hall of Fame in 1982, instrumental in the formation of the Atlantic Coast Conference. Coached the Wolfpack from 1946 to 1964 with a winning percentage of .739. A brilliant combination of coach, promoter, and a master at both inspiring his players and exciting the crowds. Before Dean Smith, Mr. Case was largely responsible for popularizing basketball in North Carolina. With a Hall of Fame resume,' Coach Case is well qualified to discuss this topic.

1. Make a more serious study of human psychology.

2. Do a better job with public relations.

3. Have a better savings plan.

4. Be more skilled in all areas of player guidance.

5. Give players more free time.

6. Have more discipline.

7. Give my family more priority.

8. Train my assistants to be head coaches.

9. Be more active in church.

10. Give more time to civic and community activities.

EVERETT CASE: Questions that need to be answered:
"What are the players you coached yesterday doing today? What are the players you are coaching today going to do tomorrow?"

"SO YOU WANT TO BE A COACH!"

ABE LEMONS - HEAD COACH
OKLAHOMA CITY UNIVERSITY, UNIVERSITY OF TEXAS

Abe Lemons was the head coach at the University of Texas. It was preseason and while in Austin, I was able to catch a Longhorn's practice. I did not know Coach Lemons. I had attended a couple clinics in which Coach Lemons had headlined. We were doing the after practice 'small talk' thing with Assistant Barry Dowd and Coach Lemons, when Abe turned to me and said let's get us some "grub" and he led me through the bowels of the Arena around stacked up tables, chairs, and other equipment. Suddenly, Coach Lemons threw open a curtain and we were in the middle of a large reception for Austin native and American League Most Valuable Player Don Baylor. We have a nice buffet meal and then we went our way. Our coaching paths never crossed again. But a neat coaching memory was created.

Abe Lemons died in 1999. He claimed (without opposition) to being the greatest Indian coach in history, a reference to the large number of players with Indian descent he coached at Oklahoma City University. An outstanding coach, who won at Oklahoma City, Texas Pan American and at the U of Texas, his intuitive coaching style and great sense of humor; made it hard for people to get past the one-liners and appreciate his abilities as an excellent basketball coach. Laughter may have been the one thing we remember about Coach Lemons; make no mistake he was a coaching genius.

- "Finish last in your league, and they call you an "Idiot", finish last in medical school, and they call you "Doctor."

- "The trouble with retirement is you never get a day off."

- "I don't jog, I want to be sick when I die."

- Abe Lemon's response to Digger Phelps talking about the pressure of freshmen playing at Notre Dame. "I bet that 18-year-old Marine with his face down in the mud, under fire at Iwo Jima was thinking to himself, 'Gee, I'm glad I'm not a freshman at Notre Dame."

- "The players getting taller is getting out of hand, what we need to do is sink the baskets into the floor at each end of the court and then recruit midgets." CONT PG 318

- Abe commenting at halftime on his center getting one rebound, "That's one more rebound than a dead guy."

- Abe Lemons talking with fellow Oklahoman and friend, MLB Hall of Famer, Johnny Bench, "Bench if you'd have come with me and forgot about baseball, you could be the principal of a high school by now."

- "When I got fired at Texas, the AD brought me in and told me, "You're fired," I looked around to see who else was in the room, wasn't anybody there."

- "When we went to New York City for the NIT they were selling two eggs and toast for $20.00 in the hotel. I told the waiter, next time we come to this tournament I'm going to bring chickens and leave some players home."

- "The words I have probably said the most throughout the years are: "There can only be five starters and you are not one of them."

- This is a story told by Jody Conradt, former Texas Women's Basketball Coach, told to her by Coach Dowd, Abe's Asst. Coach, "A player came into see Coach Dowd complaining about playing time and how he should be playing more and how he is better than all the guys ahead of him. Coach Dowd told him he would have to go and see Coach Lemons about that, the player scoffed and said, "that won't help, I've already talked to Coach, and he told me I should go and commit suicide." (Probably can't use that one anymore.)

- "Secrets of a long marriage, twice a week, a candlelight dinner at a great restaurant, corner table, fine wine, live piano serenade a fire in the fireplace. Betty Jo goes on Tuesday, and I go on Thursday."

- Pre-Game speech prior to U of Wyoming game played on the sparsely populated and windy high plains of Wyoming: "Ok, the guy who plays the worst has to stay in Laramie." CONT PG 119

"You always catch the wrong players breaking team rules, I finally fixed that, when my star player broke curfew, I brought him in and told him his punishment was he would have to start and play the entire 40-minute game without a rest."

- Doctors bury their mistakes, mine are still on scholarship.

- One year we played in Alaska, and they made us honorary Alaskans. Then we went to Hawaii, and they made us honorary Hawaiians. Next year we are going to the Virgin Islands.

- Abe at post-game press conference commenting on the referees: "That was the toughest seven-man zone we've played against all season"

- Aside from all the one liners and near comedy routines on and off the floor, **Bob Knight, the Hall of Fame Indiana coach said that Abe Lemons is <u>"One of the five best basketball minds I have encountered during my time in coaching."</u>**

- Jerry Hale, the Oral Roberts U. coach and Abe were walking back to their NYC hotel after ORU had just lost a tough game at the "Garden" in the NIT. Coach Hale lamented about the close calls, bad breaks, missed free throws, etc., ORU had suffered in the season ending loss. "Coach Hale finally turned to Abe and said, "The good Lord just was not with us tonight." To which Coach Lemons promptly chimed in, "I heard He went to the Knicks game."

Etc. John Wooden once had a disgruntled player come into his office and declare he should be playing more, he was a much better player than Joe. Coach Wooden patiently listened to the unhappy player, when he was through, Wooden said, "Yes, you are a better player than Joe. It is a shame that you are letting him beat you out."

Clinic notes – Las Vegas 2009

Coach Calipari has a college coaching record of 339 – 93 for a winning percentage of 75%

- Demand a lot and you will get a lot. Accept mediocrity, you'll get it every time.

- Try to create leadership or you must lead from the sideline.

- Teach kids to be responsible for their play, if team is 0-6 each player must own take ownership of their lack of performance.

- Getting the team to work hard is easy – getting them to love each other is much harder.

- Kid says he should be playing more, ask him who he should be playing in place of.

- Kids must be positive – kids play better when they are having fun.

- My offense is a Maserati, but I couldn't get it out of the garage - everyone was playing a zone against us. A balanced attack is important.

- If a team will not run with us-we try to steal every pass-we do not steal off dribble.

- In transition or early offense, the best for us is to get down the floor with pace – quick ball reversal and play. Offensive shooter in corner holds position until the driver is stopped – then slides /lifts to open area. By holding position, the defensive player is more likely to commit to helping the drive.

DEAN KARNAZES
"5O IN 50"
<u>A STORY ABOUT ENDURANCE</u>

Mr. Karnazes did something that normally would be called unbelievable except for the fact that it was believable because he actually did it. Beginning on Sept. 17, 2006, Mr. Karnazes, started his 50-50 challenge with the Lewis & Clark Marathon in St. Louis and finishing with the New York City Marathon on Nov. 5. If anyone is keeping score that is one marathon each day for 50 consecutive days.

It was on the morning of Marathon #19. I was on a mission to run 50 consecutive marathons in all 50 US states, and I could not get out of bed. How was I going to possibly run a marathon? Let alone 31 more in 31 days after that.

The trick I learned is don't think about the future and don't reflect about the past. Just be in the "Here and Now" and the present moment of time and do the best you can do NOW. It takes some discipline not to let your mind wander, but it is almost a Zen-like state (Zen-like is the same as the mood of a beginner; a beginner does not recognize there are no assurances, expectations.) Being in this state of mind allows you to almost endure anything. Endurance simply comes from enduring. Throw yourself into your challenges that is how you gain endurance and personal strength.

<u>What I learned is: You can't fool yourself either you look inward and say, "I deserve to be here, I paid my dues, or you say, "you know I spent too much time on the couch."</u>

THE MAKING OF A "TEAM"

"If you are battling for every point or inch for an advantage

And things are not going well, and yet your team

is getting closer and closer together

As the battle gets harder and harder

As opposed to pulling apart.

This is the very essence of

"TEAM."

Tim Tebow

Etc.: "THE DASH." None of us are going to live forever. We are born and we die. A birth date and a death date. This is a given. What really counts between your birth and death is the "Dash" - your life. It's never too late to begin working on your "Dash," until it is.

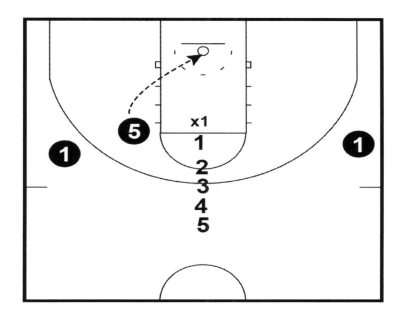

CHARLIE SPOONHOUR, HEAD COACH,
MO. STATE UNIVERSITY, ST. LOUIS U.
U OF NEVADA – LAS VEGAS

Winner of 65% on his games as a Div. 1 head coach. An excellent coach, and an extremely popular and respected personality.

A PROGRAM BUILDING REBOUND DRILL

1. 5 MINUTES ON THE CLOCK
2. Every player must complete the drill. X1 must get three defensive rebounds to complete drill
3. On an offensive rebound - play continues
4. Mgr. (black #1's in diagram) – checks off players as they get three Defensive rebounds. We come back after practice to finish up Until every player has gotten 3 def. rebounds.
5. This drill is done three times a week the first two weeks of the season.

THE MIND OF A "MASTER" FASTBREAK COACH
PAUL WESTHEAD

Coach Westhead, a coaching leader. Led the LA Lakers to an NBA Title in Magic Johnson's rookie season (1980.) Won the WNBA championship at Phoenix. A winner of 508 games in Div.1 Basketball. Finished his career as the head women's coach of U of Oregon women.

- This Fastbreak is dangerous to your job. You cannot take bits and pieces of this Fastbreak and get the same results that we had at Loyola – Marymount. You must commit to this Fastbreak concept of play.
- Run on every situation.
- We want a shot within 7 seconds of a defensive rebound.
- We are better on a made shot because we can run out of our Fastbreak alignment on makes– we can get a shot in two seconds.
- We want you to make the basket – we do not want to take a long time to figure out how to score.
- We want 100 shots a game – we do not worry about a few misses. Thus, the kids have confidence.
- We are trying to shoot the ball ahead of transition defense.
- I do not call many time outs – my best offense is when you score.
- Why should I call a timeout? Opponent fatigue is a major part of our philosophy, why give opponent rest periods. We hope you score.
- **If you ask players to do two things, they won't do either – if you demand they do one thing they'll do it.**
- In transition, we can always rise up and shoot because the defense is trying so hard to get back, they are always on their heels.
- More important than having good shooters is that your shooters think they can shoot.
  Keys to the Westhead Fastbreak:
  1.The long outlet.
  2. Getting the #3 man to run, he is a defensive rebounder. He
  CONT PG 325

must rebound and run. He must be your hardest working player.

3. **On a made basket, the #3 man can get a two-pass layup in two seconds.**

4. Offensive rebounding.

5. Do not add anything – the more you add the less you will get.

- The team must be totally dedicated to offensive rebounding for this system to work. In transition, nobody blocks out, therefore, aggressive offensive rebounding pays off.
- #5 takes ball out of bounds. By getting the ball inbounds in .25 of a second eliminates the need for a press offense.
- I believe in NO defense. Half effort is worse than NO effort because the opponent will take longer to shoot and then they will get the offensive rebound. This kills the fast break.
- #3, your runner must not leak out early. Be aware of your players always trying to cheat the system. Example: leak out early, #3 coasts and still get to the offensive rim in 2 seconds.
- A 40-minute commitment
- The break gets better as the season goes along it is similar for a game, as the game goes along the fastbreak gets better.
- We believe in opponent "TMF" = Temporary – Muscular – Failure.
- We want our opponent to say, "Coach, these guys are crazy, I quit."
- If the fast break is not working, it is because the #3 man is sabotaging the break, he is not running. Make it an honor to be the #3 player, the hardest working runner, willing to run his lane 65 consecutive times w/o getting ball.

Etc.: "Average tennis players have a great variety of shots while the great tennis players hit the same old winners." Vic Braden

TOM BRADY, THE G.O.A.T.
A UNIQUE CONDITIONING METHOD

Tom Brady attributes his physical conditioning methods for his ability to continue to perform at a high level as an NFL quarterback to a different approach.

<u>Brady does not want his muscles to be solid; he wants them to be flexible and pliant, but strong.</u>

Strength is very important. But how much strength do you need(?) You only need the strength to withstand the hits and throw the ball and make your movements being a quarterback. You need conditioning because you need to be able to do the job over a period of time. <u>You need muscle pliability, long soft muscles in order to be durable. (This is the kind of strength needed in the game of basketball.)</u>

Brady talked about pro football's obsession with building strength. When they get really strong? They lift more weight. They get even stronger. That's not Brady's thing.

What he'd like, most notably, is to play for several more years.

On Tiger Woods, whose physique changed to a more buffed strength-oriented appearance as his career unfolded and physical disabilities limited his success. "It is hard to watch Tiger Woods withdraw from a golf tournament. You are watching the greatest golfer I've seen not be able to play a sport at his age the way he would like, to me, that is hard to imagine. It's kind of sad."

DON MEYER

HAMLINE U. – LIBSCOMB U. – NORTHERN ST.
"PASSING – RECEIVING – TRANSITION IDEAS"

Coach Meyer is one of the greatest coaches at any level with 923 career wins. A basketball purist who loved the game and loved teaching and seeing young athletes grow in the game. Renowned nationally and internationally as a giant in the game. Coach Meyer was a mentor to the coaching profession. He conducted Coaching Academy's, Youth basketball camps, coaching clinics and produced a massive video library for coach's education. A great supporter and promotor of the game of basketball. (Coach Meyer died of cancer in 2014.)

PASSING:

- There aren't many great passers anymore. Most perimeter players can dribble, and some can shoot but not many can pass. It is quickly becoming a lost art.
- Great passing teams are happy teams.
- Players must understand who they are passing to and the current situation. It does no good to throw a pass to a great 3-point shooter inside the 3-point arc, and it does no good to pass to a post man that can't dribble on the break when he will have to put the ball on the floor to get to the rim.
- The bounce pass is used in tight quarters (penetrating guard using the bounce pass to the post) and can be used on cuts to the rim (example: back cut on the wing.) We don't want any bounce pass on the perimeter, and a general rule of thumb is no bounce passes anytime the player is moving away from the basket.
- We like to use the chest pass in the open court (transition) or when our guards are spaced on the perimeter (much quicker than the one-handed flick pass.)
- We tell our players if they can't successfully make solid, catchable passes to the post, they can't play. We work on post feeds a lot. On the baseline post feed, we want our players to dribble down to get the proper angle, and then we teach the CONT PG 328

players to step across with the inside foot to shield the pass from their defender (one of the only times we violate our concept of permanent pivot foot.)

On all bounce passes (including post feeds,) we want the ball to hit 2/3 of the distance from the passer to the receiver. We also want the passer to turn the wrist from inwards to outwards so that the ball digs into the floor and spins into the receiver.

RECEIVING THE PASS:

- On all catches, we want the following: "Ball in the air, feet in the air" so that we can catch with two feet and then use our permanent pivot foot.
- On all catches, we want the receiver to meet the ball (shorten the pass.) Most passes are intercepted when the receiver does not shorten the pass, allowing the defense to shoot through the passing lane.
  - "Every pass is a shot." Perimeters must believe that their pass will lead to the success or failure of the shot. A good pass in the shooting pocket will lead to a rhythm shot, where as a pass too low or too high will get the shooter out of his rhythm and may take the shot opportunity away (defense has time to react.)

TRANSITION GAME:

- In the primary 2x1 break, we teach our ball handling guard that they must attack the defense with the intent to score. They only make the pass to the receiver when the defense fully commits to their penetration.
- In the 2X1 break, we want our offensive players to split the floor into "thirds," approximately on yard outside of the free throw lane. As they get closer to the hoop, they will progressively get closer to each other. We want the ball in the inside hand of the ball handler (better angle to make the bounce pass to the finisher.) CONT PG 329

- In the 3X2 break, we want our ball handler to go towards our best shooter and away from our best finisher at the rim (ball handler must immediately recognize the strength of his teammates.) The ball handler must attack the first line of defense and occupy the defender. At that point in time, the defense must make a decision to guard the hoop or "cheat" to guard the best shooter. If the bottom defender protects the hoop, the shooter will have an open look, and if the bottom defender "cheats" to guard the Shooter, the finisher will have an open look at the rim. The key is to occupy the top defender and be able to make a quick read on the bottom defender (requires a point guard with a high skill level.)
- We want our point guard to receive the outlet as deep as safely possible. On the catch, we want his body opened up to the middle of the floor. We prefer the catch to be wide (near the sidelines) so that the angle is good to make the pitch-ahead pass to the near-side wing, or the point – to post "lob" pass to a post running to the rim. If the guard catches in the middle of the floor, there is typically a lot of traffic and passing angles diminish.
- We want our (#2 and #3) to run the wings as wide as possible. In fact, in practice, we have them run near the sidelines or even run out of bounds to emphasize running wide. Once the rebound is secured, they must immediately sprint to their lane.
- Point guards can also "cross main street," that is dribble diagonally across the floor from is reception of the long outlet pass and use the #4 man who is trailing as a moving screen. This is great way to get a quick ball reversal, which forces the defense to rotate.
- If the point guard has no options to pass the ball ahead to a teammate, we want our point guards to look to penetrate in secondary transition. We tell our point guards to "crack the shell" of the defense it is crucial that the near side wing is wide and low enough, and that the trailer stays well behind the 3-point line to space the floor and discourage help-side defense. On the penetration, the low post must drop into an alley near or behind
  CONT PG 330

the hoop to give the guard room to get to the rim or passing angles on any post help.

- If the point guard is a great shooter, we work on the pull-up "3" in transition, especially in a 2X1 or 3X2 setting. This shot is very difficult to make, but it is almost impossible to defend, without giving up an easy layup (Especially in 2X1.)

*Etc.: **"Never let your team feel like they have "Arrived."*** *Georgia Tech had just defeated the legendary University of North Carolina and their HOF coach, Dean Smith for the first time in Tech basketball history. It was a terrific win v the Tarheels and cause for great celebration: **the Yellowjackets promptly lost their next four games."***

SECTION XI

MORE FROM THE
"BOTTOM DRAW"

A LESSON DELIVERED!!!!!
(ONE FOR THE RECORD BOOK)

The University of Michigan football team lost their final two games in 1979 to end the season with a very mediocre 8-4 season by Michigan standards. In a highly anticipated 1980 season, the "Blue and Maize" led by their great head coach Bo Schembechler began with a win over Northwestern followed by consecutive losses to Notre Dame and South Carolina, being their 5th loss in 6 games.

As inevitably happens, immediately after the South Carolina loss, there is the "Come to Jesus" coaches meeting. Bo is not happy, Assistant Coach Bob Thornbladh says, "Bo we've got problems on this team. Bo slowly looks up, "Coach Thornbadh, we have lost five of our last six intercollegiate football contests. I appreciate your astute analysis. "No, it is worse than the record, Bo says, "What do you mean?"

Thornbladh, "We got guys on this team saying, <u>we practice too long</u>, <u>we hit too much</u>, and <u>the coaching staff is too tough.</u>" Bo says, "You're right, that really is a problem, who is saying these things?" Assistant Coach Thornbladh swallows hard, clears his throat (he knows what's about to happen) "Cannavino for one." Bo slams both fists on the desk and yells in disgust, "My Captain, you have five minutes to get that man in my office;"

So Cannavino shows up a big, strong, swashbuckling, Italian American guy. An All Big 10 linebacker, at this point, he hates Bo. He is ready for a showdown with Bo, Cannavino's sick of the yelling, sick of the shouting. He is ready to go "mano a mano to see who's got what. Coach Schembechler yells "SIT DOWN." "I understand Mr. Cannavino we've got guys on this team saying we are practicing too long, we hit too much, and the coaching staff is too tough. Is that accurate?" Now Cannavino is glaring right back at Schembechler with clenched teeth says, "Yes, it is." Bo, "Furthermore, I understand you are one of the guys saying that, is that accurate Mr. Cannavino? "Ya, that is true, too."

THAT IS THE LAST THING ANDY CANNAVINO SAID ALL DAY. CONT PG 334

Bo slams two meaty fists on his desk as he stands up. "Mr. Cannavino, let me tell you something, your daddy was an All American at Ohio State and Woody Hayes did not even visit your high school – he did not want you. We gave you a full ride at Michigan. The coaching staff here at Michigan has made you an ALL BIG 10 linebacker and you have the nerve, the gall, to tell me, we practice too long, we hit too much, and the coaching staff is too tough. Cannavino, I want you to stand up to all the great Michigan men who came before you, the Dierforf's (Dan), the McKenzie's (Reggie), and the Mandich's (Jim) and you tell them: you practice too long, you hit too much, and the coaching staff is too tough. And do you know what they will tell you, "GROWUP AND BE A MAN. Mr. Cannavino, WE HAVE A PROBLEM WITH THIS TEAM, AND THAT PROBLEM IS YOU AND UNTIL YOU CHANGE YOUR ATTITUDE, WE ARE GOING TO GO NO WHERE AND IT IS ALL YOUR FAULT."

(NOTE: This illustrates the common understanding no one ever walked out of a conversation with Bo Schembecler, saying, "I wonder what that was all about, boy, that man is hard to read")

Andy Cannavino got the message loud and clear his arm relaxing on the back of an office sofa came off and his hands are on his lap, shaking. Tears are coming out of this tough guy's eyes. He has made a big change in the last 60 seconds.

The staff was scared witless – Bo had just called out his Captain. Bo, for the first time, was about to lose his team.

WHAT HAPPENS NEXT?

Bo is on "fire" to get the season turned around. The staff expected that – what they did not expect, Cannavino was more fired up than Bo. He was all over his defensive guys making them do sit-ups and pushups, laps and many "Do agains." Finally, one of the defensive teammates says, "Man, Cannavino what has gotten into you, you used to be cool, man." Cannavino responded, "You know I did a lot of thinking last night and it occurred to me, I am the captain of this defense. I don't really care if you think I am popular. I only care about one thing from now on, I am not going back into that man's office ever again." CONT PG 335

334

NOW WHAT HAPPENS?

Michigan rattles off nine straight victories, undefeated in the BIG 10 including Bo's first Rose Bowl victory in about six tries. More impressive, the last 24 quarters of the season, no team crossed the Michigan goal line – not one touchdown against.

NOW HERE IS THE LESSON

1. If you have a problem with someone talk to the person you have a problem with and no one else. It is better to get it taken care of sooner rather than let it fester. If you are not willing to have that conversation, drop it. Once you have talked to the other party, the problem is not yours – it is on the other party.

2. If they solve the problem, give them all the credit, not you. And finally, when all is said and done, do not hold grudges. If you ask Bo, what was Michigan's the best defense of all time, he would say "1980." Or he would say Cannavino's defense.

3. If you asked him who was his best Captain? Bo without hesitating would say, "Andy Cannavino, not only was he the best captain I ever had, but he was also the best coach I ever had, that defense was following him – not me by the end of the year. He was the best of all time."

Cannavino and Bo were "Thick as thieves" until the day Coach Schembecler died. No one took Bo's death harder than Andy Cannavino.

Etc.: Best player penalty is huge. Top kid screwing up and paying the "fine" validates the rest of the team paying the penalty.

MICK CRONIN - UCLA
AN IRISHMAN WITH AN ATTITUDE

Mick Cronin, an eastern guy, raised in Cincinnati was named Head Coach of the legendary UCLA Bruin basketball program on April 9, 2019.

In his first meeting with the players he inherited at UCLA, Coach Cronin wanted to make one thing clear. He was not going to blame them for being on a roster he didn't recruit. He wasn't going to encourage them to go elsewhere, which is what happens during a lot of major college coaching changes. "You show up for workouts tomorrow, you're <u>"My player,"</u> he told them. Everyone showed up and we got to work. I told the guys, if you'll listen and hang in there it's not going to be easy, but you'll be able to have pride and be able to hold up your end of the bargain at UCLA.

SEE PAGE 337: "THE SEAT I SIT IN.. " FOR
MORE OF THE MICK CRONIN STORY

*Etc. Success is peace of mind which is a
direct result of self-satisfaction in
knowing you did your best to become
the best that you are capable of becoming.*
John Wooden, UCLA

"THE SEAT I SIT IN…"
MICK CRONIN, UCLA

Long recognized in the coaching profession as an outstanding basketball coach. A "grinder," who worked his way up the coaching ladder as a club coach, high school assistant, college assistant and successful head coach at Murray State and U of Cincinnati. At high profile, UCLA, Coach Cronin gained notoriety in the national spotlight as one of the elite basketball coaches in the game. The Bruins gritty, hardnosed style was a departure from recent Bruin season's performances.

*IN 2021 TWO YEARS AFTER BEING NAMED HEAD COACH, UCLA WAS IN THE "BIG DANCE."

*The Bruins charged into the NCAA tournament defeated Michigan State, BYU, Alabama, Abilene Christian, and Michigan. That brings us to the Elite Eight game to quality for the Final Four. The opponent would be the tournaments #1 seed, the Gonzaga Bulldogs. The Bruins Were a 14 to15 point underdog. This game would become an instant classic.

*It was an overtime game played at a very high level by two outstanding teams; ending in a halfcourt made shot by the brilliant Gonzaga freshman, Jalen Suggs in overtime to propel Gonzaga to the NCAA championship game and a gut-wrenching loss for a valiant UCLA team. **The following is Coach Cronin's post-game thoughts and emotions as told to CBS reporter Tracy Wolfson:**

"I just told the team we have got to leave the last shot go. We won, because as I sit in Coach Wooden's seat you must live by the things he taught, TRUE GREATNESS IS GIVING YOUR BEST EFFORT. What else can I ask of those guys. I can't ask anything more. I can ask for a different result, but my message to those guys – do not let the last shot ruin what you have done. We might not have cut down the nets, but we'll get another chance, God willing. This team gave everything I could possibly ask."

"Every possible thing that could have, happened to us, Jules Bernard was sick all last night and still tried to play tonight, to a halfcourt bank shot, it's just gone all year like that, and this team refused to give in even when we got down five points in tonight's OT, they found a way to tie it. Just an unbelievable effort by these guys. I am so proud of them."

A SHOOTING STANDARD
TO "SHOOT" FOR.

From a coaching family, Bryce Drew, presently the Head Basketball Coach at Grand Canyon University and formerly the head Coach at his alma mater Valparaiso and at Vanderbilt University. During his collegiate career at Valparaiso University, he was known as an outstanding shooter. ...

*during a shooting drill at practice Bryce Drew using one ball and a rebounder and moving constantly around the 3-point line **made 100 three-point shots in seven minutes and one second**. Truly an outstanding shooting exhibition.*

But wait there is more...

Two months later Valparaiso welcomes Czech Republic recruit Lubos Barton. Mr. Barton in the same shooting drill that Drew Brice **made 100 3-point shots in 7:01 minutes was shattered by Barton making 100 3-point shots in 6:40 besting Bryce Drew by 21 seconds**

'I did not think we'd see someone make 100 threes in less than seven minutes," said Valparaiso Head Coach Homer Drew, at the time, VU head coach and father of Bryce.

"Good shooters can do it in 10 or 11 minutes; really good shooters can do it in about 8 minutes," commented Coach Homer Drew.

Bryce, a first-round pick of the Houston played six seasons in the NBA with Houston, Charlotte and New Orleans. Another brother Scott, the head coach at Baylor University won the NCAA Championship in 2021.

What Barton did in 6 minutes and 40 seconds is a coach's dream.

The 6-7 – 230 lb. Lubos Barton, from the Czech Republic had a long and successful career in Europe.

Etc.: "We really do not have time to get into a body language discussion."

338

THE POWER OF THE CONTESTED SHOT. . .

The team with the highest field goal shooting % wins 80% (plus) of the time. The ONE thing that affects shooting percentage more than any other measurement is the contested shot. This is powerful.

The contested shot: NBA study of playoff games:
1. **Zero contest Field Goal % = 68% makes**
2. **Strong contest Field Goal % = 36% makes (a drop off 32% points)**
3. **Players make 95% of uncontested layups. Any kind of contest lowers made layup % to 49%. This is the power of the contested shot.**

When do you contest? Contest every shot regardless of distance from shooter. The defender must "jump" and extend. Every contested shot regardless of distance from shooter has a statistically positive effect on lowering the shooters field goal percentage. <u>A side benefit for the coach is that a player going "up"or not going "up" with the shooter, is a "visual" that the player either "gets it" or not (the value of the contesting shots or may need some remedial training.)</u>

<u>Contesting shots – Technique</u>

- The "Close out"- If contesting shots is Job #1 – it is unwise to concentrate on the popularly taught "stutter step" approach.
- The defender must run with speed and go up as high as possible, as close as possible and straight up. **NOTE:** this is the same thing a player does on their jump shot off a hard dribble and popping straight up – this skill translates to the defender's action when contesting shots.
- You may get some blocks, but that is not purpose. Do not be afraid of getting faked out - if you are afraid of being faked out you will not go after the contest. If you should get beat; the team defense aspect is in play.
- At every level, the contested shot is a winner, and the converse is also true. The mindset is the shooter is always going to shoot and that shot must be strongly contested.
- Do not foul on/after the shot. Fouling wastes effort and loses games.

"MY SWEET CHILDREN"
TONY GONZALES – NFL
HALL OF FAME SPEECH

Tony Gonzales, regarded as one of the greatest a tight end in NFL history, played 17 seasons mostly with the Kansas City Chiefs. A terrific athlete. Mr. Gonzales played both football and basketball for the University of California-Berkeley. Recorded below are Tony Gonzales comments at his induction into the NFL Hall of Fame.

"You will get knocked down, you will fail, and you will doubt yourself. But that is a good thing.

That my "Sweet Children," is where you will find the "Gold" in life. That is where you will come face-to-face with who you are and find out what you are truly made of.

Be fearless and go there. The fight you have is the most worthwhile fight you will have.

Life takes off on the other side of fear."

Etc.: "I was concentrating so hard on my speech to the booster club, I cut my face while shaving. My wife overheard me and exclaimed. You should have concentrated more on your shaving and cut your speech. Jim Harrick's wife, UCLA National Champions 1995

SHOOTING
A Different Kind of Drill

by Ron Ekker NCAA, NBA coach

Theory: I believe in training the mind, the body (shooting technique) will follow the mind.

My belief is that if you have the right INTENSITY, THE RIGHT MIND SET AND YOU JUST KEEP SHOOTING YOU WILL FIND THE CORRECT TECHNIQUE. It may not be the same form as the next guy – but the right technique for the individual shooter that is natural.

I believe that a lot of coaches teach things that are unnatural for a certain player. I am going to try and get across the "feeling" of how the drill works. If coaches decide to do this drill, do it exactly like I describe it and following the coaching points are very important.

Those players who shoot 600 or more shots a day, my guess is that 500 of them are just wasted. I watch those guys; they are just throwing them up. The following 7 rounds of 15 attempts with intensity that is insisted on is much more valuable. Keep track of all shots. A good shooter beginning standard is to average 8 out of 15 attempts over the course of 7 rotations or 56 makes. If the shooter averages 56 makes for 5-6 shooting sessions; he/she moves up one make to 9, then 10, 11, 12, etc. for the seven rotations for five or six consecutive days. Each 15-shot session is followed by shooting 10 free throws. This goal is to make 9 out of 10 free throws.

- The rebounder must hustle and retrieve the ball you do not want to slow the drill down.
- Distance – Begin at a very comfortable distance – always inside the 3-point arc. Depending on age and/or abilities; the beginner might start inside the block/charge arc. Expand range as shooter improves.
- As soon as the shooter finishes, they go and shoots 10 free throws – rebounder stands along lane line and not under basket. CONT PG 342

Shooting Drill – "Must Be Passionate About Coaching Points:"

1. Record all shot att./makes.
2. Each shot is a "Gem"- Do not waste shots.
3. Do not take a bad/hard shot.
4. Do not shoot, just to shoot.
5. Shooting is an "Art" – each shot is "special" that you hold onto and revere; you cannot waste a shot i.e., throw it up carelessly.
6. Don't take these "Gem" opportunities lightly.
7. (a lot of kids just shoot w/o feel and emotion regarding the importance of each shot)
8. **IMPORTANT:** If shooter catches the ball and the body and mind are not ready, or it is a poor pass - don't shoot – remember each shot is a "Gem/special" don't throw it away; pass it back to the passer. A player who begins at a 5-6-7-8 make standard never passes the ball back to the passer. BUT THE PLAYERS WHO'S STANDARD IS AT THE HIGHER 10-11-12 ETC. MAKES PER 15 SHOT ATTEMPTS WILL PASS BALL BACK TO PASSER. Those shooters have gained understanding of the importance of each shot, they did not "feel" ready – that tells me they are learning to "feel" without thinking and the shot really means something to them, and they are not going to waste a shot that does not have the correct "feel."
9. "feel" of the ball. The shooter does not shoot off bad passes. This process of "right feel" will carry over into the game.
10. "Trust" your technique" – constantly remind players of this.
11. Don't think about the shot – trust it- don't think about where your fingers are supposed to be – just trust.

Maurice Cheeks – NBA Hall of Fame player with the 76ers; averaged 12 makes per 15 shots for the 7 rounds. He worked all summer – on this drill – originally Maurice was as terrible shooter. CONT PG 343

We talked little about technique. Maurice Cheeks changed his technique primarily by himself w/o knowing it because he unknowingly had to change in order to make "shots." I gave him a standard to 8 makes. He fought to make 8; then he fought harder to make 9; then 10 and 11 and finally he was making 12. **Remember, do not move to the next "make level" until shooter has achieved five or six days of achieving his/her present level. Continually, ingrain, motivate and challenge the player the importance of making <u>this</u> basket.**

- Trust your technique, it will take you where you want to go.
- Concentrate on your "feel" for the shot.
- Concentrate on <u>THIS</u> shot being important.
- Talk to the players about concentration – you can't play worrying about what the coach-fans think. You can't play getting involved the officials. You must block all that out of your mind.
- Concentrate very deeply – especially on free throws.
- If I see a player in a drill lose concentration – I correct.
- DO NOT CORRECT DURING THE DRILL – do only minimal corrections.
- Do correcting after the session (105 shot attempts.)
- Player movement in the drill should be very quick – 15 hardworking J's will test your endurance. CONT PAGE 344

Etc.: "We really do not have time to get into a body language discussion."

A SIMPLE DRILL THAT MUST BE RUN CORRECTLY.

1. Shoot a round of 15 FG attempts followed by 10 free throws.
2. Record all shots.
3. Mental concentration and Physical quickness with purpose.
Shooter:
1. After releasing ball, shooter <u>holds</u> position until ball is retrieved.
2. At that point, shooter makes a <u>short</u> jab step (6-12 inches) in opposite direction of cut to ball. Cut is quick, run - do not slide to the next shot, hands available and shooter comes up shooting upon catch. NOTE: a short **jab step** needs to be made w/a certain rhythm and not so quick or frantic

105 SHOOTING DRILL (2)
Dick Lien playbook

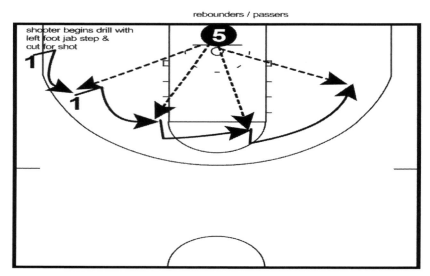

that it cannot be reacted to by defensive player.
3. Drill continues as shown in diagram.
Rebounder:
1. Quickly retrieves ball and makes a crisp "On time – On target" pass.
2. Rebounder(s) is important and must hustle to get ball to shooter.
<u>Shoot 10 free throws:</u> – make 9 - begin new rotation.

"EXPECTATIONS & EXCELLENCE"

*Jessica Shepard graduated from Fremont high school (Nebraska) and like all Nebraska's elite athletes her dream came true. She received and accepted a scholarship offer from the Univ. of Nebraska. A dominating big player at 6-4 she was a major contributor to winning the NCAA Women's Basketball championship team, however, it was **FOR** **Notre Dame's** fighting Irish and **NOT** the **Nebraska Cornhuskers.** Ms. Shepard transferred after her sophomore season, after Notre Dame - she was drafted in the WNBA's 1ˢᵗ round by the Minnesota Lynx. What went so right and then so wrong at Nebraska? In her own words she describes her experience at Notre Dame:*

"The expectations are probably higher here than at Nebraska. You are just held to a different standard. It's just excellence. Every day we practice, we come into practice, and you do it until you get it right. And you are expected to go 100% on every possession. The Coaches here (Notre Dame) get more out of you than you think you can get out of yourself."

Note: No school or coaching staff wants to be known as having lowered expectations. Conversely, everyone wants to be recognized for a culture of high expectations, excellence and winning. If you have it, keep it – if you don't, seek it.

Etc.: "IT'S ALL ABOUT THE TEAM. We are not here to tolerate our differences we are here to accept them."

PETE CARILL
PRINCETON UNIVERSITY

For 29 years Coach Carill led the Princeton tigers to more than 500 wins and 13 Ivy League Championships. A master teacher and innovator of the iconic offensive system simply known as the "Princeton Offense" an offense that relies on spacing, precision cutting, passing, and "drop dead" outside shooting and finally the renowned and feared "backdoor cut" aided by the NCAA tournament win over the defending National Champion UCLA in which the winning basket in the final seconds of the game came on a classic back cut, bounce pass uncontested layup for the winning basket. His genius is cemented in coaching lore with the compliment of a coach being told that his/her team plays like Pete Carill's Princeton's teams." The genius speaks to us:

- At Princeton, I ask a lot of my players, but at Princeton they have a lot to give.
- It has always been important to me that my players got the best of what I had. It might not be good – It was the best of what I had.
- The truth about fast players – wherever they are going they get there faster than slower players.
- We are judged by wins and losses not how well we teach.
- Nobody pays to see average.
- Be good at what happens a lot – this cannot be overstated. What happens a lot: <u>dribble</u>, <u>shoot</u>, and <u>pass</u> – be good at those skills.
- A very important part of my life has always been teaching. I read about a retiring Princeton professor he had been very demanding, always insisting on best effort, and a little cantankerous. I thought, "Hey that's me, except that I yell and swear."
- I have a lot of pride, but I never say I'm proud of myself. I don't even know what that means. If there are things to do, I just do them.

- If you have a good strong heart, you can overcome your environment, whatever it is.

THE PICK AND ROLL OFFENSE

In the NBA, Marcin Gortat sets 22.5 on-ball screens each game. Utah Jazz Rudy Gobert sets a league high 33.8 on-ball screens every game. Anthony Davis (LA Lakers) set 32.4 on-ball screens. This is approximately 1/3 of the total team possessions by an NBA TEAM. That is a lot of pick and rolls to defend. The Pick and Roll trend has affected play at all levels.

In the NBA a Good Screen: opens enough room for the ball handler to:
a. drive b. shoot c. penetrates and pass out to the open 3-point shooter. d. pass to the pick and roll screener on his cut to the basket.

Note: the NBA on ball screening technique much of the time is a fake screen (slip) or brush type action that helps game flow and athleticism and proves a momentary distraction at the "point of action" (slip screen.)
NOTE: the NBA has started tracking "Screen Assists.)

"The way the game is played today with so many great shooters all over the floor, you need that big player who can set screens, is comfortable setting screens and enjoys setting screens knowing there is a chance he is not going to get the ball, but your team is going to get a great shot. You have to be tough, you have to sacrifice your body and set the on-ball screen play after play.

The ball handler (guard) and the screener (big player) must understand where and when to set the screen. Timing and chemistry are essential.
The screener needs to force the defender on the dribbler to trail the dribbler - then the screener has done their job."

Etc.: Attention: Coaches, particularly assistant coaches: "Silence" when confronted by outside criticism of the head coach, players or the program is a form of insubordination."

QUIN SNYDER - HEAD COACH
UTAH JAZZ
"BUILDING RELATIONSHIPS"

"I think in any coaching situation you try to treat your players with respect, And to me, this is the most effective way to communicate (regardless of level of play.) I think if players know that you are **trustworthy and you do what you say**, the players will know there is earnestness about you trying to help them improve. That is the foundation of a relationship.

Etc.: "I can't tell you how to be a great coach but making excuses will immediately turn you in the wrong direction."
   Joe Dean, former coach, motivation speaker and Converse shoe sales executive
   (When Converse was the only basketball shoe on the market.)

KIRK FERENTZ - HEAD COACH
UNIVERSITY OF IOWA
23 Years as head coach of the Iowa Hawkeyes.
Winner of 182 games

The Iowa Hawkeyes were coming off a season "high" with a win over the legendary Maize and Blue, the Michigan Wolverines. As big as the Michigan win was the following week loss to Penn State plunged the Hawkeye spirits to a season low. Coach Ferentz, a master coach, was well aware of the somber mood when he addressed the team:

"You have two options. You either surrender to what just happened mope and feel sorry for yourself or you do something about it."
"Don't think that as a team we weren't thinking about these two options on that Saturday night on the way back to Iowa from the Penn State game. But it's more about how we operate, it's our culture and what our individual and collective team response would be at this tough time..."

Etc.: Coaches must lead. How?
1. Be optimistic. If you are not, your followers can not be expected to be.
2. If you do not love people. Do something else.
3. Be absolutely clear what you stand for.
Rudy Giuliani, former mayor of New York City

MATT CAMPBELL - HEAD COACH

IOWA STATE UNIVESITY

An outstanding coach who has resurrected the Iowa State football program since being named head coach in 2016. Since coming to Ames, IA. Coach Campbell has been named Big 12 Coach of the Year in 2017, 2018, 2020. **The following are Coach Campbell's post-game remarks to the team after an upset win at TCU:**

"You are teaching the world that toughness, discipline and attention to details - matters. That is your platform. It's team above self, nobody buys into that. Culture today says, "Screw the Process," I want instant gratification. But the facts say if you fall in love with process, the process loves you back."

"There are some young guys in here who are still trying to climb the ladder. You older guys who have grinded and stuck it out and fell in love with the process and now the process is loving you back. And if you younger guys want to continue, it can be a dark lonely road that comes with achieving success."

"With success, now everyone is wanting to jump on and be a part of the fun of Winning."

"But you can't buy into "easy" it is a long dark and lonely road if you want to stand on the winner's platform at the end of the process and the confetti comes down."

"Stay the course, it is hard to do. But the process of a commitment leads to experiences like what we have all just experienced out There on that football field today."

Etc.: "It's not how you teach – It is what they learn.

IT'S LEARNING NOT TEACHING
1. tell me and I will forget
2. Show me and I will remember
3. Involve me and I will learn

It was the first game of the season, and thIS true freshman had been on campus less than a month. This rookie defensive end was "going nuts," sacking the quarterback, "blowing up blockers, crushing ball carriers, and running down the plays on the opposite sideline. The color announcer, a former BIG10 head coach commented: "This guy is playing football, real football, he is playing free, all out without any inhibitions. Now the coaching staff has got to be careful and not get his mind full of coaching points which will lead to confusion, indecision, which slows the feet and diminishes his talent."

Coaches, particularly the inexperienced, but not just inexperienced coaches, tend to coach for themselves, satisfying their own ego needs. It is seen at games, practices, summer camps, et.al. It is not coaching for learning but coaching for oneself.

Many teaching demonstrations by coaches have little connection to the needs of players. The demonstrator's execution of dribble/pick and roll maneuvers, shooting, guarding, etc. is flawless but in the end what do we have, a confused, bewildered player unable to process what has just been spewed out by a well-meaning but unaware of what was needed. What's needed is simple:

- Limit the "talking part" to include only needed basics that can be understood and replicated. Coach must study and know, not only his craft but his audience to know what is needed.
- Allow the learner to figure things out on their own, based on their answers to the coaches' questions and follow-up with a series of repetitions.
- The coach takes themselves out of the process. They correct minimally and encourage to the max. This is learning without teaching.
- The well-trained coach makes a point by not telling, but by helping the player discover through questioning, observations, and suggestions. CONT PG 352

- Learning takes place through involvement, not by talking, but when given information, the player can use it to form their thoughts and actions.
- The master coach learns a lot by simply observing players. By watching, the coach will learn what to coach and how to coach the players.
- All a fine teacher does is make suggestions, point out problems, ask questions. "What do you think?" "Have you ever tried to do it this way?" "Was Joey open too? what do you think? "Did you "think" about the cut, or did you "feel" the cut?
- Athletes think with their spinal cord (reaction is not a "thinking" response to stimulus.) A popular refrain from coaches at all levels: "Read the defense" when on offense or "Read the offense" when on defense really what that means is the physical response will be "Too late" to be effective. Why is this? **A stimulus (such as a drive to the basket) evokes a corresponding reaction by the defending player. If the reacting defender interjects a thinking component in any part of his/her response to the drive – that response will slow the reaction and, in all likelihood, will be "too late."**

  What is needed is shortening or eliminating the reaction time between stimulus (drive to basket) and the corresponding defensive reaction. The learning process includes endless repetition that leads to "feeling" and playing (reacting) instinctively. This will eliminate / reduce any thinking process; with the result being a quicker player.

Etc.: The best way to teach is in the way that is most understood.

BILL SNYDER
KANSAS STATE UNIVERSITY

Bill Snyder was hired in 1988 at Kansas State University coming from Hayden Fry's staff at the U of Iowa. KSU dubbed "Futility U" by Sports Illustrated. A program that had not won a bowl game since 1934. Coach Snyder steadily improved the won-loss record until he finished his coaching career with 215 wins against 117 losses and one tie, including 19 bowl game appearances. How did this happen? Among many things was: 1. He was a notorious hard worker and demanding the same of his staff. 2. He scheduled non-conference guarantee games in Manhattan (KS) with teams that the Wildcats could defeat building program wins. 3. Distance K-State from a loser perception, as an example, he retired" Wildcat Willie" the team's furry and congenial mascot for starters, replacing him with a super- tough appearing Powercat "Wildcat." When fully analyzed, Coach Snyder's impact on K-State football has been near miraculous. The Football Stadium on campus is named Bill Snyder Family Football Stadium.

THE "16"

1. COMMITMENT – Bigger – Faster – Stronger.
1. COMMITMENT – Bigger – Faster – Stronger.
2. UNSELFISHNESS- No.1, is Team.
3. UNITY – Come together as one as never before.
4. IMPROVE – If you are not getting better, you will fall behind EVERY DAY as a player, student, person.
5. BE TOUGH – mentally and physical
6. SELF-DISCIPLINE – Do it right, don't accept less.
7. GREAT EFFORT – is a prerequisite to success.
8. ENTHUSIASM – Do what you love, love what you do.
9. ELIMINATE MISTAKES – Don't beat yourself.
10. NEVER GIVE UP – Never, never, never give up.
11. DON'T ACCEPT LOSING – If you do, it will be easier the next time.
12. NO SELF-ELIMINATORS – Expect more from yourself.
13. EXPECT TO WIN – Truly believe we will win.
14. CONSISTENCY – Do your very best every time.
15. LEADERSHIP – Set example first – then lead.
16. RESPONSIBILITY – You are responsible for your performance – there is a right way and there is an easy way. DOING THINGS, THE RIGHT WAY IS YOUR RESPONSIBILITY.

THE 3 POINT SHOT – THE EARLY DAYS

Homer Drew Valparaiso, retired, head coach, claimed to "Love the "3." However, for "Loving" the change, the below list, by today's standards, his approach was extremely modest considering the initial distance was a mere 19' 9." In 2008, the distance was extended to 21' 6" – later it was extended to the present of just slightly over 22.' This read gives an idea of Coach Drew and other coaches thoughts and opinions on the games "new long shot." It's a far less daring approach than we see in today's "Modern Game." Coach Drew's approach:

1. Puts the little back man in the game.
2. Select your 3-point shooters based on practice.
3. The "3" will shoot you out of the game – if you shoot it too soon.
4. Yet. . . the "3" can win games for you. Wait as long as you can before going to the "3." Down 7 pts. w/ 2min. is still time to drive.
5. Weight training allows a shooter to develop range.
6. Be behind the line not <u>on</u> the line.

Other well-known successful coaches of this era, had other things to say about this new "long shot" rule:

- Duke's Mike Krzyzewski considered the 3 point shot a threat to America's Puritan ethic. "You should have to work hard to get a basket."
- Dayton's Don Donoher (a Final Four coach) viewed the 19'9" shot as an example of America's declining moral climate. A disgusted Donoher described the 3 pointer, "To me it's like a game show."
- Jim Killingsworth of TCU was so distraught over the new rule that he was quoted as saying, "If you can't find me, I'll be over at the Trinity River... with a rock tied around my neck."

"THE BRAIN"
ACCORDING TO MIKE LEACH
MISSISSIPPI STATE UNIVERSITY

Mike Leach, "The Pirate," as he is known for his affection for the "Pirate way of life," gives some free medical observations and advice from the sports world as it relates to how the athlete's brain functions in competition.

"If a player is thinking about the game and what needs to be done with one side of his brain - so now you have one-side of the brain locked in, now you got one-side of the brain poised to play the game – good now we're ready to go.

However, if the other side of the brain is going off into space, "Gee, I wonder about that, I wonder about this, I hope "Coach" didn't overwork us this week, I know it is a big game, but, coach how about a little "Chill." "My game shoes feel a little funny, and on, and on."

"No, no, screw that – your whole head has got to be in the GAME."

Etc.: "We do not say "NO" enough to players." Denny Crum, U of Louisville, two NCAA championships, SIX Final Four appearances, inducted into Basketball Hall of Fame (1994)

JOE MONTANA
SAN FRANCISCO 49ERS
"IN THE ZONE"

Alias' "Joe Cool, "The Comeback Kid." Quarterbacked Notre Dame to a National Championship. Started and won four Super Bowls with the SF 49er's and was the first player ever named Super Bowl MVP three times. Inducted into Pro Football Hall of Fame in 2000. With a championship career, Joe Montana's 'IN THE ZONE' thoughts need to be studied, practiced, and replicated:

Being in the zone means a higher

state of concentration. When you

let your mind wonder, you make

mistakes. When you start thinking

about bad things that have

happened, or good things that

could happen, your focus isn't

where it should be, it should be

ON THIS PLAY - **PLAY RIGHT NOW.**

Edu.: I am good at what I love. I don't love all I am good at

DEL HARRIS (NBA) BASKETBALL COACH
FIVE LEVELS OF COMMUNICATION

Head coach of the Houston Rockets going to the 1981 NBA finals v Boston. Hired by the Los Angeles Lakers and improved the Lakers win record in his first four years with the team. Below are five levels of communicating with players. Each succeeding level requires more volume and urgency to be effective.

1. Conversational, normal Conversation, "what's happening," "how are the classes going," "What's the going on back home," etc. Conversation is needed both on good and bad days. And never underestimate the power of listening, really listening and not waiting to respond. It takes a measure of humility to do that.

2. Informational. We are teaching at this point; Teachers, preachers and coaches will raise the tone and use body language, we are teaching for understanding.

3. Encouragement / Praise. Can be tricky. Too much praise and encouragement for things that are normal and even expected or in some cases required; cheapens real achievement and pretty soon the player can't tell the difference between praise, encouragement and performance critique. Legitimate encouragement is needed but patronizing and/or constant disapproval slows progress

4. Correctional. should not be overlooked; errors must be identified and always corrected. There can be an increase in the emotion or urgency in the coach's voice. **Encouragement and correction** must be balanced against one another, too much of either is confusing to the players and team. We hear much about the process being more important than the result. However, when **"everything is not "OK"**, with the team, real life dictates in the coaching business that we are **judged primarily on results**. Eliminating mistakes and errors is the time-tested way to improved performance. In sports, the best teams know eliminating errors and mistakes is the best way to achieve winning.

5. "Go Crazy" Simply, there are times when the team needs to be reminded the coach has limits to his/her patience, and he/she has an "edge" and its "Go Crazy" time and afterward the team realizes it does not want to go through one of "These" episodes again. Most important is use your "Go Crazy" very sparingly. Don't fly off the handle once a week - the impact will become less and less and eventually you will wear down the troops and they will shut you out. Use your power wisely.

FEAR, COURAGE, INTELLIGENCE
RICKSON GRACIE
UNDEFEATED CAREER JUIJITSU CHAMPION

I believe fear and intelligence are remarkably close together. A guy who says, "I am not afraid of anything" is stupid and for me, silly. it is something that does not live in my mentality to not be afraid, I'm afraid of many things – I strive to overcome my fears.

Everyone is fearful. How do you overcome fear? Fear must be combined with intelligence to prevent yourself from getting smashed, defeated, hurt, humiliated and/or disappointed. So, it is important to be afraid – to help you cope with the circumstances fear presents.

At the same time, you must have the courage and capacity to experience mental control of fear and develop a different kind of understanding of fear. So, fear helps you to a point where you can prepare for the time when you have to "Go into action." You must make fear disappear from yourself and go forward with the training of your body, spirit, and mind.

Mr. Gracie supports deep breathing techniques which help body functions (heart, brain, lungs, etc.) Once you concentrate on your breathing you can triple the amount of oxygen that is circulating in your lungs, brain, and body. That helps you control brain and emotions and be more connected to your brain.

In addition, deeper breathing controls, your heart rate, keeping you calm through the function of complete breathing, and you will be able to assess your emotional and physical circumstances in greater detail and respond appropriately.

A casual observer of most athletic events will immediately see the various deep breathing habits that are a standard part of athletic competition. The free throw shooter in basketball, the Olympic athletes in various events. The field goal kicker, et.al. Rickson Gracie's book: "Breathing a life in the Flow" deals with this breathing phenomenon.

"You can spend seven days without food. 3 days without water but 5 minutes without air will kill you. Learning how to metabolize your oxygen in a more precise way will change your life and the way you see the world."

PAT DOUGLAS
E. MONTANA, CAL ST BAKERSFIELD,
UC IRVINE
"THINKING BASKETBALL"

An excellent basketball coach winner of three Div. 2 National Championships as the head coach at Cal State-Bakersfield. ***2018 Small College Hall of Fame Inductee. A career 573 wins (65% wins)*** *at Eastern Montana, Cal. State Bakersfield, and California-Irvine. In addition, Coach Douglas was named Coach of The Year three times by the National Association Basketball Coaches (NABC) and Big West Coach of the year once. Known as a strong believer in fundamental based play and defense.*

- Every opponent has certain fundamental and psychological weaknesses – we search for those weakness and then we work to take advantage.
- Pre-season: We do "60-30's." Run 60 yards / jog 30 yards for 25 min. daily for three weeks in the preseason. This establishes a baseline of PRIDE and WORK ETHIC and brings the team together.
- Too much knowledge slows the feet.
- The big question. what can we do to play in the NCAA Tournament? I'm going to play a style that I believe will win the National tournament.
- We do not double the post with a good player's defender – we assign the weakest offensive man's defender to double the post player.
- As you go up the ladder of competition the big difference is – INTENSITY.
- The ability to defend the post position and control the dribbler will determine the quality of your defense.
- You cannot come to practice and just EXIST, or you do not practice. We must have emotional, physical, and psychological involvement in practice.
- The "KEY" is the passer: It's not the opponent's best scorer but the opponent's best passer is who we must control.
- When there is dribble penetration know what the offensive player wants to do pass or shoot from scouting report.

359

JAMIE DIXON, HEAD COACH
TCU
"DEFENDING SITUATIONS"

One of the top coaches in the country, began his head coaching career in the "old" BIG EAST at the U of Pittsburgh, Named National Coach of the Year in 2011 by Sporting News. An intense competitor accepted the job at Texas Christian University his alma mater in 2016. Has racked up a college coaching career (Pitt & TCU) win record of 69%. **Below, Coach Dixon explains TCU's defensive techniques v. common offensive scoring situations.**

GENERAL NOTES:

v. Shooters – on screens trail (caboose) shooters – "slash" thru non-shooters. When using the "stand up" technique – standup the cutter physically early in the cut. If you are late or stay back it will be a foul. Also, in the "stand up" do not get pushed back by the cutter – hold your position.

v. Shooters – on ball screen - hedge and help on shooter - until shooter's defender can re-establish control of shooter/dribbler – then and only then go back to your player who will either roll to basket or pop out shot or reversal pass.

We switch 1-2-3 involved in on ball screen or screening away from ball.

Trap sideline and corner screens – must really sprint out of traps.

"Leveling off" – refers to a hedge (temporary switch) – the big player must stay with the ball until the little (guard) gets back and in front of their player. The big then recovers to their player with one hand up and one hand down to prevent pass to roller.

V. Screens: Trail all shooters - slash through v. non- shooters.

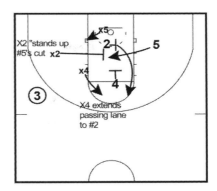

CROSS PICK

DOWN PICK

<u>Left Diagram:</u>

Positions:

#3 has ball, #2 is setting <u>cross</u> screen on X5, #4 is setting <u>down</u> screen on screener #2.
 Defense:
1. X5 goes under screen by #2 – this protects basket
2. X2 "stands up" (body checks #5 coming off #2's screen
3. X4 drops into position as shown

<u>Right Diagram:</u>
 Offense:
1. #5 is coming off #2' <u>cross pick</u>.
2. #2 after setting screen on #5 comes off the #4 <u>down pick</u>
 Defense:
1. X5 meets #5 at the "Block." Going under protects basket from a layup
2. X2 stands up #5 before recovering to #2 cutting to top of circle.
3. X4 extends the passing lane from #3 to the cutting #2

361

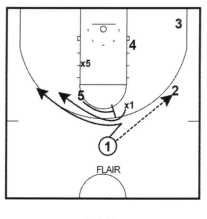

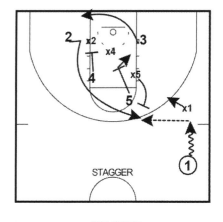

FLAIR   **STAGGER**

FLAIR - LEFT DIAGRAM

1. X1 goes over the top on the #5 screen

2. X5 really softens up getting into help position. X5 is in position to prevent the "Sweep" move by #1 driving baseline upon reception.

STAGGER – RIGHT DIAGRAM

1. Guard this action the same as guarding a double screen.

2. X5 "Stands up" #2.

3. X4 sags & plays for the "Slip" by # 5

4. X1 on pass jumps to ball to help prevent penetration by #2 / with good awareness of #1.

Etc.: Coach Popovich at NBA's first quarter time out with the Spurs off to a raggedy start, "Listen up, it is a long game, let's not get crazy.

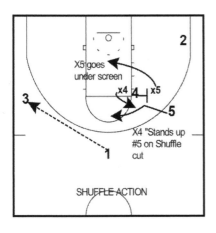

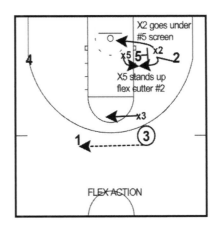

SHUFFLE CUT – LEFT DIAGRAM   **FLEX – RIGHT DIAGRAM**

1. On the #1 to #3 pass - #4 sets up the shuffle screen at the elbow.

2. X4 "Stands up (disrupts) #5's shuffle cut route.

3. X5 always goes below the screen

4. If, when #5 gets "stood up" and flops/pops back out using #4 as a second screen like a "flair" X5 comes back up on the same route as #5 – that would be over the top of the #4 elbow screen.

FLEX – RIGHT DIAGRAM

1. #3 to #1 pass - #5 sets the flex screen and X5 "stands up" #2 disrupting the flex cut. Remember: the "Stand up" technique is contact with chest, do not throw an arm.

2. X2 always goes under the screen.

3. X3 "Jumps to ball and sets up a "picket fence" with good arm action and position to retard pass to the flex cutter by #1,AND is in perfect position on #3's screen down on the Flex Offense continuity.

363

AMERICA'S PLAY – LEFT DIAGRAM

UCLA HIGH POST ACTION – RIGHT DIAGRAM

1. X3 goes under all cross picks

2. X2 "STANDS UP" #3' on cut off #2's screen

3. X4 is the protector

4. X5 extends the passing lane from #1 to #2

5. Not shown in diagram – our rule is always to trail double screens. X2 after "Standing up" cutter (#3) trails hard on #2 knowing that there is help from X5.

UCLA HIGH POST ACTION - RIGHT DIAGRAM

1. On pass from #1 to #2 - #5 "Stands Up" cutter #1

2. X1 goes on the 3 second lane side – so as not to be screened

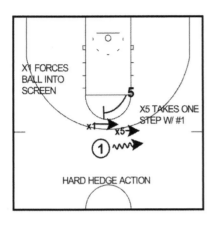

ON BALL SCREEN – "HARD HEDGE"

LEVELING ACTION – "SWITCH"

LEFT DIAGRAM

1. X1 forces ball to use the screen.

2. X1 & X5 are "foot to foot" do not allow #1 to split X1 AND X5.

3. X5 comes up with #5 at their level, or even one step higher toward midcourt line.

4. X5 slides one step with #1

5. X1 on initial force of #1 into the #5 "On ball" screen – keeps pushing up and then goes under X5 and regains defensive position on #1.

6. #5 re-locates on screen #5.

RIGHT DIAGRAM

1. #5 On ball screen, X1 forces #1 to use #5's screen.

2. X5 "LEVELS" and does not allow #1 to turn corner.

3. X1 goes over screen.

4. X3 "STUNTS" for the purpose of slowing down the ball and creating indecision.

5. #5 re-locates on the rolling or popping #5

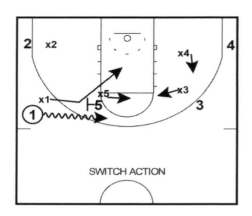

SWITCH ACTION

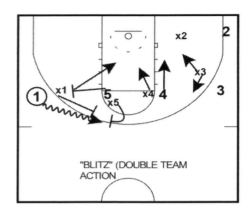

"BLITZ" (DOUBLE TEAM ACTION

SWITCH ACTION – LEFT DIAGRAM

1. X1 does not allow #1 to reject screen by #5.

2. X5 switches to #1

3. IMP. X1 switches into the "gap" as shown so that #1 will not be able to split X1 and X5 if #1 comes back to the left

4. #3 and #4 stunt. If X3 has to help on the dribbler - #4 must help and come up higher anticipating #3 getting ball.

"BLITZ" ACTION (DOUBLE TEAM) ACTION

"BLITZ" ACTION (DOUBLE TEAM) – RIG#1 HT DIAGRAM

1. X1 forces #1 to use #5's screen

2. X5 comes up aggressively and chases #1 into the Blitz (double team)

3. X4 runs to "gap" in the lane and takes #5 or first man on the "roll"

4. X2 & X3 to clean up the help side – with responsibility in diagram for #3 and #4 (must verbally communicate.)

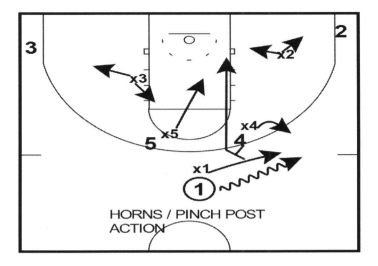

HORNS / PINCH POST
ACTION

HORNS/PINCH POST ACTION

1. X4 Hedges – assisting X1 to go over the top of #4's screen.

2. X5 drops into the middle lane "Gap" as x4 dives to the basket – defensively the rule is to not switch. We want to disrupt offense and recover back to assigned players. The "Stand Up" technique is an example of the kind of disruption that is a central tenet of our defensive approach.

3. X4 recovers to #4

4. X3, X2 have two jobs as helpers and recovering to their defensive assignment.
5. We only emergency switch

Etc.: Murray Warmth was a successful and longtime University of Minnesota Football Coach, in the 60's and 70's. After he retired, he was asked about a particularly poorly played game by Golden Gophers, Coach Warmath, responded, "The players can say all they what they want about "laying it on the line and giving everything." They may not consciously accept it, but they gave in even if they claim differently." It takes a lot of toughness and self-talk to keep fighting when things don't look good. I didn't see that. That team needs to do a lot of soul searching going forward."

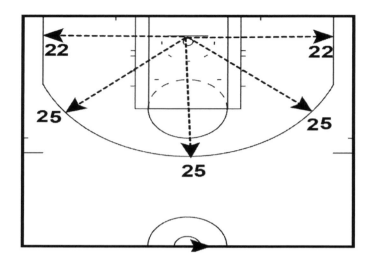

HISTORY OF THE ABL 3-POINT LINE

In 1961, the owners of the fledging ABL (American Basketball League) got together in Chicago and created a 22' three-point line. However, the powerful Abe Saperstein the League Commissioner and owner of the popular Harlem Globetrotter owner arbitrarily rejected the owners wishes. He and DePaul longtime coach, Ray Meyer one day simply walked out on a gym, eye-balled the various distances and decided 25' from the backboard (not the center of the basket) would be the distance. And that was it with no pushback from the other ABL owners, many other than Geo. Steinbrenner, the future owner of the NY Yankees knew little about basketball or running a professional sports team.

Why all this fuss over the 3-point line distance. Some owners did not want a 3-point line. But it was felt the 3-point shot was necessary to compete v. the NBA.

No one ever imagined the 3-point line would become the most powerful incentive in sports in 60 years a line that is still the same as Ray and Abe's.

"BROADWAY JOE"

Joe Namath, the brash first round draft choice of two competing leagues the NFL & AFL. The two-league bargaining drove up Joe's value ending in a huge financial windfall for Joe and his rookie contract. Many Jet players were deeply resentful not only of Joe's insane rookie salary, but his instant popularity and rookie's cocksure attitude. And this was before he even completed a pass or huddled up the team.

After Joe Namath's first practice with the New York Jets, there was a post practice meeting with the veterans detailing the way the Jets did things and what was expected of the rookies. Most everything said was in opposition to the way the free-wheeling Joe Namath lived his football and personal life and who would soon be known as "Broadway Joe." A moniker that would be earned many times over in his time as a famously beloved fan favorite of New York Jets.

But at the NY Jets first practice the sentiment toward "Broadway Joe" was completely different and boiled over into a post practice team meeting. Joe later described the meeting. "A lot of things were said and at the end of the meeting I felt I had to say something, I said, "I don't really care if you like me or not, but don't bring IT to the football field; BUT AFTER PRACTICE, IF YOU WANT TO FIGHT, I WILL FIGHT."

Joe Namath's after practice challenge, seemed to be a foretelling of the Broadway Joe era that included induction into the National Football League Hall of Fame.

"I'm convinced I'm better than anybody else.
I've been convinced of that for quite a while.
I haven't seen anything out there that I
Couldn't do and do well. . .I get annoyed
With myself for doing something wrong. . .
I tell myself, 'You're the best, Damn,
Do it right."

Joe Namath, Hall of Fame, Class of 1986.

"PRACTICE, PRACTICE, PRACTICE IS THAT WHAT WE ARE TALKING ABOUT, PRACTICE?"

(The above was said in a mocking manner by Allen Iverson at a post practice. A terrific All-Star guard for the Phila 76er's who seems to have a contrary opinion of the value of practice.)
*The great **Deion Sanders** a two time All American at Florida State, NFL Hall of Fame football phenom, and also played nine years of Major league Baseball; is presently the Head Football Coach at Jackson State University. Coach Sanders reflects on "practice," what he sees from the eyes of a coach and what his purpose was as a great player when he took the practice field.*

WHAT IS YOUR PURPOSE FOR PRACTICE?
"Right now, we just practice to practice."
That is the problem with some of today's athletes.
We do not practice to be great.
We do not practice to dominate.
What do I mean?
We practice to get through practice.
We practice counting how much time is left.
We cut deals in practice, "you go soft then
I'll go soft"
We do not practice to dominate.
When I ask you what is your purpose for practice?
You really don't have an answer.
I don't care what your endeavor in football or life
It must have purpose.
WHAT IS YOUR PURPOSE FOR PRACTICE?
I practiced to be the best ever
So, every time I walked on that field
I HAD A PURPOSE FOR MY PRACTICE,
"THE SEARCH FOR DOMINATION."

"NEED" PLAYS

What are "NEED" plays? With the of pressure of "time and score," teams call on certain practiced plays that are designed specifically for situations in close games and at the end of games.

Notes on "NEED" plays:

1. The clock determines whether there is time only for a "catch and shoot" play or is time to drive/pass.

2. "NEED" plays are used sparingly, but you must have them available.

3. "NEED" plays must be practiced. Coaches do not have to spend a lot of time practicing "NEED" plays as they do not come up that often, but team does have to learn what to do in these special situations.

4. Players need to know how to miss a free throw when the "need" calls for a miss. Harder than one would think.

Practicing 'NEED' plays:

Do not 'practice' NEED plays "live" i.e., 5x5. Bear Bryant the legendary coach at the University of Alabama never practiced special situations "live." He called it rehearsal, not practice. He did not want the play to fail. The team never witnessed "NEED" play failure. If there is doubt, there is no result. When a "NEED" play is destroyed in practice (2nd team knowing the play in advance) that play creates doubt.

Finally, coaching is a bundle of skills and coaches are evaluated in many ways: handling lineups, teaching, bench coaching, discipline and end of game coaching decisions and execution. "NEED" situations which ultimately are win/lose decisions have affected coaching careers positively and adversely. It is wise for coaches to work on having, "Something for everything." CONT PG 372

- ✓ "OK, we got time to get this done."
- ✓ Bobby is taking the ball out; can you make that pass to Grant at the top? He waits for an answer. Bobby responds, "yep."
- ✓ "Grant, can you get open and make the next pass to Laettner?" ANS. "got it coach."
- ✓ "Zion use your big body to nail the down screen for Laettner, can you do that?" ANS. "yes"
- ✓ Christian let Zion set the screen don't come off too soon, but make your cut with purpose, Grant is going to get you the ball, "knock it down and let's go home." ANS. "I'm all in."

Coach K:

1. exuded self-assurance – transferring that confidence to team.
2. Specific instructions, requiring an affirmation of understanding from each player.
3. Each player was reminded to do his job and the importance of everyone doing their job. Doing your equals team effort.

Following are "NEED" situations from actual games. This is informational only and not meant to determine whether they are good or bad plays, only examples of "NEED" Tactics.

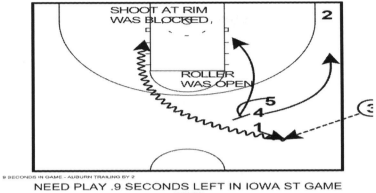

NEED PLAY .9 SECONDS LEFT IN IOWA ST GAME
AUBURN

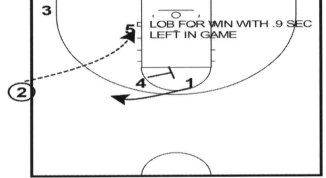

Top Diagram: Auburn is tied with Iowa State with 9 seconds remaining. After a time out Auburn runs this BOB play – It turns out to be a well planned and executed action that gives a great opportunity to put the Tigers ahead. As shown, shot is blocked at rim by X5, #5 rolling was also open. <u>Sometimes the Defense makes good plays, too.</u>

Bottom Diagram: After the blocked shot went out of bounds and another time out – Auburn must run a "Catch and Shoot" with only .9 seconds left. The lob play failed because the pass was not made so that #5 could catch and make a play. Auburn had a plan that was designed in this "NEED" situation, but was unable to execute it successfully.

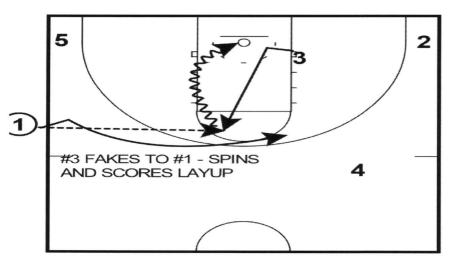

"Same game:" Iowa State v Auburn OT. Iowa State is down one point. After a TO this play won the game with basically an uncontested layup. Play was set up as shown. #3 fakes a handoff to #1 wheels and gets to the rim for the win.

Etc.: **PROCESS OVER RESULTS:**
"Evaluate the game based on what happened in the game -
Not the result."
        Brad Stevens, Boston Celtics

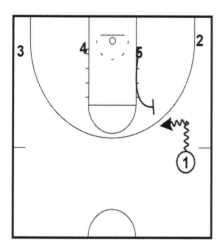

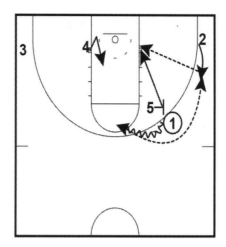

Left Diagram: This is a change of direction play or variation that has become common. Left Diagram shows a spaced-out alignment. #5 sets an on ball screen for #1 who comes hard off the screen as shown setting up the mis-direction action that follows.

Right Diagram:

#5 has set On Ball screen for #1.

#1 comes off screen hard advancing into the top of circle area– selling mis-direction area, #4 ducks in.

#2 lifts and #1 throws back to #2 with #5 rolling.

Etc.: Repetition and staying with the things you believe is very important.
Kelvin Sampson, University of Houston

375

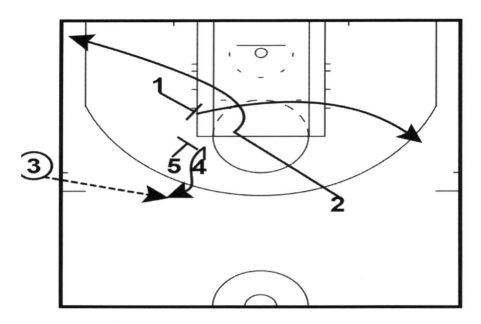

This is an NBA "NEED" – "Catch and Shoot" play for a 3-point basket.

1. #4 and #5 are big players with 3-point ability. Usually, NBA big defensive. Players are not great at getting to out to defend shooters.

2. #1 screens for #2 and #4 & #5 double screen for #1 (not well depicted on diagram.)

3. – this gives the appearance that #1 the team's best shoot is coming off the #2 back screen and #4-#5 double – but #1 fakes using the #4 - #5 double and cuts to a shooting spot as shown.

3. The play is set up as if we want to hit #1 or #2 but the play is really for #4 the better of the big player shooters – coming off #5 pin down.

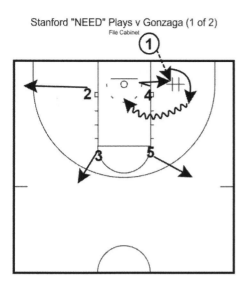

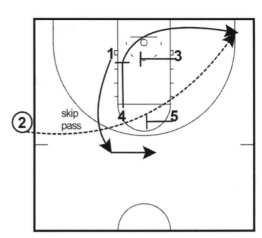

In the 18-19 season Stanford and Gonzaga women played in Spokane on Dec.2. Gonzaga won a highly competitive back and forth game 79-73.

In two "NEED" situations-trailing late in the game Stanford ran the two plays shown.

It seems that the best "NEED" plays are very simple in design relying on execution as opposed to trickery.

<u>Left Diagram:</u> #4 seals hard and pops as tight as possible. #1 who is often a player who is given less defensive attention as most defenses want to load up 5 defenders v. the 4 offensive inbounds players.

#1 follows pass and drives ball into the free throw lane area. Other 3 players space for the possible "kick out "pass to open shooters.

<u>Right Diagram:</u> Sideline-out-of-bounds play to set up a 3-point shot. The passer threw a poor "skip" pass, and the shot was never attempted.

*Etc.: Al McGuire the brilliant and eccentric head coach of the Marquette Warriors and the 1977 NCAA Champions, **"Don't be afraid of your stars." Coaches should not be coached by their players**.*

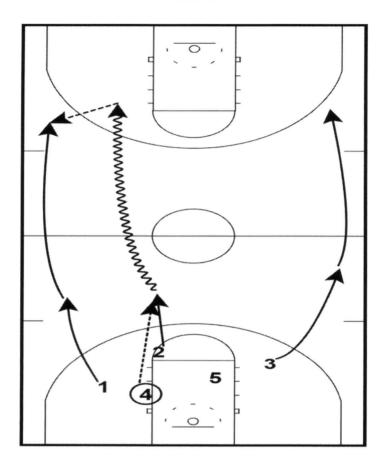

With precious few seconds remaining in the Colorado State v. Nevada-Reno; CSU, trailing by "3"gets a rebound possession and transitions up court and finishes with a penetrating (#2) and pitch back to #1 for a 3-pt." splash" and 3 pt. the lead. <u>There was no time out taken by CSU. Coaches should be aware, as CSU was, that a time out would have allowed UNR to set its defense in its strongest position i.e. 5X5." Time out v no time out is an important consideration that a coach makes in this and other similar situations.</u> CONT PG 379

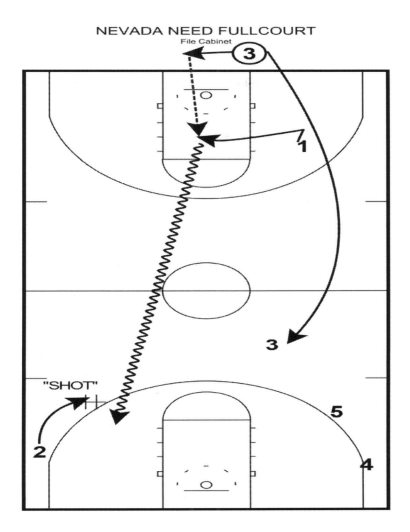

After CSU scored Nevada needs a "3" - takes a timeout and sets up the above "NEED" action diagrammed on this and the next page. Without hard pressure by Colo. State UNR speed dribbles as shown with #2 setting up for a "potential "3." See pg 380.

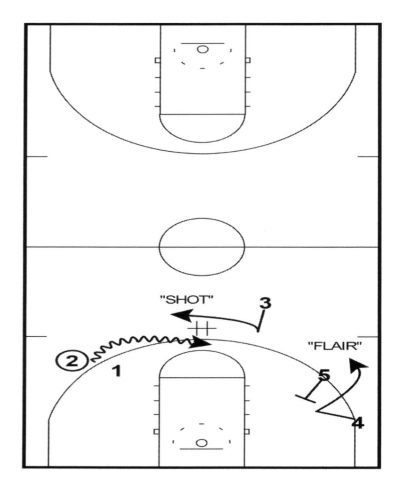

#2 was not able to get a good look - the action continues with a #2 and #3 hand off action. AND finally, a #4 and #5 on the "flair." Nevada did not get a shot as time expired QUESTION: a. too many options? b. the Nevada timeout gave CSU time to set its defense?? (Just asking?)

"IT'S THE TEAM, THE TEAM, THE TEAM!"

Everybody talks about the team. "I just love my team." "I love my coach. "I love my school." "We are going to win the Conference, "but as soon as something goes wrong: "How come I didn't start." How come coach took me out." "Why did coach yell at me, I'm not the only one that messes up." "Why doesn't he/she yell at someone else" and on and on goes the "blame game." A lot of teams are built for only good times and are incapable of digging down deep when the "Team" really needs them. There just seems to be a lot of fakery on many teams. Below is a story that describes "Team" in another way.

My friend and high school teammate, Junior (Wilkinson) had an old '51'ford that "ran" like a '41' he had "lowered" it, so it traveled close to the ground. It was "cool" to do the lowered "thing" with your "ride" back in those days. Junior's '51' Ford was about the "coolest" thing in town, and he was really proud of that car.

I rode with Junior to football practice it was a seven-mile drive. One day we were on our way home from practice the road was rough, it was always rough and going over the bumps in the road a couple of lug nuts came off one of Junior's wheels and if you know anything about cars, you know that you won't go very far without your lug nuts, and we didn't. The wheel was so wobbly that as much as Junior revved up the engine, we were stuck all because of a of couple tiny lug nuts.

Now a car is like a "team." Someone must be the steering wheel, someone is the engine, someone the battery, the ignition, the radiator, and so on down the line. Yep, and someone must be the lug nuts, too.

A team needs all its parts to be a "TEAM." Like a car, regardless of whether you are steering wheel, the engine or the lug nut you've got a job to and need to it to the best of your ability. That is the only way a car or the team goes anyplace.

What does this mean – ON A TEAM - EVERYONE HAS A JOB AND IS IMPORTANT.

.

"THE LAST GAME"
"THERE WILL BE NO CHAMPIONSHIP, THIS YEAR"

If you go online and peruse College and University Official Athletic Sites occasionally there is a column that lists "Last Game." And in basketball if there was no National Championship, listed under "Last Game" the "Last Game" was LOST. Now if you have coached awhile there is no escaping the scene that takes place in the locker room after "The Last Game."

THE LAST GAME

The game had just ended, the game was lost, the season was over, Yes, it was the last game for everyone. In the locker room, the scene is eerily like other season ending locker rooms: there is the raw emotion of a reality that cannot be denied or changed. Players masking their agony with heads buried in towels, slumped shoulders staring at the floor with a painful, "Nobody's home look," players the soft sound of a player quietly crying and the "Punch in the gut" realization of what was not thought possible only two hours earlier - a Championship was not to be this year and forever for the seniors who just played their final game losing in the Championship game.

Finally, the obligatory "Boiler plate" eulogies to the season are delivered by the coaches with sincere emotion: "I'm proud of you." "You gave me/us everything, I could not have asked for more." "I have never been prouder of any team I have ever coached," and on and on and on it goes. SEE PAGE 383

"A DIFFERENT KIND OF "LAST GAME" STORY"

"We are here, feeling the way we do in this stinking, losing locker room, because we could not make up six stinking points in the final five minutes enough to win this game and given a "life" to our pursuit of the Championship. This could have been avoided, I am steamed, angry, disappointed, disillusioned, and disgusted with everyone in this room; every player, every coach, managers, trainers, and anyone who touched this team caused this defeat. "We coaches and you players had five months to make up the points we needed tonight. We talked all season about winning this championship. Turns out what we really are good at is talking. Even in the last month, the last two weeks, if we had the gumption to back up the "talking part" we would have won tonight. All we needed was just a fraction more effort in our preparation, but we didn't have that extra needed to reach just a little higher and the result was we did not get the job done and now they'll be loading the body bags on the bus tomorrow and a toe tag with each of our names.

"Now listen and listen very carefully."

"As much I despise how this game and season ended tonight. My greatest disgust, and anger is not with the trainers, managers, you players, or the coaches. It's me. It was me; I am the one who was failed you tonight. And I really hate it. No one in this locker room failed you more than your head coach. I should have been more accountable for our practices, more individual work before and after practice, more video, more attention to scouting reports. Yes, It was your coach who allowed this awful locker room feeling. It was me.

You seniors and everyone for that matter, moving forward wherever and whatever you do there are going to be a rough "patch" or two along the way, like tonight that you will have to overcome. Remember this night and season and know it's the little things and a little bit extra that will help get you get to the other side. Never forget tonight.

PUNISHMENT??

Coach Agnus Berenato, a veteran head coach at Rider U, Georgia Tech, U of Pittsburgh, recently retired from Kennesaw State after a 33-year coach career, stated in a retirement press conference, "Together (players and coaches) we have enjoyed the journey, grew our student-athletes and experienced the thrill of victory." Her experienced outlook is worth remembering:

"Kids will do anything to avoid displeasure or pain. Kids will not do anything to achieve pleasure."

Example: If kids know that they will have to run sprints if they do not call out names of teammates in a drill – they will do it.

On the other hand, instead of a consequence, if you promise a water break for calling out the names in the same drill, they do not really care.

It has been Proven:

"Kids will be motivated to do a better job of avoiding pain than they will seeking pleasure."

Etc.: "Remember - nothing is deserved – everything is earned."

FIRST FIVE MINUTES
OF 2ND HALF

Gene Roebuck, the longtime head coach of the University of North Dakota. Winner of 628 games in his 25 years as the head coach of the then Fighting Sioux (now Fighting Hawks,) winning 13 conference championships and back-to-back NCAA Div. II championships. An excellent coach on the importance of coming out of the 2nd half fast.

The first five minutes of the 2nd half are very important. You can lose a lead, gain a lead, or even get buried if you don't come out with intensity in the first minutes of the second half.

It is easy to go into the locker room at halftime and just sit there, relax, and let your mind drift to things outside the locker room and when you come out for the 2nd half you are not loose, you are not ready to play when you hit the floor and the other team can really take it to you.

So those first five minutes of the second half is very important.

In tonight's game, the first five minutes of the 2nd half was the game for us. Even though they (opponent) fought back, we had the lead and maintained that cushion because we were able to come out of the locker room and handily win the first five minutes.

Source: Grand Forks Herald (ND)

Etc.: "What is your best play with 8 seconds left in the game."

COACH: "TELL'EM A GOOD STORY"

Great coaches are great storytellers. They shape the stories they tell themselves and the stories they tell others.

Stories represent things of importance in the program told in another way that is interesting and creates an impression and ultimately is remembered.

As a coach you are trying to reach into the players private voice, their public voice can tell you anything, but that is not how you influence them positively, you want them to buy in with their private voice (what they are saying to themselves) what you are laying down and eventually their private voice and public voice are speaking in concert with the coach.

WHAT IS A GREAT STORY?
1. Truth – the stories must be grounded in reality and is believed.

2. Direction – story needs to take you where you want to go. What is your purpose for telling the story?

3. Write out your story to the team. Review the story. Be able to tell it to the team with some theatrics and reliability.
By Jim Loehr

"GRIT"

by Angela Duckworth

What is GRIT? Grit is a passion and perseverance for very long team goals. Grit is having stamina. Gritty players are made for the long haul.

- ✓ Starting with today – day in and day out – not for weeks – but for months and longer.
- ✓ Working hard to make your future goals and needs, a reality.
- ✓ GRIT is like living life as if it was a marathon not a sprint.

How do we build GRIT?

I do not know how you build Grit? But I do know that talent does not make you gritty. There are many talented individuals who do not follow through on their commitments.

Building GRIT in players is about having a continuing "get better" mindset. The belief that the ability to learn is not fixed but connected to effort. When kids begin to understand how they can change and learn. They recognize they are more likely to persevere and when they fail, they do not feel failure as a permanent condition it is just a happening to learn from. A learning mindset that leads to growth is a great idea for making players GRITTY.

Etc.: End of game strategy:
1. Up "3" - foul
*2. **Switching** becomes more important*
3. Opponent needs basket, defensively we must:
       *A. We must **push ball out of middle***
       *B. **Front the post**.*
Kevin O'Neill, Hd. Coach – Tennessee, Northwestern, Marquette, US Marquette, USC

"SCORING PLAYS!"IN THE FOLLOWING FIVE PAGES ARE A VARIETY OF OFFENSIVE ACTIONS THAT WERE IN THE "FILE CABINET." THE ACTIONS ARE NOT MEANT TO BE SPECTACULAR OR GROUNDBREAKING INFORMATION. IN FACT, MANY ARE SIMPLE IN THEIR DESIGN AS OPPOSED RELYING ON COACHING TRICKERY.

ALL RESULTED IN MADE BASKETS.

Etc.: "Process" is a buzz word that dictates and precedes "Results." However, the scoreboard also dictates a winner and loser without regard to process. In the competitive world of sports, coaches are judged on results. It may well be an oversimplification to rely on the fall back "Process" for a poor game result. Demanding the elimination of mistakes and errors is the best way to achieve the desired "results" and at the same time advance the "process."

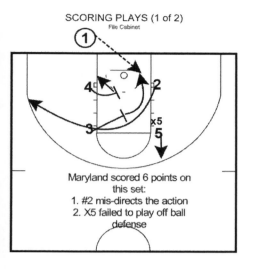

Maryland scored 6 points on
this set:
1. #2 mis-directs the action
2. X5 failed to play off ball
defense

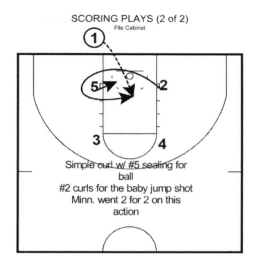

Simple curl w/ #5 sealing for
ball
#2 curls for the baby jump shot
Minn. went 2 for 2 on this
action

MARYLAND   MARYLAND

Left Diagram: As noted this play was a high value scoring action, Maryland scoring 6 points in one game on one BOB play is extraordinary. <u>Never underestimate the ability of opponents to screw-up. In this case X5 in the diagram did not properly align on defense.</u> #2 Maryland's best shooter creates a misdirection.

Right Diagram: A simple "curl" maneuver by #2, a good player. One key, #5 facilitates #2 being open; #5 real digs in, seals and "begs" for the ball - to occupy #5's defender.

Etc.: "One thing I never take into consideration is when I hear:
"THEY SAID SOMETHING."

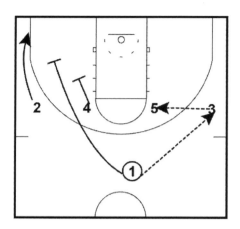
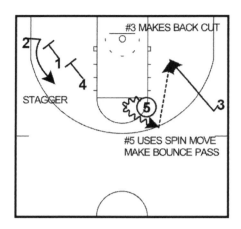

KANSAS STATE

<u>Left Diagram:</u> Although, the alignment is 1-4. This type of offensive maneuver can be run from other formations.

<u>Right Diagram:</u> This diagram high lights three possible options: backdoor, stagger action, and a 1x1 for #3 on an open half of the court. This recalls a statement attributed to Paul Westhead, who has a strong NBA, WNBA, and NCAA background. He stated, "if you give a player two things to do, he/she won't do either, give them one thing and demand the do it – they will do it."

<u>Right Diagram</u> notes three possibilities.

In this diagram, the primary option, is the backdoor to #3 must be careful not to overload #5 with too many possibilities. See P. Westhead above. #5 dribble toward the stagger action sets up the backdoor by #3 the "goal" was to get to the goal. However, this sets up a good 1x1 with an open Rt. Side of the court for #3 and / or a finishing Pick and Roll with #3 and #5

Etc.: WD > WS
(Well done is greater than well said)

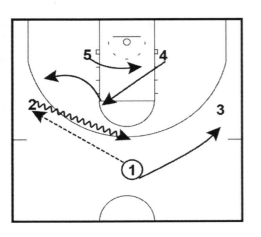 

TENNESSEE

Left Diagram: A lot of teams run this "Over the top" pass and when executed is worth psychological points as well as scoreboard points. Tennessee scored on this play on two consecutive possessions. Misdirection shown in Left Diagram is an important function

Right Diagram: The key actions: 1. The pass by #1 – the target is the corner of the board and has enough air under the ball giving #4 room to maneuver the ball to the rim or dunk ball. In addition, 2. The cutter #4 sets up the cut and cuts as shown once the ball is released by passer.

391

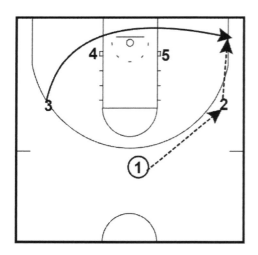 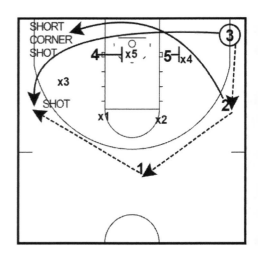

KEARNEY ST. (NEB)

This is a zone/man play and a good end of quarter/game (EOQ/EOG) play. Also, it can be used as a "NEED" play. The play is from Kearney State (NEB).

One thing that is hard on zone defenses is making their defensive "covers" if they are constantly getting screened / bumped.

Left Diagram: It helps to have a good shooter in the #1 spot. This well stretch the defense vertically. The cutters stretch the defense horizontally with the result - it opens improvisation i.e., driving lanes

Right Diagram: #3's cut stretches the defense when the ball goes to the corner and then reversed. Cuts are made by #3 and #2 after on they pass. As ball is reversed to the left side of the floor; #3 is running to shooters spot ("3") & #2 is looking to explore the short corner and not shown #4 is sealing X5. X5 andX4 are bumped as both defenders work to re-establish there cover rules Without scoring opportunity on the left side, ball is reversed through the point at the top and continuity continues to right side.

****#4 and #5 "Screen, seal and postup.

392

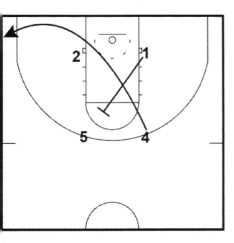

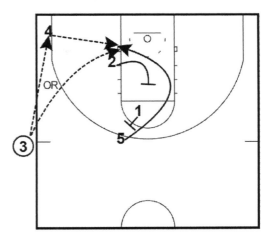

STANFORD

Stanford ran this Sideline-out of bounds that creates a staggered screen for an uncontested layup.

<u>Left Diagram:</u> The play action sets up as shown with safe passes to corner and #1 on pop up (not shown.)

<u>Right Diagram:</u> NOTE #1 by cutting a big player (#4) to the perimeter they are less likely to be denied a passing lane (Defensive big players are less likely to contest #3 to #4 pass.) NOTE #2: with the overload to the left side of the court, this could very well be a lob play with #5's cut.

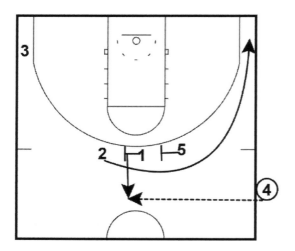
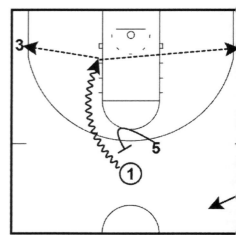

ARKANSAS

Arkansas' play to win game with a corner "3" by a wide open #2 - open shot was missed – and the game was lost.

NOTE: Without a time out to set up the sideline action, this action can be run "live" without the benefit of a timeout.

 Left Diagram: #1 screening for #2 and cutting opens initial passing lane.

Right Diagram: Action is pretty "straight up" #5's screen helps #1 get downhill and makes the play.

Etc.: Deflections result in steals at a rate of 46%. A steal is the highest scoring possession in the game at .96 pt. per possession (PPP.)

"SUSPENDED"

The 1978 Orange Bowl was being advertised as the battle to decide the National Champion. #6 Arkansas (10-1) v. #2 Oklahoma (10-1.) Oklahoma was coached by the legendary Barry Switzer, featuring the brilliant Billy Sims in the Sooner backfield. Arkansas was led by first year coach Lou Holtz. Coach Holtz had a surprise for the Orange Bowl, college football and the "Las Vegas" world when he announced that he had suspended players that represented 78% of Razorback scoring. Arkansas a heavy underdog before the suspensions; now the national press was predicting an Oklahoma embarrassment of Arkansas.

Lou Holtz, "I had just suspended 78% of our point production before the Orange Bowl. Everybody was talking about how bad we were going to get beat. Finally, I had enough, I felt it was affecting the morale of the players and if things were not addressed, we were going to get smashed by an excellent Oklahoma team."

What did Coach Holtz, a master coach do now?

Despite our desperate situation, I asked the team how we could win. One guy spoke up, "We had a great defense and there was no way we were going let the Sooners run all over us like everyone was saying." Another said, "We got a great kicking game." Another chimed in our quarterback had a good year and was a great leader." "We have good receivers." "Our team depth will keep us physically fresh," etc.

Through Coach Holtz' leadership he flipped the dialogue, drilling down on team positives to counterbalance the devastating personnel losses. Finally, the team shed the "Poor me" attitude and actually was excited to accept the challenge.

The Game: Arkansas ran out to a 24-0 lead after three quarters. The game's final score was 31-6. It was an instant Classic and lives forever famous in Razorback country and unforgettable infamy in Sooner Nation.

Etc.: During the team's discussion about why Arkansas could still beat Oklahoma. Coach Holtz said, "I was thinking the team would conclude that they had a great coach – but it didn't come up."

BENJAMIN FRANKLIN
THE DECLARATION OF INDEPENDENCE
&
PHIL JACKSON
11 NBA CHAMPIONSHIPS

Phil Jackson the great NBA Championship coach of the Chicago Bulls and Los Angeles Lakers was a deep thinker. In the Sheri L. Berto Center, the Chicago Bulls team room, Coach Jackson created an inner sanctum of Lakota Sioux Indian lore with totem poles and other symbolic objects. The holy sanctuary was where the team would come to prepare their hearts and minds for battle. This was the room where the spirit of the team was developed. Coach Jackson was also known to pass out reading material to the players on road trips that would serve to enlighten and inspire the team. One verse Coach Jackson shared with the team many times was originated by Benjamin Franklin. It was directly related to winning and losing in the athletic arena of competition – where the tiniest of details are fundamental to success and failure.

"For the want of a nail the shoe was lost,

For the want of a shoe the horse was lost,

For the want of a horse the rider was lost,

For the want of a rider the battle was lost,

For the want of a battle the kingdom was lost,

And all for the want of a horseshoe. "

Benjamin Franklin

PRESS ON

NOTHING IN THE WORLD CAN TAKE THE PLACE OF PERSISTENCE. TALENT WILL NOT; NOTHING IS MORE COMMON THAN UNSUCCESSFUL MEN WITH TALENT. GENIUS WILL NOT; UNREWARDED GENIUS IS ALMOST A PROVERB EDUCATION ALONE WILL NOT: THE WORLD IS FULL OF EDUCATED DERELICTS. PERSISTENCE & DETERMINATION ALONE ARE OMNIPOTENT.

First seen on a bulletin board in a coaches' office somewhere along the trail some 40 years ago. "PRESS ON." it was tattered and well-traveled from use. When asked about the plaque, the coach simply remarked. "I believe in the message; I believe it can help us. We present "PRESS ON" to our players and then we refer to the words as the season plays out with all its ups and downs."

"A MAGICAL BALL OF STRING!"

It was an early season team meeting. The head coach brought into the locker room a ball of string or yarn. Holding the ball of string, she told the kids what her role as the leader would be on the team, also, she talked about herself, her background where she was from, how long she had coached and her personal goals and hopes for the team. And finally, one or two things she had to work on to be a better coach.

The coach explained she was going to toss the ball to a player, and the player would tell her "Story" to the team. Initially, the first player to catch the tossed ball of string, was hesitant telling about herself, hometown, hobbies, and family. The ball of string was then tossed to the 2nd girl, then the 3rd, 4th, 5th, etc. As the ball of string made its "rounds" the stories started to change. The players talked about a hardship that was overcome; the loss of a friend, or a family member, or winning a big tournament, the pain of an injury and the rehab.

As the ball was passed around, the attention of the players increased, they were quieter as they listened, and it became a sharing atmosphere amongst the players as the conversation reached a level deeper than "happy talk and chatter."

The farther the ball travelled from player to player the more the players felt confident in sharing their feelings.

When the ball had completed its rounds to all the girls - what you saw was a mis-mash of string connecting every member of the team and coach; the visual symbolizing a group on their way to becoming a team as long as they stayed connected to each other.

This activity needs a good set up by the coach which the head coach did by "opening" herself/himself up to the team.

"REBOUNDING"
KELVIN SAMPSON
UNIVERSITY OF HOUSTON

Kelvin Sampson is a coaches – coach. The kind of coach that other coaches learn from watching his team play. Coach Sampson has been the head coach at Montana Tech, Washington State, Oklahoma, and Indiana on the college level an assistant in the NBA at Milwaukee and Houston. He assumed the head coaching position at the U of Houston in 2014. Coach Sampson has an overall coaching record of winning 2/3 of his games and at the U of Houston has an overall 72% coaching win mark. The 2020-21 Coughers team were a Final Four. A fierce competitor and outstanding teacher of the game; has always had aggressive hard-working teams that are strong on the boards.

"HOW DO YOU GET YOUR PLAYERS TO REBOUND?"

**"IT STARTS WITH THE HEAD COACH-
NO ONE ELSE CAN HOLD PLAYERS
ACCOUNTABLE LIKE THE HEAD COACH."
"IF YOU WANT TO BE A GOOD REBOUNDING TEAM –
IT HAS GOT TO BE IMPORTANT TO THE
HEAD COACH EVERY DAY NOT JUST
THE FIRST MONTH OF THE SEASON."**

OFFENSIVE REBOUNDS: "Taking Offensive Rebounds as an example: Our goal in was to lead the nation in offensive rebounding percentage. We wanted to offensive rebound 50% of our misses. What that means is if we make 20 baskets and take 40 shots. We miss 20 shots – the goal is to rebound 10 of our missed 20 shots equaling 50%.

The players buy in because we emphasize our goals and then hold the players accountable to those rebounding goals in practice."

"EVERYTHING WE DO IS TO WIN ONE GAME."
"STORMIN" NORMAN ELLENBERGER HD. COACH
UNIVERSITY OF NEW MEXICO

*"The foot-stomping, flamboyant, showman known as "Stormin" Norman Ellenberger was insanely intense, and loved to play to the crowd, dressed in all black, with western boots, partially opened shirt, traditional aqua blue, necklace and wristwatch coached at New Mexico for seven years and had a 134 -64. In 1979, Coach Ellenberger along with chief recruiter Manny Goldstein, in an attempt to recruit high school phenom Moses Malone once rented an apartment across the street from Malone's home. Later both were fired because of FBI wiretaps that showed altered high school and Jr. college transcripts. The Lobo coach was convicted on 21 counts in state court receiving probation. The Judge called Ellenberger a "victim of high-pressure college athletics" and in 1983, those convictions were later formally dismissed. Norm Ellenberger would never work as a head coach again. After New Mexico, Coach Ellenberger worked for Don Haskins at UTEP, Bob Knight at Indiana, and was an assistant in the WNBA and coached boys' and girls' basketball in the Upper Peninsula (MI). Mary Haskins, wife of the late UTEP Don Haskins probably characterized Norn Ellenberger best when she described him, "Norm was such a special person, always young at heart." The '70's and 80's was a dynamic time for college basketball, big arenas being built, dynamic personalities from the great coaches like Dean Smith, N. Carolina, Georgetown's John Thompson, Bob Knight at Indiana and many others and great players like Larry Bird and Magic Johnson. And amongst all the game's greats; Norm Ellenberger was at the center of every basketball conversation. **Following is an inside look at the intensity and drive that proved to be Coach Ellenberger' greatest strength and ultimately may have contributed to his downfall.**

This is a coaching clinic address in the fall of 1978, following a 24-4 season in 1977-78, In Coach Ellenberger's own words. He tells what he told the 78-79 team. **But first, he speaks to the coaches.** "Every meeting we have is very important. You can write all the X's and O's you want - you've got all the answers in that Medalist Notebook you've all got; you can call coaches throughout the country, go down to the library and get all kinds of books. All these things are important. But, unless you have an attitude, a feeling in your heart, and "goose bumps" don't stand up on your arms at game time - you can read all that crap you want and you're not going to be any better off than the guy down the road who didn't do anything to be a better coach. CONT PG 401

We had our first meeting a few days ago and I want to tell you a few things I said to my team. "Now we graduated four of five of the greatest basketball players in the history of New Mexico basketball led by Michael Cooper, now with the LA Lakers. So we've got a bunch and new guys on the team."

FOLLOWING IS THE 1ST TEAM MEETING: "On October 15 approximately 300 college teams are going to start practice and about five months later there is going to be one team left. The only thing I want you to think about is being that team at the end. Don't think about winning the conference, beating the Russians on Nov. 6, I want you to be thinking about winning the National championship in March. Last year we didn't get through the first game after having one of the finest basketball teams in the United States. But this year, it is different and the day you stop thinking about winning the National Championship; is the day that you become a traitor to your team. If you don't prepare yourself mentally, emotionally, and physically from this day on then you are making a big mistake.

Each of you is in this room for a different reason and it is not primarily to win for the University of New Mexico. I realize and understand that. Basically, you were recruited to come here to answer and satisfy a drive from inside ("heart".) I understand that it is a self-motivated reason, maybe you want to be a pro basketball player, I understand that and all the other reasons.

But you must understand that you cannot and will not ever will be able to satisfy your personal goals by yourself. Each of you will satisfy your own drives through this group (your teammates) and through this group only. Therefore, let's decide why we're going to win a national championship. First, it if for you to satisfy your ego and desires. Not for the UNM, but for you. #2 we are going to win for the coaches, most of you have no idea what we go through to get the job done. CONT. PG 402

And finally let's win for the University of New Mexico. We led the nation in attendance last year and have the greatest fans. Let's reward our fans. Human Nature: Everyone in this room is lazy and selfish. I've seen it in your pickup games, you're running. You are no different from any bunch that has been here before you.

You will not go anywhere without all your teammates. You may not like all your teammates. You may not like me some days. I may not like each of you on some days. I don't like everyone in the building all the time. But I darn well respect them ant that's what I expect out of you. The Black guys respect the Mexicans, the Mexicans respect the Indians and on and on. That's the way the world is made and from that we will develop an eternal love to where we will lean on each other through respect, and we will be successful.

I don't want excuses. We do not get involved with any type of excuse. Excuses require remedial situations for those remedial people who constantly need reminding. <u>NO EXCUSES. We are going to start playing games before you know it. When those games are over, and you look at the scoreboard you will not see one inch of space reserved for "COMMENT."</u>

Our game is total "run and pressure." We are going to practice for winning one game and that's the game to win the national championship. So, what does that mean? We have got to get ready to win that BIG game and the only way to do that is to make every minute you are involved with UNM basketball - PERFECT."

Etc.: We need your "Game" - not just your "Name."

"I HEARD IT SITTING ON THE FIRST ROW"

- ✓ "There are so many empty seats in the arena, I should have been a tailor."
- ✓ "Hey ref, I can I get "T" for what I am thinking? Because I think you're an SOB."
- ✓ "We are such bad passers; we are thinking about giving the first 10 rows of fans shields for personal safety.
- ✓ "I did something real innovative in the pre-game, I used colored chalk."
- ✓ "Louie is always complaining about how the ball bounces, problem is he's the guy who's fumbling it."
- ✓ "Coach, I was wide open. Son, from that spot, you are going to be open the rest of your life."
- ✓ Coaching isn't what people think: On game day the first thing I do in the morning is throw up and then coming to the game I'm hoping to get in a car wreck, so I didn't have to go to the game.
- ✓ "The good one's want a coach who is driven and focused on winning."
- ✓ "It was between, UCLA and USC, kid went to USC. He said it was easier to spell."
- ✓ "MSU was recruiting this kid, but I told him he didn't want to go to Maine."
- ✓ Heard at the grocery store, "You look just like our coach. "Yes, I do hear that a lot." "Bet that really makes you mad."
- ✓ "We had a lot of fun at practice yesterday, I am going to have to use some different drills."
- ✓ "I don't mind it so much if we fly by a guy who is shooting, the problem is we keep flying by the dribblers.
- ✓ "Hands down on Defense, Man down on defense."

CONT Pg 404

- ✓ "The idea should not be to not create offense for the other team by shooting bad shots, turnovers, and giving up fastbreak baskets."
- ✓ "The three variables we can control: 1. Defensive play. 2. Playing hard. 3. Playing as a team."
- ✓ Tom Kelly, the irascible Minnesota Twins manager won two World Series with the Twins, when asked about the team's chemistry, looked disapprovingly at the questioner and said, "I don't know what chemistry is, I flunked high school chemistry in two states. Therefore, I don't worry about it. I just tell them to go out and play their positions and do what they are told."

Etc.: "There is a big difference in <u>playing hard</u> and <u>competing</u> – Magic Johnson played very hard, but his ability to compete goes to another level, Magic's competitiveness was off the charts."

EPILOGUE

EPILOGUE – *"A short section at the end of a literary work. A closing commentary added to writing providing explanation and further information."* <u>Websters New World Dictionary</u>

I was at a book sale at a sports event having a visit with an interesting fellow from Montana. He purchased "... "The File Cabinet." In our conversation he emphasized he rarely read books, "I probably won't read your book (now that was a little concerning.) However, He went on to inform me that a buddy had put him onto the best book he had ever read, "Greenlights" by Matthew McConaughy. I was so impressed by his enthusiasm for a book and author I had never heard of. I immediately purchased it. Since buying the book I have learned that Mr. McConaughy is an Academy Award winning actor, a writer, and television pitchman for Lincoln automobiles. In addition, his name has been floated as a potential candidate for Governor of Texas. The book's jacket endorsements accurately portray the essence of "Greenlights" as being many books in one, <u>an autobiography, adventure, comedy, self-help guide, and inspiring memoir.</u>

A huge University of Texas sports fan, Mr. McConaughy presents a narrative in" Greenlights" that directly relates to many of the themes expressed in" A Coaching Journey. . ." and instantly was added to the "File Cabinets" collection of knowledge and inspiration.

<u>A ROOF IS A MAN-MADE THING</u>

FROM "Greenlights" by Matthew McConaughy

January 3, 1993, NFL playoffs. Houston Oilers vs. Buffalo Bills. Oilers are up 28-3 at halftime, 35-3 early in the third. Frank Reich (QB) and the Bills come back to win 41-38 in overtime for one of the greatest comebacks in NFL history. Yeah, the Bills won, but they did not really beat the Oilers. The Oilers lost that game, they beat themselves.

Why? Because at halftime they put a ceiling, a "roof," a limit on their belief in themselves, subconsciously. Maybe they started thinking about the next opponent at halftime, played on their heels, lost their mental edge the entire second half, and they lost.

<u>You Ever Choked?</u>

You know what I mean, fumbled at the goal line, stuck your foot in your mouth when you were trying to ask that special person for a date, had a brain freeze on the final exam you were totally prepared for, lipped out a 3 foot tournament winning putt, missed a game winning 15 ft. jump shot or been paralyzed by the feeling of "of my god life can't get any better, do I really deserve this?" CONT. PG 406

<u>I have</u>.

What happens when we get that feeling? We clench up, get short of breath, self-conscious. We have an out-of-body experience where we observe ourselves in the third person, no longer present and now not doing well what we are there to do. We become voyeurs (artificially impressed) of our moment because we let it become bigger than us, and in doing so, we just became *less involved in it and more impressed with it.*

<u>Why does this happen?</u>

It happens because when we mentally give a person, place, or point in time more credit than ourselves, we create a fictitious ceiling, restriction, over the expectations we have of our own performance in that moment. We get tense, we focus on the outcome instead of the activity, and we miss the *doing of the deed.* We either think the world depends on the result or *it's too good to be true.* But it doesn't and it isn't and it's not our right to believe it does or is.

Don't create imaginary constraints. A leading role, a blue ribbon, a winning score, a great idea, the love of our life, an All-Conference nomination, who are we to think we don't deserve these fortunes when they are in our grasp? Who are we to think we haven't earned them?

If we stay in *process*, within ourselves, in the *joy of the doing*, we will never choke at the finish line. Why? Because we aren't thinking of the finish line, we're not looking at the clock, we're not watching ourselves on the jumbotron performing. We are performing in real time, where the approach is the destination. And there is no goal line because we are never finished.

When Bo Jackson (the great Auburn University running back/MLB power hitter) ran over the goal line, he through the end zone, and up the tunnel. The greatest snipers and marksmen in the world do not aim at the target, the goal line, they aim on the other side of it. (The goal line is artificial – do not stop just because the finish line has been crossed.)

When we truly latch on to the fact that we are going to die at some point in time, we will have more presence in this one.

Reach beyond your grasp (beyond the goal line,) have immortal - lasting forever finish lines, and turn you red light-green, because a *"<u>roof is a man-made ceiling.</u>"*

"YOU HAVE BRAINS IN YOUR HEAD AND FEET IN YOUR SHOES, YOU CAN STEER YOURSELF IN ANY DIRECTION YOU CHOOSE."

Dr. Seuss

INDEX

A

B

C

D

E

F

G

H

I

J

K

THE END

Made in the USA
Middletown, DE
25 May 2022

66188651R00232